Sacred Uncertainty

Sacred Uncertainty

Religious Difference and the Shape of Melville's Career

Brian Yothers

NORTHWESTERN UNIVERSITY PRESS
EVANSTON, ILLINOIS

Northwestern University Press
www.nupress.northwestern.edu

Printed in the United States of America

10 9 8 7 6 5 4 3 2 1

Library of Congress Cataloging-in-Publication Data

Yothers, Brian, 1975– author.
Sacred uncertainty : religious difference and the shape of Melville's career / Brian Yothers.
pages cm
Includes bibliographical references and index.
ISBN 978-0-8101-3071-5 (cloth : alk. paper) — ISBN 978-0-8101-3179-8 (pbk. : alk. paper) — ISBN 978-0-8101-3072-2 (ebook)
1. Melville, Herman, 1819–1891—Criticism and interpretation. 2. Melville, Herman, 1819–1891—Religion. 3. Religion and literature. I. Title.
PS2387.Y65 2015
813.3—dc23

2014042758

♾ The paper used in this publication meets the minimum requirements of the American National Standard for Information Sciences—Permanence of Paper for Printed Library Materials, ANSI Z39.48–1992.

For Maryse

CONTENTS

Acknowledgments *ix*

Abbreviations and References to Herman Melville's Works *xi*

Introduction
The Sacredness of Uncertainty *3*

Chapter 1
Melville's Communion of Solitude: Reading and Marginalia *11*

Chapter 2
Landlessness: Religious Difference around the Globe, *Typee* to *Moby-Dick* *51*

Chapter 3
"Poor Richard Ain't a Dunker": Mapping American Religious Difference, *Pierre* to *The Confidence-Man* *99*

Chapter 4
"Conflict of Convictions": Remapping Religious Difference in *Battle-Pieces* *131*

Chapter 5
All Souls: *Clarel*, Religious Pluralism, and Unitarianism *163*

Chapter 6
"I Too Am Uncertain": The Doubtful Testament of *Billy Budd* and Melville's Later Poetry *191*

Notes *217*

Selected Bibliography *231*

Index *241*

ACKNOWLEDGMENTS

The process of thinking over the course of the past few years about Melville's representations of solitude and sociability has made the expression of my debts to other scholars and colleagues all the more meaningful. If, as I argue below, Melville desired a kind of secular global communion of saints, something of this order exists at the present time in the far-flung body of Melville scholars in locations too various and numerous to be listed. Among Melville scholars, neither my career nor my understanding of Melville could be what it is without Samuel Otter, Steven Olsen-Smith, Jonathan A. Cook, John Bryant, Wyn Kelley, Robert K. Wallace, John Wenke, Dawn Coleman, Mary K. Bercaw Edwards, Dennis Berthold, Peter Norberg, Chrisopher Ohge, Timothy Marr, Christopher Sten, Cody Marrs, and Mark McCullough. In the wider profession, I owe much to my teachers: G. R. Thompson, Kristina Bross, Robert Paul Lamb, Wendy Flory, and the late Cheryl Oreovicz, and to friends and interlocutors like Liam Corley, Steven Frye, Eric Carl Link, Tracy Collins, Kathleen Maloney, and Derek Parker Royal.

I owe thanks to so many people at the University of Texas at El Paso (UTEP) that it would be impossible to list them all here, but several colleagues have been particularly indispensable sources of wisdom and encouragement: Tom Schmid, Kate Mangelsdorf, Deane Mansfield-Kelley, Ezra Cappell, Meredith Abarca, Sandra Deutsch, and Lois Marchino. In their respective roles as dean of the College of Liberal Arts and chair of the English Department, Patricia Witherspoon and Maggy Smith have been unfailingly encouraging, as has Cheryl Torsney in her role as senior vice provost. My student Gus Cohen, who worked as an intern with *Melville's Marginalia Online*, has likewise been an astute interlocutor. UTEP and El Paso friends like Joanie Ericson, Bill and C. J. Moore, Roy Mathew, Vinny Kaur, Joseph Singh Mathew, James and Patty Lyons, Andre Ellis and Yoshie Hagiwara, Anju and Kiron Master, Sajir and Parul Haribai, and Chetan and Sadhana Moorthy have created a community in which vigorous and creative work seems to come naturally.

I am grateful to all those who have read and commented upon portions of the manuscript along the way, most particularly Jonathan A. Cook, Steven Olsen-Smith, Samuel Otter, John Bryant, Maryse Jayasuriya, and the two anonymous readers for Northwestern University Press.

At Northwestern, Henry Carrigan, Gianna Mosser, Anne Gendler, and Steven Moore have been tremendously encouraging and supportive of this project. Portions of chapter 1 have appeared in *Leviathan* and portions of chapter 5 have appeared in *Poe Studies*, and I am grateful to those journals for the permission to use this material.

My family is always at the heart of my work, so it is fitting that I reserved my thanks to them for last. My father, Willard Yothers; my sister, Heather Maraldo; my mother-in-law Yvonne Jayasuriya; my sisters-in-law Carmeline Jayasuriya and Rosanne Weerackoon; Rosanne's family: Roshan, Ranil, Rochelle, and Rushika Weerackoon; all deserve more thanks than I can possibly give them here. My mother, Esther Yothers, and my father-in-law, Leslie Jayasuriya, both died well before this book could come to fruition, but they are both here. Finally, this book is dedicated to Maryse Jayasuriya. No possible acknowledgment could express what she has meant to every aspect of my life, but suffice it to say that my scholarly work is the least part of what would be unimaginable in my life without her.

ABBREVIATIONS AND REFERENCES TO HERMAN MELVILLE'S WORKS

The standard edition of Herman Melville's works, and the one cited throughout this volume, is the Northwestern-Newberry edition of *The Writings of Herman Melville* (1968–), published by Northwestern University Press and the Newberry Library and edited by Harrison Hayford, Hershel Parker, and G. Thomas Tanselle. The specific volumes are listed below, with variations among the editors noted when relevant. They are cited in the text in parentheses by the abbreviations indicated below and page number. Since *Billy Budd* has not been published in the Northwestern-Newberry edition as of this writing, the edition used is the 1963 Chicago reading text and genetic text edited by Harrison Hayford and Merton Sealts Jr., listed below under volume 13 of the Northwestern-Newberry edition. This remains the standard edition until the publication of the Northwestern-Newberry *Billy Budd*. The later unpublished poetry will also appear in volume 13; in the interim, I have used the 1947 Hendricks House edition of Melville's *Collected Poems*, edited by Howard P. Vincent, despite the fact that it lacks the authoritative status of the other texts. For quotations from Melville's marginalia that are not yet digitized, I have used Wilson Walker Cowen's *Melville's Marginalia* (2 vols.; New York: Garland, 1987), abbreviated in the text as *MM*, and Robin Grey's *Melville & Milton: An Edition and Analysis of Melville's Annotations on Milton* (Pittsburgh, Pa.: Duquesne University Press, 2004). Marginalia that have been digitized are cited from *Melville's Marginalia Online* (ed. Steven Olsen-Smith, Peter Norberg, and Dennis C. Marnon; http:melvillesmarginalia.org/), abbreviated as *MMO*. Poetry from *Clarel*, *Published Poems*, and *Collected Poems* are cited by line number.

Typee, A Peep at Polynesian Life (vol. 1). 1968. Abbreviated as *Typee* in the text.

Omoo, A Narrative of Adventures in the South Seas (vol. 2). 1968. Abbreviated as *Omoo*.

Mardi and the Voyage Thither (vol. 3). 1970. Abbreviated as *Mardi*.

Redburn, His First Voyage (vol. 4). 1969. Abbreviated as *Redburn*.

White-Jacket, or The World in a Man of War (vol. 5). 1970. Abbreviated as *WJ*.

Moby-Dick, or The Whale (vol. 6). 1988. Abbreviated as *M-D*.

Pierre, or the Ambiguities (vol. 7). 1971. Abbreviated as *Pierre.*

Israel Potter, His Fifty Years of Exile (vol. 8). 1982. Abbreviated as *IP.*

Piazza Tales and Other Prose Pieces, 1839–1860 (vol. 9). Edited by Harrison Hayford, Alma MacDougall, and G. Thomas Tanselle. 1987. This volume includes, along with the other Piazza Tales, "Bartleby, the Scrivener," *Benito Cereno*, and *The Encantadas*, as well as uncollected prose pieces from the 1840s and 1850s, most notably Melville's most famous review, "Hawthorne and His Mosses." Abbreviated as *PT*.

The Confidence-Man, His Masquerade (vol. 10). 1984. Abbreviated as *C-M*.

Published Poems (vol. 11). Edited by Robert C. Ryan, Alma MacDougall Reising, Harrison Hayford, and G. Thomas Tanselle. 2009. This volume includes *Battle-Pieces*, *John Marr and Other Sailors*, and *Timoleon*. Abbreviated as *PP*.

Clarel, A Poem and Pilgrimage in the Holy Land (vol. 12). 1993. Abbreviated as *Clarel.*

Unpublished Writings and Billy Budd (vol. 13). Not yet published. In the interim, the standard edition of *Billy Budd* remains Herman Melville, *Billy Budd, Sailor (An Inside Narrative): Reading Text and Genetic Text*. Edited by Harrison Hayford and Merton Sealts Jr. Chicago: University of Chicago Press, 1962. Abbreviated as *BB*.

Correspondence (vol. 14). Edited by Lynn Horth. 1993. Abbreviated as *Corres.*

Journals (vol. 15). Edited by Howard Horsford and Lynn Horth. 1989. Abbreviated as *Journals.*

Sacred Uncertainty

Introduction

✦

The Sacredness of Uncertainty

Seen in its proper light, 1866 is a fulcrum of sorts for Herman Melville's career. Twenty-five years earlier, Melville had been a 22-year-old sailor, who had published some juvenilia as a student at Albany Academy and who had sailed to England as a merchant sailor and more recently joined the crew of the *Acushnet*, a whaler bound for the Pacific. In 1841 his great novels and short stories all lay in the future, but after sailing on the *Acushnet* at the start of the year, he was in the early stages of the experiences that would directly shape his first two novels and the early chapters of his third as well as his fourth and fifth, and would less directly but significantly shape *Moby-Dick*. In 1891, twenty-five years later, he would die, leaving one of the most astounding bequests in literary history, the unpublished and incomplete manuscript of *Billy Budd*, for posterity. By 1866, he had spent a dozen years as a published novelist and writer of short fiction, gone through a seeming eclipse during which he was nonetheless actively transforming himself into a poet (completing and nearly publishing *Poems* in 1860), and reemerged as a published poet whose career as a poet would be twice as long as his career as a writer of prose fiction.[1] He had lived through immense transformations in his career, his family life (with the grimmest, the loss of his son Malcolm soon to come), and his nation. He was near the age at which we see him in what is perhaps the loveliest of all of his portraits: the Joseph Oriel Eaton painting that currently hangs on the wall of the exhibits room at the Houghton Library.[2]

In this central year for Melville, he published *Battle-Pieces and Aspects of the War*, a volume that inaugurated the public portion of his career as a poet and, as part of the collection, a piece of prose that was at once uncharacteristic and broadly revealing when we consider the arc of his career. In the "Prose Supplement" to *Battle Pieces*, Melville argued for a reconciliatory policy with regard to the defeated South, and he built his argument around a fundamental set of doubts regarding history and its meaning and trajectory. In a paragraph central to his argument, Melville wrote:

> Effective benignity, like the Nile, is not narrow in its bounty, and true policy is always broad. To be sure, it is vain to seek to glide, with moulded words, over the difficulties of the situation. And for them who are neither partisans, nor enthusiasts, nor theorists, nor cynics, there are some doubts not readily to be solved. And there are fears. Why is not the cessation of war now at length attended with the settled calm of peace? Wherefore in a clear sky do we still turn our eye toward the South, as the Neapolitan, months after the eruption, turns his toward Vesuvius? Do we dread lest the repose may be deceptive? Has the crater but shifted? Let us revere that sacred uncertainty which forever impends over men and nations. Those of us who always abhorred slavery as an atheistical iniquity, gladly we join the exulting chorus of humanity over its downfall. But we should remember that the emancipation was accomplished not by deliberate legislation; only through agonized violence could so mighty a result be effected. (*PP* 185)

This passage demonstrates that Melville's nonfictional prose can reward close attention as richly as his fiction or poetry. The metaphor at the start is that of a river; benignity, the impulse and ability to do good to others is compared to the Nile, a river charged with multiple significances for Melville's purposes: as a river that connects northern and southern regions in Egypt and Sudan, is the central artery of one of world history's great empires, is a major geographical landmark in Africa, and is the source of agriculture, and indeed life, for the human communities on its banks. In the next sentence, he continues this image of a river with his reference to "glid[ing]" with "moulded words" over treacherous obstacles and then he shifts the metaphor to images of Vesuvius. What is striking here is his emphasis on contingency and a radical kind of precariousness: whether one seeks to glide over barely covered shoals in a river or to dwell in the shadow of a volcano, one lives with the threat that one's illusions can be shattered at any moment. The line "Let us revere that sacred uncertainty which forever impends over men and nations" implies a kind of respect for the precariousness of knowledge, for the ways in which differing ways of viewing the world impinge upon, conflict with, and at times even illuminate each other.

The meaning of "sacred uncertainty" for Melville has been the subject of some dispute. A common reading has been to position Melville as a moderate in the conflict over slavery and to end the discussion there, or else to proceed to an identification of the older Melville as a more conservative writer than the radical novelist of the 1840s and 1850s. As I discuss in chapter 4 of this study, these conclusions warrant some further interrogation. Suffice it to say for now that the final two sentences of the quote above suggest that Melville had not abandoned his hatred for slavery or his impulses toward racial egalitarianism, but had been profoundly shaken by the violence of the Civil War—hardly a surprising reaction for a man with strong inclinations toward pacifism. For my purposes here, the term itself merits some pressure. When Melville invokes "that sacred uncertainty which forever impends over men and nations," the term he creates pushes powerfully in two distinct directions. On the one hand, the use of the term "sacred" points broadly toward moral earnestness and a numinous sense of awe. On the other, "uncertainty" undermines the prospect that earnestness and awe can lead to either arrogance or a conclusive faith. The state Melville describes at once defers certainty and confidence and reaches after it strenuously. It is distinguished from relativism by its moral fervor, but it is likewise distinguished from orthodoxy by its deferral of settled belief. The uncertainty invoked is a blend of the personal and communal, in that it impends over individual "men" as well as "nations." This blending of the individual and the social is, as we shall see, characteristic of every stage of Melville's literary career and of his intense engagement with the works of other authors.

If for Melville in the context of *Battle-Pieces* the term "sacred uncertainty" referred specifically to the post-bellum United States and the challenges of Reconstruction, it applies broadly throughout his career. As this study will show, at each stage of Melville's literary career, he is rethinking the relationship between faith and doubt, knowledge and hope, and the underlying moral earnestness of this inquiry is intensified, not vitiated, by the note of humor that is always present in Melville's work. Melville uses this term at a moment that is a fulcrum for his entire literary life, and it casts explanatory light both backward and forward over his long career as a novelist, short story writer, and poet.

Throughout this study, I use the term "religious difference" to denote the intellectual, ethical, and spiritual issues raised by contact among various religious traditions, inside and outside of the Christian religious traditions that shaped Melville's upbringing. I use "difference" rather than "pluralism," "ecumenism," or "dialogue" (or in relation to Melville's presumptive attitude, "skepticism," "agnosticism," or "critique") because "difference" carries with it a particularly rich set of possibilities for understanding the relationships among religious traditions. I use the term in a sense closer to its usual meaning of pertaining to distinctive qualities among otherwise related items than in the technical sense proposed by deconstruction and Jacques Derrida's concept of *différance*, but in one sense I find Derrida to be helpful in thinking about my use of the term. Derrida suggests that differences are both generative of meaning and never absolute, thus leading to an endless deferral of definite meaning. Melville's treatment of the variety of faiths and doubts with which he was engaged seems to partake of this quality, and his wandering "to and fro across these deserts" of religious uncertainty as described by Nathaniel Hawthorne seems an especially apt portrait of this sort of principled deferral of faith.[3] "Religious difference," then, for this study, becomes a term that encompasses the ways in which religious traditions jostle uncomfortably with each other, on intellectual, physical, and geographical levels. When Melville looked at religion, it was with an eye to finding both contrasts and analogies, and this way of looking at belief seems to be best described by a term like "difference" with its notes of both the contradictory and the complementary.

Ultimately, my aim in the following pages is less to argue a thesis than to understand and explicate a mode of thought and being: Melville offers a rich instance of the complexity of religious and secular impulses, and defining the contours of his fluid and evolving understanding of the doubts and intuitions, the communal experiences and individual quests that define human attempts to comprehend the ineffable, seems an endeavor congruent with Melville's own leviathanic aspirations. "Sacred uncertainty" is thus the method as well as the subject matter for this study, which seeks not so much to compel assent as to stimulate inquiry.

M. H. Abrams's *Natural Supernaturalism* showed that romanticism was characterized by a curious relationship to religion. Describing the great English and German romantic poets and philosophers, Abrams wrote:

> They represented themselves in the traditional persona of the philosopher-seer or the poet-prophet . . . and they set out, in various yet recognizably parallel ways, to reconstitute the grounds of hope and announce the certainty, or at least the possibility, of a rebirth in which a renewed mankind will inhabit a renovated earth where he will find himself thoroughly at home.[4]

Melville's own relationship to religion was fraught with still further complications, in that he was drawn to the philosophical and poetic visions that Abrams associated with romanticism, but could never see more than a distant, if desired, possibility of a "renovated earth" in which humanity could be "thoroughly at home"—hence the centrality of "sacred uncertainty" to his thought and art. One aspect of Melville's authorial persona, and from what we can understand from his letters and journals and the reminiscences of his friends and family, his own character, is the sort of rebellious religious individualism that we associate with Captain Ahab, and that pushes an individual at once toward martyrdom for a personal understanding of the truth and toward a ferocious denunciation of those falsehoods and half-truths that the individual sees as being in conflict with this transcendent vision. Another, and equally potent, side of Melville's persona (and personality) is the desire to find a communion of kindred spirits, soul-friends among his contemporaries and predecessors alike who find room for similar affirmations and similar negations. My first chapter examines the various ways in which Melville interacts with the many religious and philosophical texts that helped to shape his fiction and his understanding of the relation between faith and doubt and among a variety of contrasting traditions.

I have chosen to move chronologically through Melville's career in the second through sixth chapters of this volume because this study is, finally, the narrative of a lifelong pilgrimage. The first chapter tracks Melville's reading on religious subjects, including his biblical reading, his reading from religious dissidents from Renaissance England, and his reading of his contemporaries, both those we remember now and those we have forgotten. The second chapter examines Melville's global range of engagement with religious traditions from around the world in his first six novels: *Typee* (1846), *Omoo* (1847), *Mardi* (1849), *Redburn* (1849), *White Jacket* (1850), and *Moby-Dick* (1851). For Melville in these novels, his engagement with religious and cultural traditions in contact, cooperation, and conflict, and the ways in which their analogies and differences prove mutually illuminating, is among the most important recurring strands, in terms of both form and content. All of these novels are in one way or another global and transoceanic in their geographical sweep, and the sheer diversity of Melville's treatment of world religious traditions in them continues to astonish readers today.

In the third chapter, I move to the series of novels and short stories that followed *Moby-Dick*: *Pierre* (1852), *Israel Potter* (1853), *The Confidence-Man* (1857), and the magazine fiction, much of which was collected in *The Piazza Tales* (1856). In these works from the latter portion of Melville's fictional career, the global, interreligious, and intercultural dimensions of his thought are less readily visible, but no less thoroughly present. What is of particular interest in these works relative to the questions of religious dialogue and difference that inform the study as a whole is the way in which Melville uses his earlier, global framing of religious contact and controversy in settings within the Americas, from rural and urban New

York in *Pierre*, to the Mississippi River in *The Confidence-Man*, to the slave trade throughout the Western Hemisphere in *Benito Cereno*. Even a story like "Bartleby, the Scrivener" bears the impress of Melville's interest in the interplay among religious traditions and the doubts that these systems engender.

Next, and with a continuing focus on Melville's application of international religious models to the American context, my fourth chapter turns to the most traumatic national event of Melville's lifetime, the American Civil War, and Melville's collection *Battle-Pieces*. It is a commonplace to say, as Abraham Lincoln did, that both sides in the Civil War "read the same Bible and pray[ed] to the same God," but looking at Melville's poetry in *Battle-Pieces* gives us an enriched sense of the reinterpretation of biblical exegesis that the war required and of Melville's particular application of interreligious dialogue to the challenges confronting the nation in the aftermath of the bloodiest and most consequential war in U.S. history thus far. Central to my reading of the collection is Melville's use of interreligious dialogue and conversion in poems like "Lee in the Capitol" and "The Swamp Angel" to complicate the national discussion of race and reconciliation.

In the fifth chapter, I turn to a work that deserves much more attention than it has received, and that has finally been receiving more such critical attention in the last decade, Melville's ambitious long poem *Clarel*, which in 18,000 lines of iambic tetrameter brings together the global scope of Melville's early novels with the searching application of Melville's reflections on world religions to the American context that emerges in his later novels and *Battle-Pieces*. Of particular interest here is the way in which wider social trends like religious liberalism and an increasing sense of the intellectual respectability of doubt as the result of an expanded scientific understanding of the natural world help to refine Melville's understanding of religious difference.

My concluding chapter moves through Melville's later poetry, which contains some of the most compelling instances of Melville's treatment of religious difference out of his entire career, and ends with Melville's posthumously published masterpiece *Billy Budd*. Considering *Billy Budd* in the context of Melville's later poetry means that the long-standing "testament of acceptance" debate over the substance of Melville's religious attitudes at the end of his life can be reframed in relation to the continual interest that Melville shows in religious diversity and dialogue from the earliest portions of his career.

Melville was at once a skeptic in the broadest philosophical sense and a seeker with an earnest "will to believe," to borrow William James's term.[5] The way in which Melville's skepticism and faith were interwoven throughout his career is at once highly idiosyncratic and broadly representative of modes of faith and doubt in his era, an era that in many respects still remains our own. In this, Melville resembles his own most compelling characters, figures like Ahab, Ishmael, Bartleby, Clarel, Rolfe, Billy Budd, and Vere, who are both hauntingly individual and broadly representative of central cultural impulses: in the case of Ahab, Melville explicitly describes him as a "mighty pageant creature" (*M-D* 73). Melville's genius as a religious thinker as well as a verbal artist resides in his capacity to strike this precarious balance between the solitary and the communal in examining and representing religious experience. In understanding Melville's ceaseless querying of faiths and doubts across a global spectrum of religious difference, we begin to understand our own precarious moment.

Chapter 1

✦

Melville's Communion of Solitude: Reading and Marginalia

Melville's uncertain communion begins with the solitude of reading. Melville read and annotated numerous books, and critics have devoted a great deal of energy to explicating the significance of his reading to his body of writing.[1] Despite this wide-ranging attention to Melville's reading and sources, William Rounseville Alger's *The Solitudes of Nature and of Man; or, The Loneliness of Human Life*, which Melville purchased and annotated in 1871, has been largely neglected in this regard. Melville's annotations in the volume, however, are substantial and suggestive. Alger, who was a Unitarian minister with extensive intellectual ambitions, had pieced together a compendium of human thought on the topic of solitude, drawing from the philosophers of the ancient world and the European Renaissance as well as from revered contemporaries like Ralph Waldo Emerson. If Alger's work represents a critical survey of human conceptions of solitude across historical epochs, Melville's marginalia to Alger shows precisely how much the concept engaged, and indeed often monopolized the thoughts of America's most influential novelist.

One of the lengthiest passages that Melville marked in Alger's volume was his gloss on a quotation from Goethe. Alger quoted Goethe as reflecting that "Were there but one man in the world, he would be a terror to himself" (*MM* 1.98). Alger's reflection on this remark, marked with a line in the right margin by Melville, is poignant and worth quoting at length:

> Nay, it may be added, were there but one man in the world, there would be no man in the world. In the absence of humanity, he could no more remain man than there could be an island if there were no sea. The single individual is the collective as the little column of mercury in the barometer is to the whole atmosphere. They balance each other although infinitely incommensurate. A quicksilver sea, two and a half feet deep, covering the globe, would weigh five thousand billion tons. That is the heft of the air—that transparent robe of blue gauze

> which outhangs the Andes and the Alps. Its pressure is unfelt, yet if the pressure were unfelt, all the water in the earth would immediately fly into vapor. Public opinion is the atmosphere of society. (*MM* 1.1)

I quote this in its entirety, because it seems to me to represent a tension in Melville's work that persisted from one end of his career to the other. Melville concerns himself consistently with finding the balance between solitude and sociability, with weighing the relative merits of individual belief, passion, and self-assertion against the need for community and a sense of connection to the greater mass of humankind. Although Alger is not among the more celebrated of the writers that Melville annotated, it seems clear that Melville marked this moment because he found it to be cognate with something that animated his own literary production.

Indeed, taken as a whole, Melville's markings in *The Solitudes of Nature and Man* illustrate a thoroughgoing concern with the relationship between solitude and sociability, the nurturing of the self and the meaning of selflessness that works its way through his entire body of work. Alger's method throughout the volume is to demonstrate that figures from Emerson to Goethe to Schopenhauer to Hegel to Pascal to Jesus demonstrate a powerful need for solitude to nourish their artistic creativity and their prophetic insight into the nature of humanity, a powerful urge for connection to other human beings, and a sense of the profound pain occasioned by the social rejection that enables solitude. Alger portrays Jesus himself as a misanthrope pining for human connection, citing both the bitterness of Jesus's remark from the Gospels that discouraged his followers from "cast[ing] . . . pearls before swine" and the pathos of his remark to Simon that "thou gavest me no kiss when I came in" when celebrating the kindness of the woman who anointed his feet and washed them with her tears (*MM* 1.11). Melville marked both moments in his copy, suggesting that this vision of Jesus as one both estranged from humanity and passionately drawn to it resonated with Melville. That Melville could passionately resent the arrogance of the solitary artist/intellectual as well as empathize with the pain experienced by such a figure appears in his annotation to Alger's citation of Emerson's disparaging views on the subject of "the masses." Alger had characterized these remarks with disapproval and surprise that the "kindly Emerson" could be the source of these uncharitable thoughts; Melville wrote at page bottom "These expressions attributed to the 'kindly Emerson' are somewhat different from the words of Christ to the multitude on the Mount" (*MM* 1.4). Notably, Melville preferred here, as elsewhere, the ethical demands of the Sermon on the Mount to a misanthropy informed by a selfish belief in solitary greatness.

Perhaps most telling in relation to how Melville struck the balance between solitude and society appears in his underlining and scoring with a check mark Alger's statement that "It is not aspiration but ambition that is the mother of misery in man." At page bottom under this quotation, Melville wrote his own initials, "H.M." (*MM* 1.4). This is a fine distinction, but the context in Alger's work makes the nature of the distinction for both Alger and Melville clear: aspiration is an unselfish desire to achieve the highest artistic and moral goals, and ambition is aspiration's evil twin, a desire to achieve success by contrast to others. It is precisely this distinction that informs Melville's withering annotation to the Emerson quote.

The concern with solitude that appears in Melville's markings in Alger's volume is a recurrent theme in his marginalia. In Goethe's *Autobiography*, Melville noted with a check mark the following reflection on the necessity of solitude for the literary artist: "I clearly felt that a creation of importance could be produced only when its author isolated himself"—thus illustrating Melville's sense of the necessary loneliness of the literary calling (*MM* 1.565). In the writings of Schopenhauer, to whom Melville seems to have been led by Alger, Melville marked numerous misanthropic and even suicidal remarks, suggesting an attraction to the most extreme sorts of solitude, but he also made note of Schopenhauer's reflection on the moral ambiguities of genius: "The genius, on the other hand, is at bottom a *monstrum per excessum*; just as, conversely, the passionate, violent, and unintelligent man, the brainless barbarian, is a *monstrum per defectum*" (*MM* 2.315). Even at the end of his life, as he read Schopenhauer as a man in his seventies, Melville continued to reflect on the relationship between individual genius and interpersonal connection. As is demonstrated in his careful marking of references to religion in Schopenhauer's work, from discussions of the role of Buddhism in China to discussions of Anglican support for slavery in nineteenth-century Virginia, this obsession with the relation between the self and the broader human community frequently posed itself in religious terms for Melville.

The study that follows examines Melville's engagement with religious difference, both within American culture and around the world. It is impossible to understand Melville's wider engagement with religious and cultural questions, however, without understanding the fundamental tension between self and society, self and others that underlies his work, and that is manifested in particular in the way in which he interacts with other writers. Thus, I begin by exploring the ways in which Melville interacted with the various writers and thinkers that he regarded as his truest contemporaries and interlocutors, the figures of genius from both the past and his present from whom he received, as he eloquently stated it in "Hawthorne and His Mosses" a "shock of recognition" (*PT* 249). There is almost certainly no more concrete or reliable way to get at Melville's affirmations of and arguments with these interlocutors than in the markings and annotations that appear in his copies of many of their works.

These markings square with the most famous description of Melville's approach to philosophical questions, Nathaniel Hawthorne's letter written from Liverpool during his time as a consul there, in which Hawthorne wrote:

> Melville, as he always does, began to reason of Providence and futurity, and of everything that lies beyond human ken, and informed me that he had "pretty much made up his mind to be annihilated"; but still he does not seem to rest in that anticipation; and, I think, will never rest until he gets hold of a definite belief. It is strange how he persists—and has persisted ever since I knew him, and probably long before—in wandering to-and-fro over these deserts, as dismal and monotonous as the sand hills amid which we were sitting. He can neither believe, nor be comfortable in his unbelief; and he is too honest and courageous not to try to do one or the other. If he were a religious man, he would be one of the most truly religious and reverential; he has a very high and noble nature, and better worth immortality than most of us. (*Journals* 628)

One lesson that we may draw from this is that Melville's understanding of the world and the place of his art in the world was fundamentally religious, not in the sense that he allied himself closely or exclusively with any ecclesiastical or creedal formulation, but through his constant inquiries into the very nature and meaning of existence.

Melville's solitude—his experience of it and the value that he placed upon it—helps to explain one of the fundamental facts of his career as a writer. From the beginning of his career to the end of his life, Melville's writing was shaped by ceaseless reading, and more than his contemporaries, more than his neighbors, more than his family, the writers that Melville read, both ancient and modern, formed his intellectual circle, and indeed the ideal audience for his work. Melville's markings in his own copies of books and his exchanges with contemporaries like Evert Duyckinck and Nathaniel Hawthorne on the subject of the books that he read reveal an author who is constantly seeking out new ideas to debate, refute, embrace, praise, condemn, and reevaluate. If we are to consider Melville as a religious thinker, we must engage with the fact that Melville's universal church, his communion of saints, constituted the assemblage of minds from around the world and across the ages that he encountered in his reading, from the Bible (as translated in the 1611 Authorized or "King James Version") to the scriptures of other religious traditions that he encountered in attenuated but provocative forms. The sort of existential intensity of engagement that we see in Melville's reading of the Bible and cognate texts is not limited to these few scriptures, however. It is noteworthy that Melville explicitly made a connection between one of the most heavily annotated portions of his copy of the New Testament and the works of William Shakespeare, a central literary model, remarking that Shakespeare was "full of sermons on the mount, and gentle, aye, almost as Jesus. I take such men to be inspired. I fancy that this moment Shakespeare in heaven ranks with Gabriel Raphael and Michael. And if another Messiah ever comes, it will be in Shakespeare's person" (*Corres.* 119). Melville here identifies Shakespeare with the production of scripture, even to the point of applying the idea of divine inspiration to his work. We see here that Melville regarded the writers to whom he felt the closest tie as figures of religious significance, even if the context for their writing was secular.

That Melville was a voracious reader will come as no surprise to anyone who knows his work, and his reading has been superbly documented by Merton Sealts, Jr., Wilson Walker Cowen, Mary Bercaw Edwards, and Steven Olsen-Smith. The full extent of the impact of Melville's reading on his religious thought and his aesthetic representation of that thought has not yet been fully appreciated, however. Melville's reading, marginalia, and allusions document the growth of an extraordinarily complex and engaged understanding of the religious and cultural ferment of the nineteenth century. Melville's marginalia to the Bible, Shakespeare, Milton, and Nathaniel Hawthorne form the core of our knowledge about his reading, but thanks to Sealts, Olsen-Smith, Bercaw Edwards, and a host of other Melvilleans, we have a remarkably wide sense of the issues that engaged Melville in his reading.

Acknowledging that Melville's reading was determinative for his writing raises a new series of questions: who were the writers that he found most engaging? What patterns in their writing seem to unite them? How does Melville handle them? Several points are especially worthy of note. First, Melville tends to approach his interlocutors on the printed page as good-faith seekers of truth. He argues with them ferociously at times, and he mines them vigorously for images and allusions at others, but there is a persistent sense that he and they belong to one community of thought, whatever their differences. Moreover, Melville seems to express kinship in both his marginalia and his fiction with others who share his inquiring stance and his determination to balance the artistic demands of solitude and idiosyncrasy with the ethical demands of empathy and love. Perhaps the most striking example of this tendency is the seventeenth-century physician Sir Thomas Browne.

"Crack'd Archangel": Sir Thomas Browne and Melville's Religious Renaissance

Our evidence for Melville's engagement with the writings of Sir Thomas Browne is substantial, but we do not have extant marginalia for Browne's works. Evert Duyckinck reported to his brother George that Melville had borrowed his copy of Sir Thomas Browne's *Religio Medici*, and after devouring the book with his wonted intensity, returned it, confiding to Duyckinck that Browne seemed "a kind of crack'd Archangel."[2] Like many of Melville's observations on other authors, this seems both a remarkably expressed insight into what is most essential in Browne's work and recognition of a fundamental quality of Melville's own mind and art. Brian Foley has rightly remarked that the phrase "crack'd archangel" "defies any simple explication," but I would like to probe some of the reasons for the suggestiveness of the phrase.[3] "Crack'd" clearly enough suggests insanity and thus forecasts a figure like Gabriel in *Moby-Dick*, who is clearly both named after an archangel and "crack'd" in this conventional sense, but it is not Gabriel, a single-minded religious fanatic, who corresponds most closely to Browne in *Moby-Dick*. Rather, Browne becomes most evident in the words and phrases of Ishmael, Melville's narrator and the figure who provides the novel as a whole with its witty and paradoxical blend of farce, satire, irony, introspection, and exaltation. Thus, the "crack'd Archangel" of Melville's conversation with Duyckinck seems to indicate most powerfully the idea of a fractured religious consciousness, representing a faith that is at once potent and divided. Melville himself appears to be a "kind of Crack'd Archangel," and it is precisely Browne and Melville's shared struggles with religious difference that explain why Browne's style proved so powerfully generative for Melville.

We have long known that Browne was a major influence on Melville's prose style. Noting this fact has been mandatory at least since the publication of F. O. Matthiessen's *American Renaissance*, and Brian Foley has brilliantly outlined Melville's stylistic borrowings from Browne in both *Mardi* and *Moby-Dick*, particularly at the level of the sentence, where, for example, Foley notes that Melville employs syntactical and aural doubling reminiscent of Browne in order to test the limits of expression through language. Foley also demonstrates that Browne provides a model for blending the scientific and the personal in a single disquisition, as Melville does with such success in *Moby-Dick*. John Wenke demonstrates that these formal devices are closely connected to classical models for philosophical debate, observing that "Browne's dazzling allusive technique transforms every page of *Religio Medici* into a debate among competing positions."[4] Following Foley and Wenke, the extent to which Browne becomes a part of Melville's artistic DNA throughout his career becomes more apparent once we consider the larger ways in which Melville's considerations of difference, and particularly religious difference, in *Moby-Dick* and beyond betray a high degree of conceptual congruence to Browne's treatment of difference in *Religio Medici*.

The power and fragmentation to which Melville referred in his characterization of Browne becomes evident once we consider the rhetorical self-positioning in which Browne is engaged in *Religio Medici*. Browne seeks in *Religio Medici* to define his own idiosyncratic views, situate them as part of Anglican orthodoxy, and allow for personal dialogue with the Catholic Church from which the Church of England had become separated. Melville's project, from *Mardi* to *Clarel*, can be seen as an expanded version of Browne's project. Melville's concern is not only to maintain productive dialogue between Protestantism and Catholicism in his work, but also between Christianity and the other major world religions and between numerous varieties of Protestantism and skepticism toward any revealed religion.

Unfortunately, we do not have the sort of suggestive marginalia from Melville for *Religio Medici* that we have for many of the books that Melville read. We can, however, draw certain conclusions about how Melville read Browne from his marginalia elsewhere. Melville's marginalia in the copy of *The New Testament and Psalms* (*MMO* 65) given to him by his Aunt Jean in 1846 can be especially illuminating in setting up his reading of *Religio Medici*. Melville uses the New Testament and Psalms as a resource in two central ways: as a source for artistic and rhetorical devices, and as a means of interpreting his own existential dilemmas. In the case of the Psalms and Revelation, virtually every image Melville notes with an x or a line in the margin ends up appearing in one of Melville's published works in a recognizable form. This artistic use of the Bible is tied closely to Melville's tendency to use the texts he marks as an occasion for metaphysical and personal reflections—for example, above Paul's admonition in Romans 14 to "have faith to [one]self before God," Melville writes, "The only kind of faith—one's own," and when in

1 Corinthians 7, Paul writes "I think that I also have the spirit of Christ," Melville underscores "think" and leaves the tantalizingly ambiguous notation "I too am uncertain" at the bottom of the page. Melville's marginalia to *The New Testament and Psalms*, with its merging of the artistic and the existential, points us toward his likely approach to reading a religiously inflected text like *Religio Medici*. Indeed, Browne's commentary on religious matters bears an uncanny similarity to the attitude exhibited in Melville's markings in the Bible. We see here a particularly compelling illustration of Melville's often-quoted remark from "Hawthorne and His Mosses": "For genius all over the world stands hand in hand, and one shock of recognition runs the whole circle round" (*PT* 249). What Melville recognizes in Browne is the congruence of Browne's efforts toward understanding religious difference in seventeenth-century England with Melville's own project of giving expression to the full range of religious difference in nineteenth-century America, and indeed in the "whole worshipping world" (*M-D* 88).

We might begin our consideration of Browne's traces in Melville's work by noting the substance of one of the passages in "Loomings" in which Melville establishes Ishmael as a kindred spirit to the speaker in *Religio Medici*. First the passage from Melville:

> I love to sail forbidden seas and sail on barbarous coasts. Not ignoring what is good, I am quick to perceive a horror, and could still be social with it—would they let me—since it is but well to be on friendly terms with all the inmates of the place one lodges in. (*M-D* 7)

In his notes to the Norton Critical Edition of *Moby-Dick*, Hershel Parker identifies the second part of this passage as deriving from Browne's lines "I am of a constitution so general that it consorts and sympathiseth with all things," from which he goes on to declare his lack of physical disgust at toads and vipers and his lack of antipathy on national or religious grounds. The first part, meanwhile, would seem to derive from Browne's earlier confession from *Religio Medici*, "I love to lose myself in a mystery, to follow my reason to an O altitudo!,"[5] the cadences of which it unmistakably echoes. This line begins a virtuoso performance in which Browne expresses his pleasure in exercising his faith precisely where it is most difficult. Reason performs its most vital role by reaching the point at which it can be transcended by paradox. When we consider Browne's words in relation to Ishmael's, the implicit positioning of Ishmael as a latter-day Browne becomes clear: Ishmael's physical daring in sailing unknown seas in the physical sense is paralleled by Browne's spiritual daring during a time when Browne's England, like Melville's nineteenth-century America, was marked by intense religious controversy.

Given this starting point, with its emphasis on Ishmael as a man who, like Browne, contemplates and relishes difference, it is not surprising that we find extensive congruities between Browne's treatment of religious difference and Ishmael's as the novel goes on. Browne on Catholicism comes to resemble closely Ishmael's cogitations regarding Queequeg's faith. Browne announces, "I should violate my own arm rather than a church; nor willingly deface the name of Saint or Martyr. At the sight of a cross or crucifix I can dispense with my hat, but scarcely with the thought or memory of my Savior."[6] Browne's acceptance of the religious difference emblematized by the crucifix has a hard argumentative edge to it—is he suggesting that the Reformed Englishman who rejects the crucifix altogether can "[dispense] with the thought of [his] Savior"? Similarly, when Ishmael embraces religious difference, he also subtly anathematizes those who reject the possibility of dialogue among religious traditions. When he worships Yojo with Queequeg, it is precisely on the grounds of Christ's command to love one's neighbor as oneself, and one might suppose that any "infallible Presbyterian" who attacked Ishmael for his indulgence in pagan worship would be, like the unforgiving missionary woman in *Typee*, "not sufficiently evangelized" to love his neighbor fully (*M-D* 52; *Typee* 6–7).

The invocation of Browne's work *Pseudodoxia, or Vulgar Errors* in *Mardi* where Melville praises Browne for "hug[ing] all the mysteries of the Pentateuch" (*Mardi* 39), despite being Melville's most obvious nod toward Browne in his published work, can be misleading in relation to Melville's broader use of Browne's thought unless we recognize its implications for Browne and Melville's methods for managing religious difference. It is not so much Browne's attachment to "the mysteries of the Pentateuch" that proves compelling for Melville; rather, it is his ability to maintain a balance between openness to difference on the one hand and his maintenance of his own identity on the other. In *Religio Medici*, Browne is irenic toward his Catholic contemporaries *because* of his Anglican orthodoxy, even as Ishmael is able paradoxically to justify participating in pagan worship on impeccably Christian grounds. If Browne is a partisan of the universal Christian communion against national and sectarian bigotry, Ishmael is a partisan of humanity as a whole against Christian exclusivism.

In light of these arguments, a reasonable question might seem to be, given that both Melville's reading and direct stylistic appropriation of Browne has largely been associated with *Mardi* and *Moby-Dick*, where then does the "crack'd Archangel" so evident in *Mardi* and *Moby-Dick* go during the latter portion of Melville's career? Can Browne best be understood as a shadow that inflects Melville's work during the most ambitious phase of his prose and then flits away, displaced by other models? For an answer, I suggest that we turn to Melville's most ambitious and comprehensive post-*Moby-Dick* work, *Clarel.*

In the canto "Of Rama," Melville enters a sector of religious experience that Browne simply dismissed as "Paganism." Melville devotes the canto to a meditation on the Hindu deity Rama, who becomes associated in *Clarel* with Rolfe, a figure often regarded as a stand-in for Melville himself. Indeed, Rolfe is the figure who most resembles Browne's *Religio Medici* persona in the body of Melville's work after *Moby-Dick*. He voices skepticism while admiring the moral possibilities contained within a range of faiths, and his mixture of irony, aspiration, and melancholy makes him the truest successor to Ishmael in Melville's later work. Repeatedly in *Clarel*, Rolfe plays the role of the keen-eyed observer who is able to draw together disparate strands in his fellow travelers' arguments, and to listen to a broad range of views with sympathy and respect. It is noteworthy as well that the use of paired words and concepts that Foley identifies as a sign of Browne's influence in *Mardi* and *Moby-Dick* appears repeatedly in this stanza: in describing Rolfe as a nineteenth-century avatar of Rama (himself an avatar of Vishnu), Melville's narrator states regarding Rolfe and others like him: "Theirs be the thoughts that dive and skim / Theirs the spiced tears that overbrim / And theirs the dimple and the lightsome whim" (*Clarel* 1.32.35–37.) Melville thus reproduces one of the syntactic arrangements he derived from Browne while describing a character whose personality resembles the persona that Browne developed in his prose. Significantly, Rolfe's resemblance to Rama provides evidence of his sanctification in Christian terms: we are told that Rolfe has "never the Holy Spirit grieved"—thus suggesting both Rama's balancing of the human and divine in Hindu terms and suggesting in Christian terms that Rolfe is among the elect rather than the reprobate. The use of the Hebrew and Christian scriptures and Christian doctrine as a framework for embracing rather than assaulting religious difference continues even after *Clarel*, as in his late poem "Buddha," Melville ties the first chapter of the Epistle of James to central elements within Theravada Buddhism.

Melville's relation to Browne, then, is not simply that of a pupil to a master of literary style. Rather, Melville found in Browne an intellectual model for the engagement with questions of religious difference that characterized Melville's entire career. Along the way, Melville increased the scope of both Browne's questioning of his own faith and his empathy for other faiths far beyond anything Browne would have recognized (or perhaps even desired). Nonetheless, Browne continued to provide a model that could allow Melville to perform a precarious balancing act among multiple modalities of faith and doubt. The "shock of recognition" that Melville experienced upon reading Browne's *Religio Medici* led not merely to imitation, but to a lifelong endeavor to define the contours of Melville's own fractured belief. The larger question of the substance of this fractured belief is most clearly addressed in Melville's biblical marginalia, especially strikingly in the copy of *The New Testament and Psalms* that he was given by his aunt Jean Melville early in his career as a writer, but also in the Hebrew scriptures and in the Apocrypha.[7]

Reading the Bible: Religious Difference and Sacred Texts

Melville's reading of the Bible is vast in its implications, and it is worth beginning our consideration of this aspect of Melville's religious and creative engagements with a representative moment of reflection on the act of reading itself. In Melville's seventh novel, *Pierre, or the Ambiguities* (1852), as Pierre Glendinning is wrestling in vain with the task of producing a book that will measure up to the titanic ambitions of his soul, Melville's consistently intrusive narrator breaks in to meditate on the meaning of nature for the novelist:

> Say what some poets will, Nature is not so much her own ever sweet interpreter, as the mere supplier of that cunning alphabet, whereby combining and selecting as he pleases, each man reads his own peculiar lesson according to his own peculiar mind and mood. (*Pierre* 343)

If we substitute "Scripture" for "Nature" in this formulation, we have a fair understanding of the approach that Melville took to reading the Bible. Melville's reading of these sacred texts is shaped neither by the submissiveness of the conventional religious reader, nor by the titanic skepticism and scorn of some of his own most famous characters. Rather, Melville's reading of the Bible is shaped by sometimes competing, sometimes complementary methods of analyzing, rearranging, interpreting, and questioning the narrative and poetic structures, ethical and dogmatic assertions, and personal and social resonances in the texts at hand.[8]

More than anything else, Melville's markings of his copy of the New Testament and Psalms make clear how inextricably his personal religious thought is intertwined with his sense of vocation as a novelist and a poet. First, in his reading of the Gospels, particularly in relation to Jesus's parables and the development of Jesus's character, Melville's markings show a novelist who is intent on both developing his craft and justifying his particular methods of communicating the truth through fiction. Second, in his markings of the Sermon on the Mount and the Epistles, Melville is revealed to be strongly attracted to the most uncompromising ethical doctrines associated with Christianity, and this passionate concern with ethics is reflected throughout Melville's fiction and poetry. Third, in his markings of the Psalms, the Gospel of John, and the Pauline Epistles, Melville demonstrates a strong interest in natural theology and in the capacity of human beings for comprehension of and absorption into the divine, revealing that although Melville is sometimes regarded as a misanthrope, he can perhaps best be described as a wounded lover of humanity, at times ungodly precisely because of his passionate belief in the godlikeness of men and women. Fourth, throughout his markings of *The New Testament and Psalms*, Melville reveals that his reading of these texts is intensely personal, addressing concerns about money and relationships, fears about his own sanity and spiritual status, and, quite frequently, feelings of hurt and resentment at the rejection he experienced from his audience and the machinations of his personal enemies. Each of these strands gives us a unique insight into Melville as a man and as a novelist.

The Craft of Writing and the Stories of Jesus

Melville marks the Gospels far more heavily than any other portion of the New Testament. Among the synoptic Gospels, he demonstrates a strong preference for Matthew, the longest of the three, and the Gospel that contains the fullest statement of many of the parables and of Jesus's social ethics as expounded in the Sermon on the Mount. Melville also marks the Gospel of John heavily, with particular attention to the contrast between exclusivist messages of judgment and damnation and inclusivist messages of universal love and human dignity.

What becomes very evident in Melville's annotations to the Gospel of Matthew is that he is very concerned with the person of Jesus on two levels. First, he is very interested in the development of Jesus's character throughout the Gospel accounts. The portrait of Jesus that emerges through Melville's annotations is that of the heroic outsider who dares to speak the truth and is willing to express bitterness at the ways in which the truth is frequently betrayed. Jesus becomes for Melville both a model for the most desirable traits in many of his characters and a plumb line against which to measure the possibilities of humanity. Second, Melville is interested in Jesus as a fellow teller of stories. Melville scores Jesus's parables frequently, and even more than the parables themselves, Melville focuses on the moments when Jesus discusses his method as a teller of parables.

In the first passage from Matthew that Melville marks, Jesus's courage and personality are paralleled by those of his forerunner, John the Baptist. Melville scores both the reference in Matthew 3.3 to John as "a voice crying in the wilderness" and the description of his idiosyncratic manner of dress (camel's hair and a leathern girdle) and diet (locusts and honey) in Matthew 3.4. Here we see Melville making use of the "cunning alphabet" provided by the New Testament to inspire characters for his fiction, because the description of the mad prophet Elijah in *Moby-Dick* draws heavily on the description of John here (*M-D* 91–94). Moreover, when Melville describes the relation of "Vivenza" (a thinly disguised allegorical portrait of the United States) to the rest of the world in *Mardi*, he also draws on the imagery in this verse:

> Or Vivenza might be likened to St. John, feeding on locusts and wild honey, and with a prophetic voice crying to the nations from the wilderness. Or, child-like, standing among the old robed kings and emperors of the archipelago, Vivenza seemed a young Messiah, to whose discourse the bearded Rabbis bowed. (*Mardi* 472)

Notably, Melville connects this imagery of America as John the Baptist to imagery of America as the young Jesus instructing his elders in the temple of Jerusalem (a passage not marked in Melville's New Testament). This connection is developed in Melville's markings of the narrative of Jesus's life, and particularly in his concern with Jesus's personal authority, and the contrast between this personal authority and the institutional authority of the scribes with whom he argued.

Melville's concern with Jesus's character and authority becomes evident even before the reader of the marginalia turns to the Gospels themselves. On the inside flyleaf, Melville has inscribed a lengthy quotation, which James Duban and Clare Spark have recently and independently identified as being from Thomas Carlyle's translation of Goethe's *Wilhelm Meister's Travels*.[9] The quotation is worth considering in its entirety, since it sheds much light on both Melville's view of Jesus and his view of the ideal form of humanity:

> In life he appears as a true Philosopher—as a wise man in the highest sense. He stands *firm to his point; he goes on his way inflexibly*; and while he exalts the lower to himself, while he makes the ignorant, the poor, the rich, partakers of his wisdom, of his riches, of his strength, he, on the other hand, in no sense conceals his divine origin; he dares to equal himself with God; nay, to declare that he himself is God.
>
> In this manner is he wont from youth upwards *to astound his familiar friends*; of these he gains a part to his own cause; irritates the rest against him; and shows to all men, who are aiming at a certain elevation in doctrine and in life, what *they have to look for from the world*.
>
> And thus, for the nobler portion of mankind, his walk and conversation are even more instructive and profitable than his death; for to those trials every one is called, to this trial but a few [italics indicate passages Melville underscored]. (*MMO* 65)

This inscription is highly instructive. The quotation is ambiguous in its relation to the orthodox Christian doctrine of the Incarnation, but it clearly indicates that Jesus is a model to be followed by "the nobler portion of mankind." The first excerpt that Melville underscores emphasizes the degree to which Jesus was a nonconformist, a characteristic that Melville bestows on all of his most interesting characters, those who possess religious faith, those who reject it, and those who remain uncertain. The lines "he stands firm to his point; he goes on his way inflexibly" could be applied to a devout character such as Father Mapple, but they could also be applied to a daemonic character such as Captain Ahab. Figures who are associated entirely with neither faith nor blasphemous rebellion also partake of this trait: Bartleby, Billy Budd, and characters such as Celio and Ungar, in *Clarel*. Jesus's capacity to "astound his familiar friends" and to show humans "what they have to look for from the world" is derived in part from his divine inflexibility.

Melville's interest in Jesus's capacity to "astonish" appears clearly in his response to Matthew 7.28–29, when the people are "astonished" by the fact that Jesus taught "as one having authority, and not as one of the scribes." Melville marked this passage with an "x" and wrote annotations in both the top and bottom margins. That these annotations are potentially scandalous is evident from the fact that the top and bottom margins to this page have been clipped out of Melville's New Testament. The fact that the annotations have been clipped out obviously means that any attempt to recover Melville's observations will be guesswork, but I would suggest that the annotations in this case might likely reflect a sympathetic identification with Jesus's "authority" as a teacher, and a particularly vitriolic dismissal of contemporary "scribes" such as pedantic and self-righteous book reviewers. Throughout the Gospels, Melville continued to mark passages that relate to the sense of authority that Jesus projected through his teaching and the contrast between Jesus's teaching and that of his more established contemporaries.

Melville's markings reveal, in addition to an interest in Jesus's authority, a strong interest in Jesus's humanity. Particularly in the Gospel of Matthew, Melville marks passages that seem to show Jesus behaving in odd or idiosyncratic ways. For example, Melville makes a point of scoring the moment in Matthew 21.18–19 when Jesus curses a fig tree because it does not have any fruit. Cursing a fig tree simply because it lacked fruit seems like a petulant act, rather than the sort of thing that one would expect from either God incarnate or the "true Philosopher" described in the flyleaf inscription. Nonetheless, Melville's emphasis on Jesus's divine inflexibility as described in the inscription seems appropriate here. The Jesus that appears in this passage is not a figure who can be easily tamed by the expectations of the pious; rather, he remains a figure with the capacity to surprise and disturb readers.

This interest in Jesus as a character becomes even more pronounced in Melville's marginalia to the events leading up to the crucifixion. In Matthew 26.45, Melville underscores the moment when Jesus says to his disciples "Sleep on now, and take your rest," and writes at the top of the page, "This is ironical." Melville's interest in Jesus's use of irony in this passage is significant. Melville was a consummate ironist himself, and at this particular moment, he seems to identify strongly with the sarcastic tone with which Jesus expresses his disappointment in his disciples. In the penultimate canto of *Clarel*, Melville refers to Jesus as "our pure exemplar," and notations such as this one help to clarify what sort of exemplar Melville regards Jesus as being (*Clarel* 4.34.21). Melville's Jesus is susceptible of imitation precisely because of his readily evident humanity—his divine inflexibility is wedded to an emotional life that includes loss and frustration, and in giving this interior life expression, he manipulates verbal tropes expertly.

Jesus's status as an author of verbal texts as well as a person of authority becomes especially important in Melville's marginalia to passages relating to Jesus's parables. Given Melville's interest in double meanings, and his admiring description of Hawthorne's writing as intended to "deceive, egregiously deceive, the superficial skimmer of pages" (*PT* 251), it is not surprising that he marks passages relating to Jesus's parables in Matthew 13.10–11 heavily. The passage asserts that only some of Jesus's listeners could know "the mysteries of the kingdom of heaven," a gift that is closely correlated to the knowledge available to Melville's desired "eagle-eyed reader." Later in the same chapter (Matt. 13.34–35), Melville again scores a passage that discusses the nature of the parables:

> All these things spake Jesus unto the multitudes in parables; and without a parable spake he not unto them: That it might be fulfilled which was spoken by the prophet, saying, I will open my mouth in parables; I will utter things which have been kept secret from the foundation of the world.

Taken together, the two passages from Matthew 13 identify a parable as a story that conceals as much as it clarifies. The parables here are simultaneously hyperbolically revelatory (extending even the "things which have been kept hidden from the foundation of the world") and deliberately obscure (it is only to the disciples that it is "given" to know "the mysteries of the kingdom of heaven"). The image of Jesus that Melville's markings point to is of a storyteller who bewilders much of his audience precisely because he chooses to do so. *Imitatio Christi* may seem like an unlikely source for Melville's often perverse strategies for bewildering and estranging his audience, but Melville's markings in the Gospel of Matthew suggest that he regards Jesus's use of parables as a model for his own complex and sometimes off-putting narrative strategies. One of Melville's markings in the Gospel of John encapsulates this emphasis particularly well. In John 10.24, Jesus's interlocutors say to him, "How long dost thou make us to doubt? If thou be the Christ, tell us plainly." Melville has underscored the first sentence once and the second sentence twice, and drawn a line in the side margin. He has also written an annotation underneath that has since been thoroughly erased. The cadence of the first part of this verse is reminiscent of the line "Wherefore ripen us to pain?" from the epilogue to *Clarel* (21) and the line "How long dost thou make us to doubt?" is quoted directly in *Clarel* 1.13. The second part of the verse can be read in relation to Melville's own religious doubts and uncertainties. It can also be read as the irritable cry of an audience tired of ambiguity, with Melville identifying himself with Jesus as an author who refuses to be unambiguously plain. The epistemological uncertainty that forms such an important part of Melville's work, both thematically and in terms of his authorial strategies, is thus closely correlated to Melville's reading of the Gospels.

Melville's interest in Jesus's rhetorical strategies and in the theme of uncertainty associated with the parables extends as well to the scenes in the Gospels in which Jesus answers questions posed for him by his disciples. In John 9.2, Jesus's disciples ask him whether a man's blindness is the result of his own sin or that of his parents. Melville's marginal comment is that "This leading question seems evaded in the following verses." Melville's interest seems to be piqued particularly by the questions that Jesus does not answer directly and the places where he leaves room for doubt and interpretation. Melville reads *The New Testament and Psalms*, then, in large part as a novelist as well as a religious seeker, and his attraction to both the writers of the Gospel and to Jesus himself has at least something to do with their status as masters of narrative. Melville's focus on the person of Jesus is directly concerned as well, however, with the ethical precepts that Jesus taught.

The Scales of the New Testament: Ethics and Radical Christianity

Melville's resistance to being confined by a particular religious orthodoxy is rightly acknowledged by many scholars. This acknowledgment, however, can at times obscure how deeply engaged Melville was by the ethical precepts of Christianity. This engagement is evident in Melville's extensive markings of the Sermon on the Mount in Matthew and of the ethically directed moments in the Epistles.

Melville marks the Sermon on the Mount (Matt. 5–7) at regular intervals, focusing on Jesus's strong words on divorce, wealth and poverty, and what Melville calls in *Pierre* the "gratuitous return of good for evil" (*Pierre* 215). Melville's markings are heaviest in Matt. 5, where he marks verse 22, which equates anger with murder; verses 27–28, which equate lust with adultery; verse 32, which equates divorce with adultery; verses 33–37, which condemn the swearing of oaths and command listeners to "let your communication be Yea, Yea; Nay, Nay"; verses 38–39, which reject the older saying "an eye for an eye, a tooth for a tooth" in favor of the command to "turn the other cheek" when attacked; verses 40–42, which command generous giving; and finally verse 44, which concludes "Love your enemies, bless them that curse you, do good to them that hate you, and pray for them that despitefully use you."

Melville was hardly the first or the last to be drawn to this severe and compelling code of ethics, nor was he the first or last to remark on the seemingly insuperable difficulties involved in living up to it. The degree to which he incorporated this chapter of the New Testament into his writing is striking, however. In *Typee*, Melville refers to a missionary woman who was "insufficiently evangelized" to return good for evil after being humiliated by islanders in the Marquesas (*Typee* 7). In *Mardi*, the philosopher Babbalanja interrogates the devout follower of Alma (who stands in for Jesus in the Mardian archipelago) who converses with Taji's band of travelers on the island of Serenia about the congruence between his community's beliefs and their lives:

> "Tell me not of your endeavors, but of your lives. What hope for the fatherless among you?"
> "Adopted as a son."
> "Of the one poor, and naked?"
> "Clothed, and he wants for naught."
> "If ungrateful, he smite you?"
> "Still we feed and clothe him." (*Mardi* 626)

Melville's emphasis on the ethics of the Sermon on the Mount is spelled out clearly in this passage. Babbalanja gives priority to ethics over dogma with his opening question, and he presses the follower of Alma to demonstrate his faith by means of actions that correspond to Jesus's specific commands in Matthew 5. The description of community life in Serenia parallels as well Acts 2.44–45, which is marked with a single line in the side margin, and which states, "And all that believed were together, and all had things in common; And sold their possessions and goods, and parted them to all men, as every man had need." Melville again places the Sermon on the Mount at the center of Christian belief in his fifth novel, *White-Jacket*, this time in the service of a frankly pacifist argument:

> Say on, say on; but know you this, and lay it to heart, you war-voting Bench of Bishops, that He on whom we believe *himself* [Melville's emphasis] has enjoined us to turn the left cheek if the right be smitten. Never mind what follows. That passage you cannot expunge from the Bible; that passage is as binding upon us as any other; that passage embodies the soul and substance of the Christian faith; without it, Christianity were like any other faith. And that passage will yet, by the blessing of God, turn the world. But in some things we must become Quakers first. (*WJ* 320)

In this passage, as in the passage from *Mardi* and even the humorous aside in *Typee*, human beings are shown to be "evangelized" precisely insofar as they are prepared to return good for evil. These passages make clear that when Ishmael refers to "the scales of the New Testament" in the opening chapter of *Moby-Dick*, the reference is to the strict measurement of virtue that Jesus has provided in Matthew 5. Moreover, Ishmael's moral reasoning, particularly when he chooses to worship Queequeg's idol Yojo, is drawn explicitly from the sort of ethical commands that Melville marks so heavily in the Gospel of Matthew. *Moby-Dick* is threaded with oblique references to the Sermon on the Mount, usually in relation to the Quaker doctrine of non-resistance. In chapter 81 of *Moby-Dick*, "The Pequod Meets the Virgin," Ishmael notes ruefully that the aged whale that Flask sadistically kills "must die the death and be murdered, to light the gay bridals and merry-makings of men, and also to illuminate the solemn churches that preach the inoffensiveness of all to all" (*M-D* 357). The "solemn churches" here can stand in for all of Christianity, but most specifically, they are the historic peace churches, such as the Quakers, Dunkers, and Mennonites, who reject violence altogether on the grounds of Jesus's words in the Sermon on the Mount. That Melville's interest in Christian pacifism extended beyond the Quakers is clear from his mention of the Dunkers, a small Pennsylvania German denomination that eschewed warfare, lawsuits, and the swearing of oaths, in *Israel Potter*, when he has Potter say, "Poor Richard ain't a Dunker, that's certain," in reference to Benjamin Franklin's worldly wisdom (*IP* 54). Interestingly, in light of Melville's mention of the Dunkers, he marks John 13.14–16 with a single line in the margin. These verses contain Jesus's command to the disciples to wash each other's feet, and foot-washing at every communion is a central element of Dunker practice.

The most extensive meditation on the code of ethics expounded in the Sermon on the Mount appears in *Pierre*. Melville continues to represent the Sermon on the Mount as a touchstone of moral wisdom, but he also includes an extensive critique of its applicability to contemporary life in the form of Plotinus Plinlimmon's pamphlet and the material prefatory to Pierre's reading of it. Melville's narrator begins by reflecting on a troubling contradiction: that the putatively Christian nations of Europe and America are the "most Mammonish" parts of the world. To comprehend this, he turns directly to the Sermon on the Mount, to which he refers as "the greatest real miracle of all religions" (*Pierre* 207–8). The narrator argues that the sublimity of the Sermon on the Mount makes the entire world seem false by comparison. Plinlimmon's pamphlet, then, seeks to comprehend the relationship of the Sermon on the Mount to the everyday world, and to discover whether one or the other must be a lie. Plinlimmon argues that the Sermon on the Mount can be true in a heavenly sense, while a "virtuous expediency" is the best code of ethics available for the modern world, and he suggests that the history of bloodshed within Christianity demonstrates that "the chronometrical gratuitous return of good for evil" cannot be considered true in the context of the modern world (*Pierre* 214).[10]

Plinlimmon's skepticism about the possibility (or even advisability) of living according to the standards of the Sermon on the Mount during the nineteenth century is dramatized in the closing scenes of *Pierre*, when Pierre chooses vengeance over the "gratuitous return of good for evil" when he confronts his cousin Glen. When Glen literally strikes Pierre on the cheek, leaving a "half-livid and half-bloody brand," Pierre not only fails to turn the other cheek, he fails by a wide margin to conform even to the older standard of "an eye for an eye," taking disproportionate vengeance by murdering Glen (*Pierre* 359). Pierre falls short of the standards of "virtuous expediency" in this case precisely because he has tried so hard to transcend them throughout the novel, but it is noteworthy that even in his miserable demise, Pierre is presented as a more admirable character than a figure like Reverend Falsgrave, who simply excuses himself from adhering to the demands of the Sermon on the Mount.

In Melville's copy of *The Holy Bible, with Apocrypha*, he likewise attends closely to matters of violence, warfare, and peacemaking. In the book of Judges, two patterns emerge: Melville marks moments where the Israelites credit God with gaining them military victory, and he marks repeatedly with check marks Samson's riddles that he directed toward the Philistines, and the Philistines' perplexed response to them, paralleling his interest in the parables of Jesus in the New Testament. Melville's concern with moments in the biblical text that appear to endorse violence fits closely with his general interest in pacifism and religious rationales for and critiques of pacifism. In Exodus 15.3, Melville underlined the sentence "The Lord is a man of war," a passage that would become a refrain for a poem in *Battle-Pieces* (*MM* 1.269). This interest in the tension between warfare and peacemaking, between the human capacity for both violence and the finding of divine approval for violence and the human capacity for peace and forgiveness, forms a major strand in Melville's work throughout his career.

"Bartleby, the Scrivener" and *The Confidence-Man* both engage the ethical precepts of the New Testament that Melville marked as well, and both seem to indicate Melville's pessimism about the possibility of applying the law of love to the nineteenth century. The narrator of "Bartleby, the Scrivener" recognizes that, according to the Gospel of Matthew, his obligation to look after Bartleby is as absolute as it is impractical according to the contemporary standards of Wall Street. Much of the pathos of the story is derived from the narrator's inability to synthesize the values of commercial society with the demands of the Sermon on the Mount. *The*

Confidence-Man begins with an invocation of 1 Corinthians 13, which spells out Paul's definition of Christian love, and asserts the primacy of love over even faith and hope. Melville marked the summary at the beginning of this chapter with a triple check mark in his New Testament.

This overriding concern for ethics appears as well in Melville's marginalia to Paul's Epistle to the Romans and the Epistle of James. Both Paul and James consider the relationship between faith and works using the example of Abraham as determinative for a proper understanding of the relative priority to be given to these two elements in Christian life and doctrine. Melville marks both of these moments, and his reaction is instructive. James 2.14, which rhetorically asks whether faith without works can save (and strongly implies that the answer is "no"), is marked with a check mark and a curved line in the side margin. James 2.18, in which the author concludes "shew me thy faith without thy works, and I will show you my faith by my works," is also marked with a curved line and a check mark. There is no indication here that Melville is expressing anything other than approval of the logic of the argument. Romans 4 is a different matter. Melville marks verse 5, which argues that someone who "worketh not but believeth on him that justifieth the ungodly, his faith is counted for righteousness" with a double line in the side margin. Melville marks verse 6, which describes the "blessedness of the man unto whom God imputeth righteousness without works" with an "x," and his comment on this verse at the bottom of the page has been erased. The evidence here suggests that Melville prefers James's emphasis on works to Paul's emphasis on faith. This decision to emphasize the importance of works to demonstrating the very existence of faith puts Melville on the Catholic side of the sixteenth-century controversies over justification (the Council of Trent's formulation was "faith working in love" as opposed to Martin Luther's "faith alone") and on the Arminian and Unitarian side of the nineteenth-century arguments over the same issue. This preference becomes particularly relevant to any reading of *Clarel*, a poem that expresses considerable sympathy for Catholic doctrine through the figures of the Dominican monk and Ungar.

The ethical precepts of the New Testament, which Melville marked with such consistency and thoroughness in his personal copy of the New Testament, are thus woven into Melville's fiction and poetry throughout his career. Melville's use of these precepts takes the form of an increasingly complex and nuanced series of thought experiments that explore whether these precepts can be applied consistently in the nineteenth century and beyond. Melville's attitude toward this portion of the New Testament seems to be one of admiration mixed with pessimism, and this pessimism increasingly shapes the tone and the mood of his later works. Melville resists concluding that the most rigorous ethical teachings in the New Testament are obligatory for nineteenth-century individuals, but he also resists classifying anything that falls short of adherence to these teachings as a true or meaningful form of Christianity. This resistance shows sympathy with both the "counsels of perfection" associated with Roman Catholic and Eastern Orthodox monasticism and with the strand of perfectionism within Protestantism associated with the Radical Reformation.

Humanity, Thou Strong Thing: The Incarnation and Humanism

Melville's fascination with the person of Jesus and with the content of his ethical teachings can best be understood in light of how he relates Jesus to the rest of humanity. Two passages from Melville's work are especially pertinent here. In *The Encantadas*, Melville relates the story of Hunilla, an abandoned widow whose sufferings and faithfulness rise to Christlike proportions. At the climax of Hunilla's story, Melville's narrator cries out, "Humanity, thou strong thing, I worship thee, not in the laurelled victor, but in this defeated one" (*PT* 157). In this story, the trope of redemptive suffering from the Gospels is applied to all of humanity, and most specifically to those who are among the "defeated." This extension of Christlikeness to the great mass of human beings is repeated emphatically in *Clarel*. Ungar, a Catholic ex-Confederate soldier of Cherokee descent, reflects on the meaning of the crucifixion:

> This type's assigned
> To one who, sharing not man's mind
> Partook man's frame; whose mystic birth
> Wrecked him on this reef of earth
> Inclement and inhuman. Yet,
> Through all the trials that beset,
> He leaned on an upholding arm—
> Foreknowing, too, reserves of balm.
> But how of them whose souls may claim,
> Some link with Christ beyond the name,
> Which share the fate, but never share
> Aid or assurance, and nowhere
> Look for requital? Such there be
> In by-lanes o'er the world you see
> The Calvary faces . . . (*Clarel* 4.10.34–47)

Ungar links the "Calvary faces" of all those who are suffering with Jesus's suffering on the cross, and suggests that because they lack the "balm" of foreknowledge of ultimate victory, their plight may be even more severe. Melville's narrator reinforces this connection between Jesus's sufferings and the suffering of humanity in the penultimate canto of *Clarel* when he catalogs the assortment of Christians, Jews, and Muslims who are making their way through the streets of Jerusalem and refers to them as "cross-bearers all" (*Clarel* 4.34.44). Similarity to Christ's glory and pain, then, becomes the common fate of humanity, not the exclusive preserve of a particular branch of humanity.

Melville's markings reflect his reverence for humanity in two major ways. First, he tended to show suspicion and even anger in his marginalia to messages of Christian or Jewish exclusivism. Second, he frequently marked passages that emphasized the dignity of humanity and passages that suggested that salvation could be open to those outside the specifically Christian community. If Melville seems enamored of the ethical and social dimensions of Jesus's thought, as well as of Jesus's storytelling and personality, he is distinctly less attracted to messages of dogmatic exclusivism, as expressed frequently in the Gospel of John, the Epistle to the Romans, and the book of Revelation.

Perhaps the strongest expression of Melville's repugnance toward dogmatic exclusivism appears at the end of the book of Revelation. Melville's markings in the earlier portions of the Revelation do not clearly indicate whether he marks them out of agreement, skepticism, or simply as a possible source of imagery, but Rev. 22.19, the last verse of the New Testament, is a different matter entirely. The verse states that anyone who "shall take away from the words of the book of this prophecy, God shall take away his part of the book of life." Melville has drawn a box around the verse, drawn five vertical lines through the verse, and drawn a large X across the verse. His annotations at the bottom of the page have not merely been erased; rather, they have been cut out of the Bible with scissors. Melville's reaction to this passage was clearly intense and fiercely negative. Since there are only a few instances of marginalia being clipped out of the New Testament, it is worth asking why this passage elicited such a violent response. Notably, this passage appears to make salvation or damnation dependent not on an individual's actions or good will, but rather on his or her reaction to one particular element within Christian dogma. Melville's violent response to the verse can thus be correlated both to his preference for ethics over dogma, as expressed in his markings of James and Romans, and to his desire to find a message of hope in the Bible for those who were not explicitly members of the Christian faith. Similar moments appear in Melville's markings of the predestinarian passages in Romans 8–10, all of which lead to annotations that have been erased.

The converse of Melville's mix of fear and anger in regard to dogmatic exclusivism is his attraction to passages that exalt the moral and intellectual capacities of human beings. Whatever Melville's tendencies toward misanthropy, among the most salient aspects of Melville's religious thought that his markings in *The New Testament and Psalms* reveal are his profound reverence for human beings and his hopefulness that salvation is not restricted to those conventionally designated as Christians. This hopefulness is most evident in his numerous markings of passages that suggest that human beings may be able to derive the information required for salvation from nature and reason and of passages that comment explicitly on the dignity of human beings.

In the Psalms, Melville marked Psalm 8.3–5, a passage that eloquently considers the splendor of the universe and exults in the prominent position that God has given to human beings, identifying the position of humans as "a little lower than the angels." He also marked the summary at the beginning of the chapter, which reads, "God's glory is magnified by his works, and by his love to man" with triple check marks. Perhaps even more significantly for an understanding of Melville's humanism, he also marked Psalm 19.1–5 with a single line in the side margin. The verses read:

> The heavens declare the glory of God; and the firmament shewest his handy work. Day unto day uttereth speech and night unto night sheweth knowledge. There is no speech nor language where their voice is not heard. Their line has gone out through all the earth, and their words to the end of the world. In them hath he set a tabernacle for the sun, Which is as a bridegroom coming out of his chamber, and rejoiceth as a strong man to run a race. (*MMO* 65)

This passage serves as a basis for believing that human beings can know a great deal about the divine from observing the natural world, and it strikes a universalistic note by suggesting that observation of the natural world transcends language and culture.

These markings in the Psalms are paralleled by several important markings in the New Testament. Melville scored Matthew 12.42, which compares the "queen of the south" favorably with the "present generation," with a check mark. The queen of the south, also known as the Queen of Sheba, is significant for her decision to seek out King Solomon because of his reputation for wisdom. She was not a member of the Israelite nation, but her earnest seeking after truth is honored by Jesus in this passage. Melville develops his own satirical version of this contrast between the virtuous unbeliever and the vicious believer in *Moby-Dick* when he writes, echoing Jesus's words in Matthew 10.15:

> I tell you it will be more tolerable for the Feejee that salted down a lean missionary in his cellar against a coming famine; it will be more tolerable for that provident Feejee, I say, in the day of judgment, than for thee, civilized and enlightened gourmand, who nailest geese to the ground and feastest on their bloated livers in thy pate-de-foie-gras. (*M-D* 300)

The idea that nature, reason, and the earnest pursuit of truth can lead to valid knowledge about the divine is also expressed in Romans 1.19–20, which Melville marks with the single line in the margin: "For the invisible things of him from the creation of the world are clearly seen, being understood by the things that are made." In the Gospel of John, the source of many of the most exclusivist passages that Melville scores, and at times argues with (for example, in his reference to Jesus's words "Salvation is of the Jews" in John 3.22 as "a partisan hope"), Melville marks John 12.47, which reads, "And if any man hear my words and believe not, I judge him not: for I came not to judge the world, but to save the world." Melville's ecumenical sense appears in his markings in the Hebrew Bible as well. In his copy of the *Holy Bible with Apocrypha* that he was given in 1846, Melville wrote with regard to the robes of the Aaronic priesthood as described in the book of Exodus, 39.23, "Like the chasuble of the Catholic priest to day" (*MM* 1.271). Melville's interest in tracking the congruities between two religious traditions (modern Catholicism and ancient predecessors for modern Judaism) that could be seen as alternatives to modern Protestantism proved to be highly characteristic throughout his career.

Melville also seems to have been strongly drawn to New Testament passages that connected the preaching of the apostles to pre- or non-Christian philosophers. He underlined and marked Paul's reference in Acts 17.28 to "your own poets" with an "x" and a note at the bottom that identified Aratus as the poet to whom Paul is referring. Melville also identified the "prophet of their own" who is quoted in Titus 1.12 as saying that "Cretians [*sic*] are all liars" as Epiminedes. Nathalia Wright and Mark Heidmann have both confirmed that the identities of these two figures were widely available in nineteenth-century biblical commentaries.[11]

What seems of particularly compelling interest, however, is the fact that Melville bothered to track these references down. In light of both his markings in the Bible and his favorable descriptions of the South Seas islanders in general in *Typee* and *Omoo* and of Queequeg in particular in *Moby-Dick*, Melville's interest in the presence of classical philosophers and poets in the New Testament can serve as yet another instance of his impulse toward inclusivism.

Melville's inscription on the back flyleaf of his copy of *The New Testament and Psalms* is immensely helpful in understanding this strand in his marginalia, and indeed, Melville himself points to the back flyleaf in his marginal notations on John 10.34–6, where he writes, "See the flyleaf at the end." The reader who takes this hint and turns to the rear flyleaf finds the following: On the flyleaf itself, there is an inscription in ink that reads:

> Who well considers the Christian religion, would think that God meant to keep it in the dark from our understandings, and make it turn upon the motions of our hearts.
>
> St. Everemont [*sic*]

This is followed by a longer inscription, which James Duban has identified as coming from Thomas Carlyle's translation of Goethe's *Wilhelm Meister's Apprenticeship* on the inside of the back cover:[12]

> If we conceive it possible, that the creator of the world himself assumed the form of his creature, and lived in that manner for a time upon the earth, this creature must seem to us of infinite perfection, because susceptible of such a combination with his maker. Hence in our idea of God man [*sic*] there can be no inconsistency with our idea of God: and if we often feel a certain disagreement with Him & remoteness from Him, it is but the more on that account our duty, not like advocates of the wicked spirit, to keep our eyes constantly on the nakedness and wickedness of our nature: but rather to seek out every property & beauty, by which our pretension to similarity with the Divinity may be made good. (*MMO* 65)

This quotation makes the Christian doctrine of the incarnation of Christ the grounds for the godlikeness of humanity. It prefigures the more stirring moments in nineteenth-century Unitarian sermons such as William Ellery Channing's "Likeness to God," where Channing argues that the foremost duty of human beings is to recognize and develop the glimmerings of divinity within their own souls, and it parallels Ralph Waldo

Emerson's claim in "The Divinity School Address" that Jesus's greatness consists in his status as a representative of human possibility.[13] The fact that Melville bothered to include this inscription in ink at the end of his copy of *The New Testament and Psalms* indicates that he found the ideas expressed in it appealing. Any conclusions about Melville's agreement with the passage must, however, be tempered by the fact that he wrote an annotation at the bottom of the back cover that has since been erased so vigorously that no words or even individual letters have been recovered. Both the Melville who was sufficiently attracted to this passage to reproduce it in ink and the Melville who added an annotation that was sufficiently scandalous that a conscientious family member eradicated it completely appear in the pages of Melville's novels.

Melville's writing on religion in *Mardi* illustrates the grounds for his affinity with the quotation from Goethe through the words of the old man from Serenia, who expounds his faith in Alma, who allegorically represents Jesus in the Mardian archipelago:

> All that is vital in the Master's faith, lived here in Mardi, and in humble dells was practiced, long previous to the Master's coming. But never before was virtue so lifted up among us, that all might see; never before did rays from heaven descend to glorify it. But are Truth, Justice, and Love the revelations of Alma alone? Were they never heard of till he came? Oh! Alma but opens unto us our own hearts. Were his precepts strange, we would recoil—not one feeling would respond; whereas, once hearkened to, our souls embrace them as with the instinctive tendrils of a vine. (*Mardi* 626)

The relationship between the old man's words and the quotes from Saint-Évremond and Goethe and the marked passage of John 10.34–36 is evident. The old man sees the greatness of Alma in his ability to dramatize the strains of goodness already present in the human heart. In John 10.34–36, Jesus argues that he cannot be accused of blasphemy for referring to himself as the Son of God because those "unto whom the word of God came" are referred to as gods in the law. This passage downplays the absolute distinction between Jesus and other men of good will that is built up at many other places in the Gospel of John, and with which Melville's markings often seem to argue. For example, earlier in the same chapter (John 10.8), Jesus says "All who came before me are thieves and robbers." Melville underscored the word "All," and wrote a comment at the bottom of the page that has been thoroughly erased, perhaps indicating that he took exception to the verse in a way that a family member might have regarded as impious. The juxtaposition of these two passages is helpful in understanding Melville's view of Jesus. Melville was attracted, as the front flyleaf indicates, by Jesus's divine inflexibility and godlikeness, but he also was drawn to the humanist position exemplified in the quotation on the rear flyleaf of seeing Jesus as a great exemplar who opens up the human heart to its own possibilities. It is noteworthy, however, in light of the erased annotation at the bottom of the passage from Goethe, that the travelers in *Mardi* ultimately do not remain with the followers of Alma, and that many portions of Melville's work, including Plotinus Plinlimmon's pamphlet and the characterization of Claggart in *Billy Budd*, stress the malignity of human nature alongside its more divine propensities. If Jesus's example reflects something of the grandeur of human moral possibilities, Melville is nonetheless unable to omit what in "Hawthorne and His Mosses" he calls "something, somehow like original sin" (*PT* 243). This tendency, which is at least partially antithetical to Melville's tendency to highlight the divinity of humanity, appears in Melville's frequent markings of Psalms that deplore the treachery and cruelty of the psalmist's enemies. The fact that Melville's reverence for human possibility coexists with a lively sense of the human capacity for cruelty and exploitation helps to explain why he so often, as in the case of Hunilla and the multi-religious "cross-bearers" in Jerusalem, uses the suffering of the innocent to bridge the gap between humanity and divinity.

The ambivalence toward America that surfaces so frequently in Melville's work is also closely related to the ambivalence about human nature that is reflected in the marginalia. For Melville, reverence for the godlike possibilities of humanity and American nationalism were closely related in the early portions of his career. In his more pessimistic moments in his later work, his critique of American hypocrisy easily slid into a sense of disillusionment with humanity as a whole. Melville draws heavily on New Testament tropes for redeemed humanity in his paeans to America in *Mardi*, *White-Jacket*, *Redburn*, and *Moby-Dick*. In *Mardi*, as noted above, Melville makes "Vivenza" both John the Baptist and the potential Messiah among the nations of the imaginary archipelago that serves as the setting for most of the novel. In *White-Jacket*, Melville continues this messianic imagery with a frequently quoted rhetorical flourish:

> Long enough have we been skeptics with regard to ourselves, and doubted whether, indeed, the political Messiah had come. But he has come in *us*, if we would but give utterance to his promptings. And let us always remember that with ourselves, almost for the first time in

> the history of earth, national selfishness is unbounded philanthropy; for we cannot do good to America but we give alms to the world. (*W-J* 151)

This faith in America's relation to the best possibilities within humanity is echoed as well in *Redburn*, when Melville refers directly to Acts 2.5, which he had marked with a single line in the side margin in his New Testament. The verse reads, "And there were dwelling in Jerusalem Jews, devout men, out of every nation under heaven," and the context is the descent of the Holy Spirit and the granting of the gift of tongues to the apostles. Melville applies this moment to the future of America in *Redburn*:

> Then shall the curse of Babel be revoked, a new Pentecost come, and the language they speak shall be the language of Britain. Frenchmen, and Danes, and Scots; and the dwellers on the shore of the Mediterranean and regions round about; Italians and Indians and Moors; there shall appear to them cloven tongues as of fire. (*Redburn* 169)

These passages, taken in concert with Ishmael's invocation of the "great democratic God" in *Moby-Dick*, indicate that in his early years Melville saw democracy in general and America in particular as an embodiment of the sort of human possibility that he found in *The New Testament and Psalms* (*M-D* 117). That he revised this view later in his career can be seen from Ungar's pessimistic conclusion to his meditation on America in *Clarel*: "To Terminus build fanes / No new world to mankind remains" (*Clarel* 4.22.157).

Melville's marginalia to Romans 13 may be of help in understanding his more restrained response to human possibilities in his later years. In this chapter, Paul exhorts the Romans to be obedient to even unjust state authority, emphasizing in verse 4, a passage that Melville scored with an "x" in the margin, that the magistrate is "the minister of God, a revenger to execute wrath upon him that doeth evil." Melville's poetry gives us reason to suspect that this chapter was resonant for him. In one of Melville's grimmest Civil War poems, "The House-Top," Melville revisits the question of authority and seems to approve, however ambivalently, of the policy modeled on "wise Draco" that subdues the mobs of rioters who have been committing atrocities on the streets of New York, and he concludes by acknowledging the "grimy slur on the Republic's faith implied / Which holds that man is naturally good, / and—more—is nature's Roman, never to be scourged" (*PP*, *"The House-Top,"* lines 25–27). In

Clarel, Ungar's argument in defense of the Catholic Church is based in no small part on the need for civil order, and Melville's final work, *Billy Budd*, probes the relationship between wisdom and authority relentlessly. The reverence for human possibility implied by the quotation from Goethe and numerous of Melville's markings in the New Testament is set against a stark acknowledgment of the actual failings of human beings.

This chastened sense of human possibility is all the more evident in Melville's Old Testament markings. Job and Ecclesiastes are two of the most frequently marked books from the Hebrew Bible for Melville, a pattern which forecasts Melville's high level of engagement with wisdom literature in *Moby-Dick*. The patterns derived from Job are quite central to *Moby-Dick* and have frequently been noted. The reflections in Ecclesiastes on the vanity of human desire and existence are woven more subtly into the text, but they predominate in such passages as the reverie on Solomonic wisdom at the conclusion of the "Try-Works" chapter, and it seems fair to say that Ishmael combines a Stoic and a Solomonic sense of human limitations and of the vanity of much of human desire and pleasure.

"The Only Kind of Faith—One's Own": Melville's Spiritual Autobiography

Taken in relation to his fiction and poetry, Melville's marginalia to *The New Testament and Psalms* form a compelling and illuminating chapter in his spiritual autobiography. Melville's annotation to Romans 14.22 is significant in this regard. Melville underlined the sentence "Hast thou faith? Have it to thyself before God" and wrote in the top margin, "The only kind of Faith—one's own." Melville's markings in *The New Testament and Psalms* contribute greatly to our understanding of his own faith and how it related to his personal life.

Melville's markings in the Psalms are in many cases intensely personal. He frequently marks the "cursing Psalms"—Psalms that express an often ferocious wish for the judgment of God to befall the psalmist's enemies. Melville's interest in these particular Psalms may seem to contradict his admiration for the Sermon on the Mount and his reverence for the god-like possibilities of humanity, but the contradiction is one that Melville himself acknowledged in his letters. In May 1851 Melville wrote to Nathaniel Hawthorne, "It seems an inconsistency to assert unconditional democracy in all things, and yet confess a dislike to all of mankind—in the mass. But not so" (*Corres.* 191). Melville's markings of Psalms that condemn the treachery and wickedness of the psalmist's enemies demonstrates that his humanism was tempered by a clear realization of the cruelty and malignity of which humans are capable.

That personal treachery attracted Melville's attention frequently is evident from his careful marking of the story of Judas Iscariot in the Gospel of John. Melville marked John 12.4–6, a passage in which Judas suggests that the ointment that a repentant woman has used to perfume Jesus's feet should have been sold in order to give the proceeds to the poor. The passage concludes that the real reason for Judas's philanthropy is that he intended, as the treasurer for the disciples, to embezzle the money for his own use. Melville also marked John 13.29, this time with an "x" and a subsequently erased notation. In this passage, the disciples speculate that Judas's exit from the Last Supper is for the purpose of distributing alms to the poor. The case of Judas highlights the fact that for Melville, questions of enmity and treachery are often closely related to financial matters.

Melville is also strikingly consistent in marking for comment passages related to marriage, divorce, and family life. This feature of his marginalia sheds light both on some of the most hotly debated biographical questions about Melville and on a strand of passages connected with these matters that runs through his work. As noted above, Melville scored Jesus's prohibition of divorce in the Sermon on the Mount, and he also scored 1 Corinthians 7, which deals with the relative benefits of marriage and celibacy. The markings and annotations for 1 Corinthians 7 are especially tantalizing. Melville marks 1 Corinthians 7.40, which comes at the end of an extended argument that those who are unmarried ought to remain so. Melville scored the last clause of this verse, "I think also that I have the spirit of God." Melville underlined the words "I think" and marked the end of the sentence with an "x." Most of the annotation at the bottom of this page has been obliterated, but the words that are still visible are "I too am uncertain." Given the content of the chapter as a whole, Melville must have been drawn to this passage by the discussion of the relative merits of celibacy and marriage. The moment he marks, however, is richly suggestive. Is Melville's comment directed toward his uncertainty about his own marriage? Toward the institution of marriage in general? Or, perhaps, is this a moment in which Melville acknowledges the anguish that comes with uncertainty about whether one truly possesses the "Spirit of God"? It may well be that all of these elements are behind Melville's partially erased annotation, but without a doubt this annotation illustrates Melville's concern with passages dealing with the advisability of marriage, a concern that is significant in light of Melville's own marital difficulties.

Perhaps the most poignant markings to be found in Melville's copy of *The New Testament and Psalms* are those that deal with loss and comfort. He marks the psalmists' pleas for comfort, Jesus's promise of a comforter to be sent after his ascension, and the promise that in the New Jerusalem every tear will be wiped away. In both Matthew 23.37–38 and Luke 13.34–35, Melville marks heavily the moments at which Jesus weeps over Jerusalem. In these passages, Jesus weeps over a Jerusalem "which killest the prophets" and expresses longing to gather "thy children together as a hen doth gather her brood under her wings." Melville's close attention to these verses is characteristic of both his concern with matters of suffering and solace, and his pessimism about the possibility of communicating truth to the wider public, which is largely distinguished in the passages that Melville marks in the Gospels by its eagerness to do away with prophets.

These markings throughout the Bible, with their powerful personal allusiveness, open the way for Melvilleans to ponder what Melville's response to the biblical text suggests about the contours of his own religious thought. I would suggest the following tentative conclusions. First, readings of Melville's religious thought that portray him as either an unambivalent skeptic or as an ultimately reconciled believer seem incomplete in light of the complexity of his marginal responses to scripture. A careful reading of Melville's marginalia to the New Testament and Psalms suggests that Ishmael's famous description of the interdependency of faith and doubt as consisting of "doubts of all things earthly and intuitions of some things heavenly" might indeed be of profound autobiographical significance for Melville (*Moby-Dick* 374). Second, it is perhaps impossible to draw the line where Melville the individual wrestler with faith and doubt ends and Melville the artist begins. Melville's reading of the Bible is integrated thoroughly with his fiction and poetry, and his marginalia reflect the same oscillation between reverence and blasphemy and hope and despair. Third, Melville's markings in the New Testament reflect the same fascination with and careful attention to religious and cultural difference that plays such a vital role in his writing. Melville marks numerous passages that serve as flash points of controversy between Catholicism and Protestantism, Calvinism and Arminianism, magisterial Protestantism and Anabaptism, and Unitarianism and Evangelicalism. Ultimately, Melville's marking of these passages seems to point, not to a definitive choice of one of these theological and philosophical options, but rather to Melville's ability to manipulate contradictory understandings of Christianity as part of the spiritual "alphabet" that he uses in crafting his fiction and poetry. Finally, Melville's religious thought, with all the instabilities and inconsistencies that are illuminated by reading the marginalia in relation to his fiction and poetry, contributes immensely to any compelling portrait of his personality as an author or as an individual. Melville himself hints at this in *White-Jacket*:

> Yet though all this be so, nevertheless, in our own hearts, we mold the whole world's hereafters; and in our own hearts we fashion our own gods. Each mortal casts his vote for whom he will to rule the worlds; I have a voice that helps to shape eternity; and my volitions stir the orbits of the furthest suns. In two senses, we are precisely what we worship. Ourselves are Fate. (*WJ* 320–21)

From the markings and words of Melville's marginalia to *The New Testament and Psalms*, and from the resultant echoes in his vast oeuvre of fiction and poetry, we begin to descry the contours of Melville's "own faith" and "own gods." Melville's deeply personal and idiosyncratic reading of the Bible becomes still more pronounced in its particularity when we turn to his markings in the Hebrew Bible and the Apocrypha.

Alternative Gospels: Melville's Interlocutors across the Centuries

The Apocrypha play, as we shall see, a very significant role in the concluding chapters of *The Confidence-Man*. It is perhaps not surprising, then, that Melville marked his copy of the Apocrypha heavily, most especially the Wisdom of Solomon and the Wisdom of Jesus the son of Sirach, or Ecclesiasticus. As in Job and in the New Testament book of Titus, Melville demonstrated his awareness of biblical criticism by referring to the philosophical components of the thought of the authors, noting in the case of the Wisdom of Solomon that "this admirable book seems partly Mosaic & partly Platonic in its tone. Who wrote it I know not. Some one to whom both Plato and Moses stood for godfather" (*MM* 1.315). In Ecclesiasticus (Sirach), meanwhile, Melville marks heavily those passages dealing with friendship, and in 2 Esdras those passages dealing with the sea. It is plain that Melville ransacked these books with a promiscuous eye for his favorite themes, and it is equally plain that religious syncretism was among those he looked for most carefully.

Melville's interest in the degree to which syncretism inhered in seemingly undiluted religious traditions is quite evident here: if Plato and Moses can both stand for the godfather of a biblical writing, then Christianity is mingled in its very origins with other religious and philosophical traditions. Melville's awareness of the schools of biblical criticism that demonstrated that the genealogy of the Hebrew and Christian scriptures included Greek and Egyptian sources has been well documented, and in his journals from his voyage to Egypt, he comments quite explicitly on his speculations regarding the genesis of monotheism:

> I shudder at the idea of the ancient Egyptians. It was in these pyramids that was conceived the idea of Jehovah. Terrible mixture of the cunning and the awful. Moses learned in all the lore of the Egyptians. The idea of Jehovah born here. . . . Only people who made their mark, both in their masonry & their religion (through Moses). . . . Pyramids still loom before me—something vast, indefinite, incomprehensible, awful. These the steps Jacob lay at. (*Journals* 75–76)

These fragmentary notes point to Melville's ongoing attempts to understand the origins of his own hereditary faith, forming the backdrop for many of Melville's reflections on the genesis of Judaism and Christianity in *Clarel* and elsewhere in his later poetry. Melville's work is characterized by a consistent search for the roots of the religious traditions that he encountered throughout his life, and his reading formed his most important tool for seeking out the genesis of the religious traditions of humanity. Melville's interest in a broad array of religious traditions led him to seek out alternative scriptures from a variety of written sources.

Melville's seemingly violent reaction to the final passage that he marked in the book of Revelation thus points us toward a crucial fact about his religious thought. Like Thoreau, Emerson, and many of Melville's contemporaries, Melville recognized and was energized by the thought that there were more scriptures available to humanity than the Hebrew and Christian scriptures, and his reading demonstrates that he cast his nets as widely as possible as he searched for new scriptures to explore. In some cases, Melville interacted with sources that drew heavily upon the Hebrew and Christian scriptures, most notably Milton's *Paradise Lost*; in other cases he looked at texts which described other world religions or ancient classical religious or philosophical options.

Melville's reading of Milton demonstrates his interest in the reinterpretation of Hebrew and Christian sacred texts. The work that Hershel Parker and Robin Grey have put into identifying and commenting upon Melville's marginalia on Milton means that we can now draw some rather precise conclusions with regard to Melville's use of Milton and the way in which Milton fits into Melville's broader understanding of religious difference.[14] Several patterns stand out in Melville's markings in *The*

Poetical Works of John Milton. Melville marked the biographical note at the beginning of his copy of Milton heavily; his sense of kinship with Milton and the importance that he ascribed to his own reading is shown by his marking of the passage reading "Milton's immense reading extended over the whole field of literature, and in every direction, and it required all his learning, collected by painful study during the best years of his life, long deposited in his memory, and remoulded by his genius, to build up his immortal poem."[15] In the biographical note, Melville also seemed particularly concerned with Milton's reasons for non-attendance at any church and his practice of diligent Bible-reading: Melville marked with a double line the speculation that Milton's non-attendance stemmed from "a dislike of their uncharitable and endless disputes, and that love of dominion, or inclination to persecution, which he said was a piece of popery, inseparable from all churches."[16]

Once he turned to reading *Paradise Lost* itself, Melville showed a consistent interest in reading the poem against the grain, commenting on Andrew Marvell's confession that he had "misdoubted" Milton's intent in writing the poem, "It is still 'misdoubted' by some. First impressions are generally true too, Andrew."[17] Melville adopted this sort of sardonic tone in relation to Milton's own lines at times, querying Milton's line 1033 of book 2, which states that some mortals "God and good angels guard by special grace" with the remark, "Hints this at that theological fiction ycleped Election, otherwise a species of nepotism?"[18] (Melville's anachronistic use of "ycleped," a Middle English term meaning "named," contributes to the ironic humor in the annotation.) A comment like this should give pause to anyone inclined to attribute too great a nostalgia for the Dutch Calvinism of his youth to the adult Melville.

Throughout the poem, Melville marked moments that suggested heterodoxy or idiosyncratic religious beliefs on Milton's part, and he is especially interested in moments that comment on the virtues of defiant courage, in relation both to Satan and to one of the angels on the side of the Godhead, Abdiel. With regard to Satan, Melville remarked (in an annotation that was subsequently erased and later recovered): "The is one of the many profound atheistical hits of Milton. A greater than Lucretius, since he always teaches under a masque, and makes the Devil himself a Teacher & Messiah."[19] In Abdiel's case, Melville marked his defiance of Satan and his affirmation of the necessity to join creative power to goodness and truth: "For strength from truth divided and from just / Illaudable, naught merits but dispraise / and ignominy."[20] It is noteworthy that the relation between Satan and Abdiel here is not unlike the way in which Ahab and Father Mapple are positioned in *Moby-Dick*: both are admirable in their defiance, but neither is fully free. Mapple and Abdiel defy lesser powers because of their obedience to God; Ahab and Satan defy God but are nonetheless ruled by their own internal compulsions.

That Melville's Milton is in large part the Milton of the romantics can be seen in his annotations of Shelley's "A Defence of Poetry," where he marked with a double line Shelley's assertion that "Milton's Devil as a moral being is far superior to his God, as one who perseveres in some purpose which he has conceived to be excellent in spite of adversity and torture, is to one who in the cold security of undoubted triumph inflicts the most horrible revenge upon his enemy" (*MM* 2.514). If Melville's Milton seems an infidel through the prism of his markings in Shelley, his Shelley ends up being a forthrightly religious thinker. Later in the "Defence of Poetry," Melville marked a passage that showed Shelley's description of the artist, and particularly the verbal artist in poetry, as an alternative sort of prophet:

> But it exceeds all imagination to conceive what would have been the moral condition of the world if neither Dante, Petrarch, Bocaccio, Chaucer, Shakespeare, Calderon, Lord Byron, nor Milton, had ever existed; if Raphael and Michael Angelo had never been born; the Hebrew poetry had never been translated; if the revival of the study of Greek literature had never taken place; if no monuments of ancient sculpture had been handed down to us; and if the poetry of the religion of the ancient world had been extinguished together with its belief. (*MM* 2.514)

Melville's reaction to these lines illustrates his concern with a broader conception of religion than is characteristically applied at the present time. The major artistic and literary figures of European culture are viewed as alternative sources of inspiration, and Melville and Shelley share the intuition that art is related to morality in a manner analogous to the role of religion in relation to morality.[21]

As was the case for Milton and Shelley themselves (in their widely divergent ways), Melville often tended to put classical sources in conversation with biblical ones and philosophy into conversation with theology. Melville's markings in Aristotle's *On Rhetoric* likewise points toward a desire for alternatives to the Christian scriptures in a manner that mirrors Shelley's. As discussed above, Melville annotated the Sermon on the Mount heavily in his copy of *The New Testament and Psalms*; when reading Aristotle, he marked precisely those passages that seemed to contradict the ethics of the Sermon on the Mount. Most strikingly, alongside Aristotle's argument that "revenge is honourable" because "to compensate is just, and what is just is honourable," Melville drew a cross, indicating the contrast between Aristotle and Jesus in these lines (*MM* 1.12). This alternative understanding of vengeance as potentially virtuous has a great deal of meaning with regard to the creation of a character like Captain Ahab, who is defined spiritually by his quest for revenge. For Melville, the classical world provided a robust ethical alternative to the self-sacrifice associated with the Sermon on the Mount, to which he was drawn even as he found its demands implausible in any world he could imagine. Here Aristotle provides Melville with a framework in which those aspects of human nature that do not accord with peace and self-sacrifice can be acknowledged without hypocrisy.

Reading Melville's Contemporaries: From Emerson to Schopenhauer

Melville was not alone in regarding the act of reading widely and well as a moral, ethical, and religious act. One of his contemporaries whose view of reading may have been most congenial to Melville's was Henry David Thoreau, who wrote in *Walden* that those who limited themselves to reading only the Hebrew and Christian scriptures and denied themselves access to the wider body of the "Bibles of mankind" had cut themselves off from an essential part of the human inheritance.[22] Like Thoreau, Melville was energized by world religions as well as by the presence of alternative scriptures within the ambit of Western civilization. In his copy of Schopenhauer's *The World as Will and Idea*, for example, Melville checked Schopenhauer's speculation that "the influence of Sanscrit literature will penetrate not less deeply than did the revival of Greek literature in the fifteenth century" (*MM* 2.327). Melville's writing of *Mardi* and *Moby-Dick* substantially antedated his reading of Schopenhauer, but this marking confirms a lifelong sense for Melville that contact with the great religious and literary works of Asia would produce a substantial advance in human culture around the globe. This sense intensifies especially in *Clarel* and Melville's later poetry. An important piece of Melville's sense of a literary communion of saints, and of the tension and uncertainty created by his reading, was shaped by his capacity to contemplate those Hindu, Buddhist, and Islamic texts that he was able to access with the same intensity that characterized his contemplation of the Hebrew and Christian scriptures.

The power that Melville's reading exerted upon his imagination, and the anxiety associated with his acknowledgment of this power, is expressed poignantly by one of Melville's annotations in Richard Brinsley

Sheridan's *The Rivals*. Melville marked with a double check and two overlapping single lines the sentences "Faded ideas float in the fancy like half-forgotten dreams; and the imagination in its fullest enjoyment becomes suspicious of its offspring, and doubts whether it has created or adopted" (*MM* 2.515). This acknowledgment of the author's uncertainty about the originality (and metaphorically the paternity) of the author's own work is recast by Melville in *The Confidence-Man* as a meditation on the very nature of both authorship and identity. In the forty-fourth chapter of *The Confidence-Man*, whimsically titled "In which the last three words of the last chapter are made the text of discourse, which will be sure of receiving more or less attention from readers who do not choose to skip it," Melville writes about the concept of originality:

> As for original characters in fiction, a grateful reader will, on meeting with one, keep the anniversary of that day. True, we sometimes hear of an author who, at one creation, produces some two or three score such characters; it may be possible. But they can hardly be original in the sense that Hamlet is, or Don Quixote, or Milton's Satan. That is to say, they are not, in a thorough sense, original at all. (*C-M* 238)

Here we have a particularly strong statement of writerly anxiety about the possibility of originality; as with Sheridan's "faded thoughts," the characters created by all but the greatest literary artists are inevitably derivative. The writer must remain forever in doubt of which of his or her ideas is ultimately original, illustrating that the boundary between the individual of genius and the broader human community is necessarily a vexed one for Melville.

Having made this rather depressing claim, however, Melville moves to a discussion of literary genius and inspiration that seeks to transcend all of these anxieties about originality. Melville's positive statement on originality makes this attribute positively deific:

> Furthermore, if we are to consider, what is popularly held to entitle characters in fiction to being deemed original, is but something personal—confined to itself. The character sheds not its characteristic on its surroundings, whereas the original character, essentially such, is like the revolving Drummond light, raying away from itself all round it—everything is lit by it, everything starts up to it (mark how it is with Hamlet), so that, in certain minds, there follows upon the adequate perception of such a character, an effect, in its way, akin to that which in Genesis attends upon the beginning of things. (*C-M* 239)

Here the literary artist, like the Hebrew and Christian deity, is able to bring light into existence through words. The question becomes, however, whether one is part of the elect group of literary artists who resemble the Drummond light, or whether one is part of the larger majority of writers who fall short of this standard. This question of literary election versus reprobation is one that can rival in its intensity the very question of the salvation of one's soul itself, and for Melville it seems to carry precisely such a degree of psychological and spiritual weight.

The title of this chapter suggests that Melville's version of the Christian ideal of the "Communion of the Saints" is realized through his broad and diverse reading and his alternately reverent and contentious engagement with the various scriptures of humanity and with works that he identified as communicating degrees of truth comparable to those of major scriptures. Melville's reading, and his struggle to create a community of solitude through his reading, must necessarily shape our understanding of his career, as this element is the thread that never ceases to tie together every portion of Melville's literary achievement. The quality that constantly characterizes Melville's work and his reaction to his reading is the interplay of faith and doubt, both in grand religious narratives and in the artistic qualities of the works that he reads and those that he writes.

The hallmark of Melville's career is his ability to read both sympathetically and with resistance, alternately embracing and questioning the views with which he interacts. In the "Prose Supplement" to Melville's first collection of poetry, *Battle-Pieces*, Melville provided a prescription for his divided nation that perhaps mirrored his own method for dealing with his divided self. Referring to the question of how to reunite the nation after the war, Melville wrote, "Let us revere that sacred uncertainty which forever impends over men and nations" (*PP* 185). (We might notice, incidentally, that the structure of this sentence echoes that of his earlier invocation of Sir Thomas Browne in *Mardi*: "Be Sir Thomas Brown[e] our ensample, who, while exploding 'Vulgar Errors,' heartily hugged all the mysteries in the Pentateuch" [*Mardi* 39].) Melville's embrace of sacred uncertainty and of Sir Thomas Browne ultimately come to much the same thing: a precarious balance is being struck between faith and doubt, with the crucial desideratum always being a truth that is independent of party or faction. It is noteworthy that the "sacred uncertainty" that Melville invokes in the *Battle-Pieces* passage is an uncertainty that is derived quite specifically from the tension between individual conviction and larger social consensus that formed the thematic core of his markings in Alger several years later. Melville derives the sacredness of uncertainty precisely from the conflicted sense of humankind about ethical and moral matters, and from the simultaneous moral imperatives to choose an ethical stance and to refrain from excessive self-congratulation or persecuting zeal in enforcing that stance. As in Hawthorne's famous description, both complacency in belief and complacency in unbelief are rejected on a fundamental level, and courage and honesty are the traits which keep one from resting.

As the foregoing demonstrates, Melville's sense of this "sacred uncertainty" can only be understood in the light of his networks of reading and his ambivalent relationship to so much of the work that he read. My discussion of Melville's reading above represents only a preliminary demonstration of how profoundly his marginalia and discussions of his reading must shape our understanding of his career. Ongoing projects like Steven Olsen-Smith's *Melville's Marginalia Online* are continuing to illustrate the breadth and diversity of Melville's reading and the significance of this reading to his literary, philosophical, and religious imagination, and the heroic labors of Melville's biographers from Raymond Weaver to Hershel Parker continue to shed light on Melville's imagination.[23] This process will continue for the foreseeable future, so our own understanding of Melville's religious thought necessarily continues to partake of the very uncertainty he invoked, even as its contours become progressively clearer. We turn first to the works which provided the foundation for Melville's career, his early novels of sea voyages and cross-cultural contact and dialogue, culminating in *Moby-Dick*.

Chapter 2

✦

Landlessness: Religious Difference around the Globe, *Typee* to *Moby-Dick*

Melville's career from *Typee* (1846) to *Moby-Dick* (1851) is marked by an intensifying and broadening concern with the varieties of religious difference from nearly every portion of the planet. Beginning with the confrontation between Western and indigenous religious traditions in the South Seas and expanding to include religious traditions from Asia and North Africa, Melville brought North American Protestantism into dialogue with a staggering range of world religions in his works published between 1846 and 1851. Melville engaged in this dialogue with his characteristic idiosyncrasy, but he also was behaving in a manner that was deeply representative of his age and nation—embodying, as would be so often the case throughout his career, the tension between solitude and individual aspiration on the one hand and the yearning for communion on the other. Melville's engagement with religious and cultural currents from around the globe in his first five novels had the effect of both reflecting and intensifying the multicultural religious ferment of his own time period.

The decades prior to the publication of *Typee* in 1846 had been characterized by a remarkable level of religious ferment. The Second Great Awakening had invigorated older Protestant denominations in the United States and created new ones. The Transcendentalist movement had brought an Evangelical sense of voluntarism to Unitarianism and had provided a heart to the drily intellectual New England liberalism associated with Unitarianism. An important part of both Evangelicalism and Transcendentalism was their increasing engagement with the entire globe. In the case of Evangelicalism, the overseas missionary movement in the United States had begun in the decade before Melville's birth with the so-called Haystack Revival and had by the 1840s become a vital element in American religious culture, one which contributed a sense of connection to international Protestantism and produced numerous publications representing cultures—Asian, African, Polynesian—that seemed unfathomably distant and exotic. Moreover, the missionary movement intersected powerfully with the major reform movements of the nineteenth century: temperance, with which the overlap with the missionary movement was almost absolute, and abolitionism, which divided the missionary movement in unexpected ways.[1]

The Transcendentalist movement, meanwhile, provided a sort of mirror image to Evangelicalism in relation to Asia: if Evangelical missionaries sought to convert Jews, Muslims, Hindus, Buddhists, and adherents of indigenous faiths to Christianity, Transcendentalist thinkers sought to supplement the moral and ethical teachings of Christianity with insights from world religions. Where the Evangelicals sought to convert, the Transcendentalists sought to become converted.[2] Like the Evangelicals, Transcendentalists immersed themselves in moral reform, but with an important difference. For many Evangelicals, moral reform was an important step toward realizing the kingdom of God on earth; for Transcendentalists, moral reform was a step toward the perfection of the self, the goal of "self-culture" as defined by the great Unitarian minister William Ellery Channing. A profoundly moral impulse was at the root of both movements: if the sense in which Transcendentalists were seeking the salvation of their souls was somewhat more metaphorical than the Evangelicals' quest for salvation from the world, the flesh, and the devil, it was no less real or earnest.

None of this religious complexity was absent from Melville's early work. A reader who tracked Melville's career from the publication of *Typee* (1846) through *Omoo* (1847), *Mardi* (1849), *Redburn* (1849), *White-Jacket* (1850), and *Moby-Dick* (1851) would have encountered missionary and anti-missionary arguments within Protestantism, controversies between Catholicism and Protestantism, contact among the religious traditions of Pacific Islanders, ideas on ethics and dogma from around the globe, treatments of the new historical modes of biblical criticism, religious traditions from every corner of Asia and Africa, and the application of religious and theological inquiry to the great social and political questions of Melville's day. This astonishing range of inquiry was conducted with an attitude that ranged widely from the whimsical to the reverent to the frankly blasphemous, with the author's own views remaining consistently elusive—so much so that later readers have confidently and frequently identified Melville with a range of widely contrasting religious positions.

If Melville's religious stance is protean, it is not, I would suggest, unknowable, and if we are to understand the extent of its influence on his artistic and intellectual choices, we must begin with the development of his representations of religion and culture from his earliest works, *Typee* and *Omoo*. Although these works have typically played a secondary role in Melville scholarship, far behind *Moby-Dick*, *Billy Budd*, *Benito Cereno*, and "Bartleby, the Scrivener," it is worth remembering that they were the most popular of his literary works during his own lifetime, and the ones by which he believed (and feared) he would be remembered—commenting in a June 1851 letter to Hawthorne that he would be known as the "man who lived among the cannibals" (*Corres.* 193). Beyond the significance of these works as nineteenth-century cultural barometers due to their relative popularity, they also provide a number of central formal and thematic patterns that continue to develop throughout Melville's literary career.

The Missionary Encounter in the Pacific: *Typee* and *Omoo*

Most recent discussions of *Typee* and *Omoo*, Melville's two first and most autobiographical novels, have focused on questions of race, imperialism, sexuality, and the body, and the effect of such considerations has been to revive attention to these novels more generally.[3] What pulls together these strands from these two novels is Melville's sometimes anguished, sometimes comic, consideration of the confrontation between indigenous Polynesian religious beliefs and those of Christian missionaries. Alongside this concern with relations between Christian and non-Christian faiths is an oblique discussion of the relationships among the varieties of Christian belief, particularly between the Protestantism of American and British missionaries, and the Catholicism of French missionaries, and the less pious varieties (indeed, often thoroughly impious varieties) of both practiced in the breach by sailors from a variety of nations.

A recurring motif throughout Melville's career is his representation of internecine strife among Christian denominations. This element in Melville's work becomes especially pronounced in *Clarel* (1876), which highlights a host of debates among Christians and meditates on the tendency of these debates to turn violent. Both Melville's own narration in *Typee* and *Omoo* and the accounts of his contemporaries reveal that the pugilistic approach to interreligious dialogue was alive and well among Europeans in the Pacific. For example, Titus Coan, an influential missionary leader in Hawaii and the Pacific more generally, recounts a confrontation that he had with a Jesuit priest during the early days of missionary activity in Hawaii:

> The priest kept right before me, with hands quivering, and voice roaring: "*Who is the head of the church? Who is head of the church?*"

> For a long time I made no reply, but quietly tried to work my way along, till at last I spoke out in full and clear tones, "The Lord Jesus Christ, He is the head of the Church." Immediately the priest roared out at the top of his voice, "That is a lie, Peter is the head of the Church." . . . When this assertion of Peter's headship thundered from the priest, one of the men named Samson, a bold and powerful man, could hold in no longer, and with the voice of a giant and the arm of Samson of old, he cried out, "Clear the road and let my teacher pass," and with the word came the act, and with his strong arms he scattered the mob to the right and the left.[4]

Coan, by all accounts among the more irenic American missionaries, presents us with a scene in which a Catholic priest attempts to force a debate with his Protestant counterparts by means of mob violence, and the supporters of the Protestant minister respond with violence of their own.

Melville registers this tense religious environment when he writes in *Typee* and *Omoo* about a series of conflicts among Protestant and Catholic missionaries and Pacific Islanders. At times, Melville seems to reflect typical Protestant anti-Catholicism, as when he criticizes the French colonizers in the Marquesas quite sharply. It is worth noting, however, that what Melville objects to here is not precisely the "idolatrous" French devotion to Popery that his Evangelical contemporaries would have denounced, but rather the arrogance of the colonial mission itself, an arrogance paralleled directly for Melville by the arrogance of Protestant powers like the United States and Great Britain. Indeed, it is not entirely surprising that the Catholic press in the United States in some cases welcomed *Typee* on the grounds that it pointed out the hypocrisy of Protestant missionary societies. In the concluding portions of *Typee*, which Melville dedicates to a discussion of the influence of the American missionaries sent by the American Board for Commissioners of Foreign Missions (ABCFM) to the Sandwich (Hawaiian) Islands, meanwhile, he highlights the conflicts between the American missionaries and the Church of England and the British more generally on the islands.

Melville's own experiences were far from being the only sources for Melville's first two novels. We have long known that Melville drew upon a number of late eighteenth- and early nineteenth-century texts on the South Pacific in constructing his early novels. Most notably, these included accounts by William Ellis, C. S. Stewart, and David Porter. Ellis was the author of *Polynesian Researches* and was himself a British missionary in the South Pacific, while Stewart was an American missionary with the

ABCFM. Porter, meanwhile, was a naval officer who played a substantial role in establishing an American presence in the Pacific and whose violence toward the islanders was criticized directly by Melville. All three provided substantial background for Melville's narration in *Typee* and *Omoo*, as scholars from Charles R. Anderson on have demonstrated, and indeed, as the scholarship has demonstrated over the years, Melville's level of dependence on these sources could be quite high indeed.[5] What is less frequently acknowledged is the structural principle that this dependency perhaps helps to create in Melville's work: consistently throughout his career, the duality represented by the Prince of Peace and the man o' war is a source of Melville's most fruitful paradoxes and ironies. Throughout the discussion of the Marquesas provided by Tommo, the narrator and a loosely autobiographical version of Melville himself, this tension provides the text with its shape in both formal and conceptual terms.

Tommo's first mention of the Marquesas in *Typee*, often and rightly quoted as an example of the exotic vision of the Marquesan islanders of which Melville makes use throughout the text, reaches its climax with italicized language drawn directly from Christian missionary appeals for the conversion of indigenous peoples. Upon hearing that his ship will be steering for the Marquesas, Tommo exclaims:

> The Marquesas! What strange visions of outlandish things does the very name spirit up! Naked houris—cannibal banquets—groves of cocoa-nut—coral reefs—tattooed chiefs—and bamboo temples; sunny valleys planted with breadfruit trees—carved canoes dancing on flashing blue waters—savage woodlands guarded by horrible idols—*heathenish rites and human sacrifices*. (*Typee* 5)

The imagery here moves back and forth between exotic visions of plenitude—the coconut palms, the breadfruit trees, the flashing blue waters—and images of cultural and religious difference—tattooed chiefs, bamboo temples, horrible idols—culminating in the italicized phrase designed to produce the highest level of *frisson*: *heathenish rites and human sacrifices*. Here the superstition believed to characterize indigenous religions is brought together with the ultimate ethical trespass: the murder, in the name of religious practice, of other human beings, and the viscerally shocking act of devouring their flesh. By making religious practice and belief the climax of Tommo's initial expectation of the Marquesas, Melville sets the tone for a text that will increasingly question the presumed gap between Christian love and "heathenish" violence and superstition.

Both this presumptive gap and those elements of the encounter between European and American Christianity and the indigenous customs and faiths of the Marquesas that undermine this gap become evident in the portions of *Typee* that discuss the recently founded Protestant missionary effort in the Marquesas. *Typee* includes the fiercest and most direct attack on the very idea of Christian missions of any portion of Melville's body of work. One of the most characteristic and telling scenes in this regard in the entire novel appears early on, in the form of a curious diptych fashioned out of the contrasting stories of a Protestant missionary woman and an indigenous queen. Tommo first relates the story of the Protestant missionary woman in terms that highlighted central elements in the Evangelical religious culture of the antebellum years:

> An intrepid missionary, undaunted by the ill-success that had attended all previous endeavors to conciliate the savages, and believing much in the efficacy of female influence, introduced among them his young and beautiful wife, the first white woman who had ever visited their shores. The islanders at first gazed in mute admiration at so wonderful a prodigy, and seemed inclined to regard it as some new divinity. But after a short time, becoming familiar with its charming aspect, and jealous of the folds which encircled its form, they sought to pierce the sacred veil of calico in which it was enshrined, and in the gratification of their curiosity, so far overstepped the limits of good breeding, as deeply to offend the lady's sense of decorum. Her sex once ascertained, their idolatry was changed into contempt; and there was no end to the contumely showered upon her by the savages, who were exasperated at the deception which they conceived had been practiced upon them. To the horror of her affectionate spouse, she was stripped of her garments and given to understand that she could no longer carry on her deceits with impunity. The gentle dame was not sufficiently evangelized to endure this, and, fearful of further improprieties, she forced her husband to relinquish his undertaking, and together they returned to Tahiti. (*Typee* 6–7)

This passage is quoted at length because it deserves some thorough unpacking. On one level, it works as an extended joke on the model of the tradition of "tall tales" typically associated with the American West. Tommo exploits the gap between the shocking behavior being described and his own rather refined mode of description for humorous effect, and he also makes the fastidiousness associated in much western American writing with a feminized version of civility part of the humor of the scene.

So much is evident, but what could easily be missed is Melville's play off the specific expectations for gender and piety that nineteenth-century Evangelicalism was in the process of cultivating. The virtuous missionary wife was rapidly becoming a standard trope of Evangelical discourse (all the more so if she heroically died on the mission field, as did, for example, Harriet Newell and Harriet Winslow, both of whom became the subjects of extensive memoirs by grieving husbands), so Tommo's placing of the female missionary at the center of his story is particularly apt. Two years after the publication of *Typee*, a Protestant minister named Rufus Wilmot Griswold (better known to the twenty-first century as the perfidious literary executor of the works of Edgar Allan Poe) published "The Heroism of the Knights Errant and of the Female Missionaries of America," an essay that expressed exactly the sort of panegyrics on the virtue and courage of the women on the mission field that Melville knew would be in the back of his readers' minds when confronting Tommo's anecdote.[6] Here, the celebration of missionary virtue expressed by Griswold is turned on its head: the missionary woman is, it is true, subjected to an unconscionable humiliation at the hands of the islanders, but the point of the remark that she is "not sufficiently evangelized" to accept these indignities is to remove the ethical demands of Christianity (turning the other cheek, returning good for evil, giving freely to anyone who asks) from a comfortable identification with European culture. To be fully evangelized, presumably, is something that is both morally admirable and as beyond the missionaries who are bringing the Gospel to the islanders as to the islanders themselves. By placing the missionaries at odds with their own Gospel, Melville effectively relativizes Western claims to owning Christian ethics, a strategy he continues to apply throughout his early novels.

In a curious diptych that Melville constructs employing the story related above, the converse of the insufficiently evangelized missionary woman is the tattooed queen whom Tommo describes next, making an explicit connection with the missionary's mortification. If the missionary woman defines her sense of dignity in part by physical modesty, the "Island Queen" of Nukuheva glories in physical display, with discomfiting results for a group of French sailors. After admiring the numerous tattoos of one of the sailors' own number with admiration, the queen, "eager to display the hieroglyphics on her own sweet form, bent forward for a moment, and turning sharply round, threw up the skirts of her mantle, and revealed a sight from which the aghast Frenchmen retreated precipitately, and tumbling into their boat, fled the scene of so shocking a catastrophe" (*Typee* 8). It is worth remembering here that the charge that the Marquesans seem to raise against the missionary woman in the previous anecdote is that of duplicity: because of all the clothes that she wears, she appears to be something she is not. The island queen, meanwhile, is distinguished precisely by her candor. Her nudity in this scene is a means of being precisely as she appears to be, thus making her, in the very act of engaging in behavior that horrifies her Christian interlocutors, an example of Christian candor (and Protestant simplicity) in her "heathen" state. We thus see a modest Christian woman and an immodest non-Christian woman being contrasted in a manner which calls attention to the ways in which the ethical standards of the Gospel relativize both cultures, not just the indigenous cultures of the Marquesas.

This style of contrast (what Father Mapple might call a "two-stranded" mode of storytelling) persists throughout *Typee* in relation to religious questions. Tommo's story and commentary tends to alternate anecdotes about the Typee with anecdotes about Western missionaries and sailors, frequently to the benefit of the former and the detriment of the latter. Melville is throughout particularly interested in the ways in which Christians in the Marquesas seem "not sufficiently evangelized" to live according to the standards of the Sermon on the Mount and the corresponding ways in which the society of the "heathen" Typees can appear to be surprisingly Christlike in its social arrangements and its generosity. It is unnecessary to dwell upon every example of this phenomenon in the novel, but there are a few instances that are especially instructive.

As the contrast between the missionary woman and the island queen illustrates, sexual ethics form an important part of the contrast between Marquesan and European cultures for Melville. Repeatedly throughout *Typee* and *Omoo*, Melville invokes the introduction of sexually transmitted diseases among the islanders as a synecdoche for all the ways in which European influence could be anything but benign. In *Typee*, Melville points out that European and North American sailors could be guilty of "the grossest licentiousness and the most shameful inebriety," leading him to conclude that "thrice happy are [islanders] who, inhabiting some yet undiscovered island in the midst of the ocean, have never been brought into contaminating contact with the white man" (*Typee* 15). Notably, Melville uses the rhetoric of temperance and moral reform to rebuke the European Christians in this scene—contact with Christendom has been a kind of fall for Pacific Island societies, he suggests, and he hints that this fall has been specifically sexual in its content. His later description of Fayaway as using the "primitive and summer garb of Eden" as her attire further emphasizes this idea of pre-contact Marquesan sexuality as an unfallen state, juxtaposed uncomfortably with the iniquities of allegedly "civilized" sexual behavior (*Typee* 87). Melville's commentary on the decimation of the Marquesan population (and indeed the Polynesian population more generally) by venereal disease makes clear that he blames the lascivious behavior of European and North American Christians for this fall.

If sex provides one angle Melville can use to reverse the presumed hierarchy between Christendom and heathenism, violence provides an even more telling reversal. In passages that portend Mark Twain's later criticisms of American policy in the Philippines and European policy in China, Tommo exclaims "How often is the term 'savages' incorrectly applied!" after observing the tendency of Western Christians to "burn, slaughter, and destroy" in response to acts of violence by indigenous Pacific Islanders (*Typee* 27). He revisits this note with an extended discussion of the same matters a few chapters later, echoing Montaigne's critique of European notions of superiority from "On Cannibals" with a catalog of tortures carried out in European nations that exceed even cannibalism in their horrors. What Melville was to identify in *Pierre* as the central principle of Christian ethics, "the gratuitous return of good for evil," is manifestly rejected by avowed Christians in these scenarios (*Pierre* 215). This Christian violence, when combined with Tommo's observations of Marquesan virtues, leads him to conclude that:

> when I consider the vices, cruelties, and enormities of every kind that spring up in the tainted atmosphere of a feverish civilization, I am inclined to think that so far as the relative wickedness of the parties is concerned, four or five Marquesan Islanders sent to the United States as Missionaries might be quite as useful as an equal number of Americans dispatched to the Islands in a similar capacity. (*Typee* 125–26)

This emphasis on the tension between the theory of nonviolence and the practice of violence within Christendom recurs throughout Melville's career, and is especially highlighted in the discussions of Quakers in *White-Jacket* and *Moby-Dick*. Through Tommo, Melville compares the genocidal history of war and Indian Removal in the early United States, asserting, "The Anglo-Saxon hive have extirpated Paganism from the greater portion of the North American continent, but with it they have likewise extirpated the greater portion of the Red race" (*Typee* 195). Melville's argument is consistently against the spreading of Christianity and European modes of civilization through violence, and the argument amounts to a sharp indictment of the faith and morals of the European world.

As with the matter of sexual ethics, Melville provisionally accepts standards drawn from Christian sacred texts and then demonstrates that in fact, cannibals are quite often better Christians than those who attempt to convert them, and Christians betray some disconcertingly cannibalistic qualities of their own. By the middle of the twentieth century mainstream Protestant missionaries like Lesslie Newbigin would be writing books about the tendency of the Gospel to relativize cultures shaped by Christianity as well as cultures shaped by other traditions; Melville was making this point strenuously and repeatedly as a young man in his late twenties and early thirties writing in the nineteenth century.[7] Even in moments of humor in *Typee*, Tommo gives voice to the idea that the Typee people are better exemplars of Christian love and classical philosophy alike than their would-be proselytizers, as when in response to Toby's accusation of cannibalism against the Typees, Tommo responds, "Granted . . . but a more humane, gentlemanly, and amiable set of epicures do not probably exist in the Pacific" (*Typee* 96).

Melville's interest in the tension between the communal ideal and individual aspiration, which plays such an important role in his marginalia throughout his adult life, is highlighted at a number of moments in *Typee*. When Tommo is considering the differences between life in the Typee Valley and life in the nineteenth-century United States, he remarks particularly on the Typee devotion to collective activity and effort when he considers the construction of a dwelling in the Typee village:

> There was one admirable trait in the general character of the Typees which, more than anything else, secured my admiration: it was the unanimity of feeling they displayed on every occasion. With them there hardly appeared to be any difference of opinion on any subject whatever. They all thought and acted alike. . . . Everyone contributed something to the work; and by the united, but easy, and even indolent, labors of all, the entire work was completed by sunset. The islanders, while employed in erecting this tenement, reminded me of a colony of beavers at work. To be sure, they were hardly as silent and demure as those wonderful creatures, nor were they by any means as diligent. To tell the truth, they were somewhat inclined to be lazy, but a perfect tumult of hilarity prevailed; and they worked together so unitedly, and seemed actuated by such an instinct of friendliness, that it was beautiful to behold. (*Typee* 203–4)

This is a crucial dimension in Melville's contrast between Marquesan and Western life styles, and we miss perhaps what is most central to the allure of the Pacific Island world in Melville's novels if we do not see the powerful urge toward community that such moments represent. Consistently in Melville's body of work, the need for the individual to find a point of connection with the wider community is highlighted, from Ishmael's various connections with Queequeg and his fellow sailors to the meetings of the minds that occur as the pilgrims in *Clarel* travel across Palestine. The fact that this connection to the efforts of others on a level so profound as to be unconscious plays such a significant role in *Typee* again demonstrates how thoroughly Melville's early novels adumbrate his major themes—and not Melville's only: Whitman's loafing speaker in *Song of Myself* and Thoreau's reflections on the penances undergone as part of middle-class life in Concord reflect a similar impulse away from regimented, individualized modes of labor.[8] Melville suggests that there is at least a possibility of harmony between solitude and sociability, however much tension frequently exists between these impulses.

This exaltation of the communal values of the Marquesans connects directly to Melville's critique of the imposition of a labor system not unlike slavery onto Polynesia, and particularly onto the Hawaiian Islands. When Tommo refers to the Hawaiian Islanders as having been "civilized into draught horses and evangelized into beasts of burden" by the missionaries, he is objecting to the transformation of Polynesian time from a kind of organic model into the industrial model that was in the process of emerging in North America and western Europe (*Typee* 196). In one sense, the satire against the missionaries in these texts is also a lament for a sense of time that has only recently been lost—or is indeed in the process of being lost in Melville's own society. In these passages Melville also accomplishes something quite unexpected in relation to the religious culture of his time: he takes the critique of slavery, a critique which was associated regionally with New England, and connects it to a critique of foreign missions, when the missionary endeavor was also a particularly New England regional emphasis.

Melville's attempted analysis of Typee rituals consistently comes up against an epistemological dead end, however. As Tommo acknowledges, he can observe the religious rituals in the Typee Valley, but their significance is usually opaque to him. He confesses his "entire inability to gratify any curiosity that may be felt with regard to the theology of the valley" (*Typee* 171). He further suggests that most likely the Pacific Islanders "have no fixed and definite ideas whatever on the subject of religion" (*Typee* 177). Tommo does not suggest that they have no religious ideas, of course; what he does note, with seeming approval, is that these ideas do not seem to be susceptible of a creedal formulation. In this sense, the

Typees themselves constitute an earlier example of the reverence for a kind of "sacred uncertainty" for which Melville was to call in his "Prose Supplement" to *Battle-Pieces*.

This absence of a discernable creed in the Typee religion (according to Tommo, at least) helps to contribute to the humorous appreciation that Tommo evinces for Typee society. One of Tommo's more clever extended jokes on religious topics is his jocular application of the jeremiad to the context of the Typee religion. After observing his Typee friend Kory-Kory physically beating one of his idols, Tommo reflects, "In truth, I regard the Typees as a back-slidden generation. They are sunk in religious sloth, and require a spiritual revival. . . . The wood-rot malady is spreading among the idols—the fruit on their altars is becoming offensive—the temples themselves are in need of re-thatching—the tattooed clergy are altogether too light-hearted and lazy—and their flocks are going astray" (*Typee* 179). American readers would have readily recognized the language of revivalism in this passage, here applied, not to earnest North American Christians seeking to return to a former state of virtue, but to the very people the missionaries North American Christians sponsored were trying to convert, and on behalf of the indigenous religions the missionaries sought to replace.

Tommo's commentary on the conflicts among the Typee, Happar, and Nukuhevans also has an important reference point in relation to European and American religious cultures. It would occur to Melville's more perceptive nineteenth-century readers rather swiftly that the accusations leveled against each other by these three groups resembled the national and religious prejudices of nineteenth-century Americans and Europeans: just as the Happar and the Typee leveled accusations of the worst sort of atrocities against each other, so also (for example) the British and the French. When in Nukuheva Bay, Tommo finds that the Happar "disclaimed all cannibal propensities on their own part, while they denounced their enemies, the Typees, as inveterate gourmandizers of human flesh" (*Typee* 25). In a neat parallel, when Tommo falls among the Typees, he reports that they insist with fervor that the Happar are cannibals, and that the Typees themselves are not. Melville presents his readers with a parallel case in the Marquesas to the dueling martyrologies and charges and counter-charges regarding persecution and atrocity that obtained between Catholics and Protestants in European and North American culture, a parallel he revisited in his third novel, *Mardi*.

It is within this attempt to interrogate the variable abilities of European, American, and Marquesan society to realize the moral vision of the Sermon on the Mount that Melville's withering critique of Christian missions in the later portion of *Typee* can most fruitfully be understood. As discussed in the first chapter, Melville marked the Sermon on the Mount with particular care in his copy of *The New Testament and Psalms*, and we see the importance of these passages to Melville's moral vision much more frequently than is typically acknowledged. Love, community, and the return of good for evil are the ethical standards by which Melville measures a civilization, and it is on precisely these grounds that he prefers many aspects of Marquesan civilization to its European and North American counterparts.

Difference as Taboo: The Example of Marnoo

In addition to developing contrasting social and cultural models in Tommo's narration of *Typee*, Melville also developed a model for his characters and for his use of physical space that would prove determinative for much of his career, and here as in the case of the community, religious difference comes to the fore. The concept of taboo and the character of Marnoo did more to shape Melville's future literary production than is frequently acknowledged. Tommo introduces taboo in a variety of comical or serious contexts throughout the novel, but there is an especially telling moment in his discussion of a Typee religious site when he describes the most sacred one that he is allowed to enter in terms associated with the romantic sublime and the gothic:

> Here were situated the Taboo groves of the valley—the scene of many a prolonged feast, of many a horrid rite. Beneath the dark shadows of the consecrated bread-fruit trees there reigned a solemn twilight—a cathedral-like gloom. The frightful genius of pagan worship seemed to brood in silence over the place, breathing its spell on every object around. Here and there, in the depths of these awful shades, half screened from sight by masses of overhanging foliage, rose the idolatrous altars of the savages, built of enormous blocks of black and polished stone, placed one upon another, without cement, to the height of twelve or fifteen feet, and surrounded by a rustic open temple, enclosed with a low picket of canes, within which might be seen, in various stages of decay, offerings of breadfruit and coconuts, and the putrefying relics of some recent sacrifice. (*Typee* 91)

Melville would revisit this sort of scene later, in a chapter of *Moby-Dick* entitled "A Bower in the Arsacides," and revise it considerably, but for now, it is worth noting the representational strategy that he employs here

The imagery is highly congruent with nineteenth-century gothicism, medievalism, and anti-Catholicism, calling to mind as it does the mysterious twilight frequently attributed to continental cathedrals in English gothic novels.[9] The scene inspires awe and a sense of the numinous at the same time that it trades on the representation of any religious systems less rationalized than liberal Protestantism in the nineteenth century as backward and superstitious and hints darkly at the cannibalism that Tommo frequently attributes to his Typee captors. When he refers to the "rustic pulpits, from which the priests harangued their devotees" that are constructed out of tree trunks and canes, he calls to mind both the images of the Catholic priesthood as fanatical and superstitious from gothic novels and anti-Catholic polemic alike and the revivalist sermons being preached in Melville's own time by Evangelical ministers associated with the Second Great Awakening. In this way, the taboo space allows for questions to be posed about the range of cultural and religious traditions meeting in the Marquesas.

The power of taboo spaces as locales at which the normal rules of life and society cease to apply becomes reflected in the attribution of this sort of power to certain individuals within and on the margins of Marquesan society. A central example of the "taboo" individual is Marnoo, a man who is described in terms of physical beauty and power and is regarded with reverence by his fellow Marquesans. Marnoo is a figure who is empowered by his taboo status, and the way in which Melville presents him forecasts numerous of Melville's future protagonists. He is a physically beautiful and impressive figure, a forerunner to the magnificent physical specimen Billy Budd in his appearance. He moves easily among the Typee, Happar, and Nukuhevan peoples, making him a diplomatic go-between among a variety of Marquesan nations. What allows him to do this is his specifically religious status: the fact that he is considered "taboo" means that he can be greeted and accepted by groups of people who are otherwise mortal enemies. Marnoo's insider/outsider status connects him to Tommo himself, in that Tommo is an outsider to Marquesan culture whom the Typees are attempting to absorb into themselves. It likewise connects him to Ishmael, who is an intermediary between faith and doubt, land and sea, the educated and the illiterate, and any in a series of other oppositions that could be adduced from Melville's most central novel. Still later in his career, when writing the 18,000-line verse novel *Clarel*, Melville would create a character named Rolfe, a philosophically inclined sailor whom many critics, beginning with Walter Bezanson, would identify with Melville himself. As discussed in the first chapter, Melville would explicitly compare Rolfe in the poem to the Indian deity

Rama, but Marnoo also seems a clear model for Rolfe's status as a frequent go-between in relation to the varying theological and cultural positions developed in Melville's longest poem. One conclusion that can be drawn from this is that Marquesan culture itself provides a structural principle that defines Melville's body of work, and that this structural principle is most essentially characterized by religious ambivalence and multiplicity. Melville further develops this kind of hybrid protagonist in *Omoo*, using the idea of the narrator as a "taboo kanaker"—someone who travels among the various Polynesian Islands without being exclusively tied to one—to solidify the idea of the traveling figure who moves between and among cultures as Melville's ideal hero (*Omoo* 14).

Omoo extends Melville's critique of Christian missions by setting up a series of incidents that illustrate the tension between missionary ideals and practice. Indeed, *Omoo* is in a sense framed by representations of missionaries in the South Seas: it begins with some remarks directed toward criticisms of *Typee* by missionary publishers, and it concludes with material relating to a trial in Polynesia held by missionary standards. In the preface to *Omoo*, Melville defends his work in *Typee* against its critics in the religious press:

> In every statement connected with the missionary operations, a strict adherence to fact has, of course, been scrupulously observed; and in some instances, it has even been deemed advisable to quote previous voyagers, in proof of what has been offered as the fruit of the author's own observations. Nothing but an earnest desire for truth and good has led him to touch upon this subject at all. (*Omoo* xiv)

This defense establishes a very important pattern for Melville's work as a whole: the truth consistently is his defense against attacks on his work, and he frequently employs the category of truth as his criterion for evaluating the work of others. Having stated this defense, Melville continued to press his critique of missions in *Omoo*, pointing again to the clashes between Protestant and Catholic missionaries—with a particularly pointed caricature of anti-French sermonizing in the chapter entitled "A Missionary's Sermon; with Some Reflections." His conclusion remains much the same as those in *Typee*: "In view of these things, who can remain blind to the fact, that so far as mere temporal felicity is concerned, the Tahitians are far worse off now, than formerly; and although their circumstances, upon the whole are bettered by the presence of the missionaries, the benefits conferred by the latter become utterly insignificant, when confronted by the vast preponderance of evil brought about by other means" (*Omoo* 192).

Typee and *Omoo* were both met with vigorous counterattacks from the missionary press. As Hershel Parker and Brian Higgins have detailed, these works were attacked as being anti-mission, anti-Protestant, and indeed anti-Christian.[10]

The tension between pro-missionary and anti-missionary elements had much to do with internal power struggles among differing American interests and the various interests associated with British and French imperialism in the South Seas. In particular, many American businessmen resented the missionaries because they interfered with the businessmen's economic goals in Hawaii. Some missionaries, of course, responded to these concerns by emphasizing the centrality of Christian conversion to the success of the businessmen's frankly imperialistic aims: Henry T. Cheever, for example, writing in 1851, argued that Christianity was a foundational necessity for commerce and civilization, suggesting that if the business interests would but recognize it, the missionaries were their best friends. Cheever's crassly materialistic approach to missions was emblematic of one tendency within the missionary movement, but a counterbalancing tendency was the pro-temperance, anti-tobacco, and Sabbatarian element within the movement, which tended to inhibit profits. British imperial interests also tended to conflict with the missionaries, and at times there were strategic alliances between British officers and clergy and American business interests. As Leon Howard pointed out in his pioneering biography of Melville in 1951, during his brief stay in Hawaii, Melville tended to ally himself with the businessmen and the British rather than the missionaries.[11]

What conclusions might we draw regarding Melville's treatment of the missionary encounter in the South Pacific? It is not hard to understand why a young man who had experienced an exhilarating sense of cultural (and likely sexual, if we are to believe his own narratives and certain gossipy barbershop relations in his old age) liberation in the Pacific would find the austerity of the missionaries unpleasant. At the heart of these first two novels is a romantic desire to dispense with institutions and their tyranny over individual impulse and energy, and the missionaries saw the redirecting of impulse and energy into directions in keeping with their understanding of Christianity to be central to their task. Conversely, however, Melville's attachment to the indigenous communities of the South Pacific had something to do with the emphasis on collective well-being and the sense of the community as prior to individual self-aggrandizement. The question of how to balance solitude and society in a morally satisfying way thus was a crucial element even in these first two novels.

Anti-missionary sentiments also had political implications on the mainland. Overwhelmingly, American missionaries, both to the indigenous peoples of North America and to overseas destinations, were New Englanders who were Congregationalists, Presbyterians, or Methodists in religion, and Whigs (or, earlier, Federalists) in politics. Anti-mission sentiment was identified with the antebellum Democratic Party, with which Herman Melville was closely connected through his brother Gansevoort. It is noteworthy, however, that Melville's own critique of missionaries was a reversal of the more standard critique of missions that was often heavily flavored with the racism of large sectors of the antebellum Democratic Party. Although Melville never identified himself as an abolitionist, he consistently made antislavery remarks throughout his career, from the 1840s through the post–Civil War period. Melville's fractured stance—anti-mission and antislavery—is revealing in that it corresponds to a similar fracturing that was taking place in the missionary movement itself in the 1840s.

Since its founding in 1812, the American Board of Commissioners for Foreign Missions had dominated the field of American foreign missionary activity. After the *Amistad* trial of 1839, the board was divided, with the staunchly abolitionist American Missionary Association leaving the ABCFM in protest against its vacillation on the subject of slavery. In an earlier decade, resistance to slavery and resistance to missions might have seemed paradoxical, but by the 1840s, the missionary movement could be charged, and often was, by its own most fervent members, of duplicity in its own ethical and moral standards.[12]

The general animosity between Melville and the ABCFM missionaries should not obscure the fact that not all missionaries condemned Melville, and Melville maintained cordial relations with at least some missionary families. In his 1881 memoir, Titus Coan, an evangelist on the Big Island of Hawaii and a leader in the broader American Pacific mission, refers several times to Melville's early work, and never with contumely. Coan refers to Melville as a "gifted" and "romantic" author, although he also suggests gently that Melville's knowledge of Marquesan geography as expressed in *Typee* was less than exhaustive.[13] Coan's son Titus Munson Coan visited Melville in 1859, and was one of the forerunners of the 1920s Melville revival in his estimation (uncommon in the late nineteenth century when Melville was writing) of Melville as a major American author.[14] Perhaps the religious context of the 1840s can provide us with some insight as to why the Coans did not share in the general effusion of vitriol toward Melville on the part of missionaries and their supporters. Titus Coan had become convinced of his missionary calling under the preaching of the leading figure in the Second Great Awakening, Charles Grandison Finney. Although Finney was an enthusiastic Christian revivalist and Melville was a frequent critic of missions, revivalism, and at times Christianity itself, there are certain congruities between their understandings of the world that can prove mutually illuminating.[15]

Finney was an attorney who experienced a dramatic conversion as a young man. In his memoir, he relates the story of how as a young lawyer he found himself experiencing divinity in the midst of nature. Finney wrote that as he experienced the descent of the Holy Spirit, "I could feel the impression, like a wave of electricity, going through and through me. Indeed it seemed to come in waves and waves of liquid love, for I could not express it in any other way. It seemed like the very breath of God. I can recollect distinctly that it seemed to fan me, like immense wings."[16] In this passage, Finney demonstrates that his brand of evangelical Protestantism is not far removed from romantic veneration of nature and anti-institutionalism. Finney's general approach to his evangelistic endeavors was to emphasize the human role and the role of feeling in his sermons, as against the traditional Calvinist doctrines and rhetoric of predestination. If Melville attacks the missionary movement vehemently, he also shows affection for the sort of "heart religion" Finney advocated, and he shows this most directly in his references to the Sermon on the Mount as the core of what he finds compelling in Christian ethics and in the passages where he stresses the importance of affection and fellow-feeling, such as the opening paragraphs in the chapter in *Moby-Dick* entitled "A Squeeze of the Hand."

What is most noteworthy about these early novels is that they proceed by means of a fairly simple triangular model for understanding religious difference: one side of the triangle is formed by hypocritical missionaries and Christian sailors; another side is formed by unjustly maligned but still menacing indigenous peoples, with religious traditions that are better than their libelers would suggest but still imperfect and unsettling; and a third side is formed by Melville, his narrators, skeptical sailors, and Melville's sympathetic readers, all of whom mock the foolishness and are appalled by the hypocrisy of the missionaries and all of whom are ambivalently attracted to the Edenic lifestyles of the islanders, but who proceed with a remarkably low level of self-doubt and self-examination relative to Melville's later protagonists.

Melville's engagement with religious questions is clear in these early novels, but it has not attained the level of subtlety that Melville would reach in his later treatments of religious difference. Moreover, Melville's anti-missionary stance in the novels (and indeed the vitriol directed at Melville in the missionary press) may have been a bit of a pose: one of the more interesting aspects of Melville's nineteenth-century reception is the fact that Titus Coan could write with seeming approval of Melville's South Seas tales, and that Coan's son, Titus Munson Coan, felt comfortable visiting Melville a decade and a half after Melville's initial novelistic success at the expense of the missionaries. Indeed, Titus Munson Coan reported dissatisfaction that Melville seemed unwilling to talk at length about his time in the Marquesas—not a likely response if he saw Melville solely as a libeler of Coan's own family's enterprise. Melville is perhaps thus best imagined, not as an enemy of the missionaries, but as an ambivalent if highly critical interlocutor.

Melville's Turn to Asia: *Mardi*, *Redburn*, and *White-Jacket*

Melville's third novel of the South Seas, *Mardi*, takes a more philosophical approach to exploring the problems of religious difference.[17] On one level, the confrontation between Christian and indigenous religious traditions from the earlier novels is continued. On another level, Melville defamiliarizes Christian traditions by describing them in the proto-anthropological terms used by missionaries and diplomats reporting back from the South Pacific. Melville's incorporation of religious difference becomes still more profound as a result of his reading of discussions of Hinduism, Buddhism, and Islam by Western scholars who had become immersed in these traditions as a result of the presence of British colonialism in South Asia. *Typee* had initially been published in Murray's Home and Colonial Library; now the intellectual fruits of the British colonial encounter in South Asia were appearing in Melville's body of work.

The United States engagement with Asia has frequently been underestimated in scholarly considerations of the development of American cultural identities, but we have become increasingly aware that Asia was an important presence in American culture throughout the nineteenth century. As early as 1963, Dorothee Metlitsky Finkelstein found that Melville had woven Asia into his work throughout his career. More recently, studies by Malini Johar Schueller and Timothy Marr have reinforced the importance of the American encounter with Asia for the context in which Melville wrote. Unlike such locales as the Marquesas and Palestine, Melville never traveled to India, but his reading served to make him more familiar with Indian cultural and religious attributes than we might otherwise have reason to expect.[18]

Melville's reading on Hinduism and other South Asian religions drew, as we now know, on several important and widely circulated English-language studies of the subject. H. Bruce Franklin identified numerous

Melville allusions and sources to South Asian religions in his 1962 study *The Wake of the Gods*, which is still seminal reading for anyone serious about Melville's treatment of non-Western religious traditions, but he ultimately regarded these allusions as being peripheral to the major thrust of *Moby-Dick*, suggesting instead that Egyptology was at the core of Melville's use of mythology in the novel. Following a hint initially suggested in Howard Vincent's *The Trying-Out of Moby-Dick* (1949), Franklin suggested that the works that contributed most to shaping Melville's representations of Hinduism in *Moby-Dick* were Thomas Maurice's *Indian Antiquities* (1793–1800) and *A History of Hindostan* (1795–98), and the fact that he did so helped to solidify the consensus that South Asia formed an important background for Melville's writing of *Moby-Dick*.[19]

Mardi ultimately makes the celebration of religious difference as a fundamental human value even clearer than it is in *Typee* and *Omoo*. In a chapter entitled "Dreams," Taji, the narrator, reflects on the ways in which a panorama of religious difference can go into the makeup of one human being:

> I list to St. Paul, who argues the doubts of Montaigne; Julian the Apostate cross-questions Augustine; and Thomas a Kempis unrolls his black letter for all to decipher. Zeno murmurs maxims beneath the hoarse shout of Democritus; and though Democritus laugh loud and long, the hoarse sneer of Pyrrho be seen; yet, divine Plato, and Proclus, and Verulam are of my counsel; and Zoroaster whispered me before I was born. . . . My memory is a life beyond birth, my memory, my library of the Vatican, its alcoves all endless perspectives, eve-tinted by the cross-lights from the Middle-Age oriels. (*Mardi* 367–68)

We see Catholic and Protestant, Christian and pagan, materialist and idealist, skeptic and believer all coinciding in one mind, and we notice that the mechanism through which this occurs is the reading of books. As argued in the previous chapter, Melville's most important co-religionists are the figures whose work he reads, and Melville imagines himself as sharing in the communion of all those who assert faith and all those who wrestle with doubt. The content of the faith and doubt, meanwhile, is pertinent but not decisive: with regard, for example, to the question of the Trinity, Melville has Samoa assert, "But let us not turn upon friends, confounding them with foes. For dissenters but assent to more than we. Though Milton was a heretic to the creed of Athanasius, his faith exceeded that of Athanasius himself" (*Mardi* 296). The "faith of Athanasius" is of course that of orthodox Trinitarian Christianity; the Unitarianism of many of those Melville loved in the flesh was heretical by its standard, and yet here Melville makes Milton's dissent a sign of his great faith. As was to appear elsewhere in his works, fervency and courage, and engagement with the possibility of doubt, constitute the faith that matters for Melville, and correctness of doctrine does not.

If *Mardi* represents a sort of climax for the development of religious difference as a central theme in Melville's early novels, the next two novels, *Redburn* and *White-Jacket*, might seem to indicate a decrease in Melville's interest in these matters, as the direct confrontation between the theological and ethical arguments of competing religious traditions is not a central component in these works. A closer look, however, indicates that Melville's probing of the ethical dimensions of religious experience has only intensified in these two works. Meanwhile, in a muted but substantial fashion, Melville continues in these works to explore rival religious and cultural perspectives and to demonstrate his keen powers of observation in relation to cultural difference.

That Melville's interest in Asian culture had not disappeared in the period between *Mardi* and *Moby-Dick* is apparent from his treatment in *Redburn* of the title character's experience aboard an Indian vessel at port in England. Redburn relates in some detail his observations of the *Irriwaddy*, out of Bombay. When he observes the Lascar sailors aboard the ship and their fellow sailors from all around South and Southeast Asia, he observes:

> The Lascars were on the forecastle deck. Among them were Malays, Mahrattas, Burmese, Siamese, and Cingalese. They were seated round "kids" full of rice, from which, according to their invariable custom, they helped themselves with one hand, the other being reserved for quite another purpose. . . . They were a small-limbed, wiry, tawny set; and I was informed made excellent seamen, though ill adapted to stand the hardships of northern voyaging. (*Redburn* 171)

This moment is an important one to remember, because it makes clear that Indians and Indian thought are not just a part of Melville's mythological background for novels like *Mardi* and *Moby-Dick*, but rather concrete actors in his experience as a sailor. Melville does not simply read about Hinduism in books like Maurice's *Indian Antiquities* and *The History of Hindostan*; he considers Indian sailors as concrete actors in his stories, and his discussion reaches a level of specificity that includes recognizing dining and grooming habits and distinguishing among a variety of Asian nationalities. His praise for the sailing capacities of the various South Asian nationalities represented in the above passage suggests that when he brings Indian sailors into *Moby-Dick*, they are not simply being employed as tropes, but as representatives of a concrete group of people within the transnational society of whale men. This is a significant part of the distinction between Melville's treatment of South Asia and those by contemporaries like Emerson and Thoreau: for Emerson and Thoreau, South Asia is a locus for ideas, whereas for Melville, with his experience as a sailor, South Asians are flesh and blood individuals, who have their own specific traditions for the functions of daily life down to the details of their dining habits, and his expression of their religious and philosophical ideas is connected to his experiences with them as individuals who exist in the material universe, not just a textual one.

Melville's ongoing interest in Asia appears in *White-Jacket* as well, in this case in his description of the ship's library, where he notes that among the captain's books is:

> another venerable octavo, containing a certificate from Sir Christopher Wren to its authenticity, entitled, *Knox's Captivity in Ceylon*, 1681—abounding in stories about the devil, who was superstitiously supposed to tyrannize over that unfortunate land: to mollify him, the priests offered up buttermilk, red cocks, and sausages; and the devil ran roaring about in the woods, frightening poor travellers out of their wits; insomuch as the islanders bitterly lamented to Knox that their country was full of devils, and consequently, there was no help for their eventual well-being. Knox swears he himself heard the Devil roar, though he did not see his horns, it was a terrible noise, he says, like the baying of a hungry mastiff. (*WJ* 168)

The tone here is clearly jocular, but as in *Redburn*, Melville acknowledges the inevitable contact with religious difference implied by life at sea, and once again, he makes the encounter between Asia and the English-speaking world crucial to this contact. Robert Knox had been, like Melville himself, a sailor who had been captured by non-European peoples, in this case the people of the Buddhist kingdom of Kandy in seventeenth-century Ceylon (present-day Sri Lanka). Knox's *An Historical Relation of Ceylon* had been among the more popular captivity narratives of the late seventeenth century in the English-speaking world, and it addressed directly the difficulties faced by a Puritan Englishman who found himself in captivity in a non-Christian culture that he admired, but to which he was unwilling to assimilate. The reference to the devil in the passage quoted is of particular interest, as it shows the integration of pre-Buddhist religious practices of propitiating malevolent spirits into the popular religion of the Buddhist Kandyan kingdom, thus offering a kind of parallel to the syncretic elements Melville noted in Christianity.[20]

Although Melville dismissed *White-Jacket* and *Redburn* as books written to order, his profound ethical interest in the Sermon on the Mount is given substantial expression in these, the last two works that he published before *Moby-Dick*. In *Redburn*, this becomes most clear in the portions of the text set in Liverpool, where Redburn observes almost unimaginable poverty. In *White-Jacket*, it is the sheer violence of life at sea that brings Melville and his readers into contact with the most profound sorts of ethical questions. In one sense, *White-Jacket* was among Melville's most efficacious works during his own lifetime, in that it was read on the floor of Congress and contributed to the banning of corporal punishment as a means of discipline on naval ships. This social contribution to the conscience of the nation is no accident. The novel is full of ethical reflections, many of them directly in dialogue with the demands of the Sermon on the Mount. *White-Jacket* is, after all, the account of life aboard a man o' war, and consistently we find Melville reflecting on the ways in which war is at odds with the more uncompromising Christian ethics associated with the Sermon on the Mount.

Another way in which *Redburn* and *White-Jacket* anticipate *Moby-Dick* (and indeed *Billy Budd*) is with regard to the question of moral evil on the individual level. In both novels, Melville creates characters who seem to embody all of the worst possibilities of human nature. In *Redburn*, this role is played by Jackson, a sailor who distinguishes himself by his malice and provides a premonition of the role of Claggart in *Billy Budd*. In *White-Jacket*, a similar role is played by Captain Clarett, a dictatorial ship's captain who foreshadows Captain Ahab's role in *Moby-Dick*. The presence of these two characters in the novels that immediately precede *Moby-Dick* points toward an increased urgency in the relation of difference to moral and ethical questions, and it is to this high point in Melville's career that we now turn.

The Howling Infinite: The Proliferation of Religious Difference in *Moby-Dick*

In each of Melville's first five novels, his narrators challenge the proprieties of nineteenth-century American religious cultures, especially through their critique of the missionary movement and of the involvement of the

Christian churches in violence. Melville never, however, fully stakes out an independent religious position prior to *Moby-Dick*. In his most ambitious and profound novel, he is simply up to something much more grand than he has been willing to attempt or capable of attempting previously. He makes the approach to questions of faith and meaning plain in Ishmael's soliloquy on Bulkington following his death:

> Know ye, now, Bulkington? Glimpses do ye seem to see of that mortally intolerable truth; that all deep, earnest thinking is but the intrepid effort of the soul to keep the open independence of her sea; while the wildest winds of heaven and earth conspire to cast her on the treacherous, slavish shore?
>
> But as in landlessness alone resides the highest truth, shoreless, indefinite as God—so better is it to perish in that howling infinite, than be ingloriously dashed upon the lee, even if that were safety! For worm-like, then, oh! Who would crawl craven to land? Terrors of the terrible! Is all this agony so vain? Take heart, take heart, O Bulkington! Bear thee grimly, demigod! Up from the spray of thy ocean-perishing—straight up, leaps thy apotheosis! (*M-D* 107)

This passage serves as a manifesto of sorts for the treatment of religious difference that will obtain throughout the novel, arguing as it does for the need to escape from the comforts of inherited certainties.

The cultural, doctrinal, and ethical dimensions of religious difference coalesce spectacularly in *Moby-Dick*. The tension between varying epistemological and axiological approaches to the world is evident even before we reach the line "Call me Ishmael" at the opening of the first chapter, and from this opening line, Ishmael both embodies and interrogates religious difference. *Moby-Dick* begins with an extended comment on the act of interpretation that is focused quite specifically on the religious and theological dimensions of interpretation. First, we read seriocomic reflection on the ecumenical qualities of books. In the "Etymology" and "Extracts" that begin *Moby-Dick*, Melville presents us with a "pale consumptive Usher" who has collected names for the whale from a variety of European and non-European cultures, and a "poor devil of a sub-sub" librarian who has "gone through the long Vaticans and street-stalls of the earth, picking up whatever random allusions to whales he could anyways find in any books whatsoever, sacred or profane" (*M-D* xv–xxviii). The goal of both the usher and the sub-sub is to find an approach to truth about the whale by cataloging its representations; throughout *Moby-Dick*, Melville is engaged in a similar quest with regard to the divine.

The central characters of the novel are fraught with religious complexity. Ishmael is by his very name associated with the nexus of the three Abrahamic religions: Judaism, Christianity, and Islam. This son of the "infallible Presbyterian Church" also sees himself in terms provided by Greco-Roman philosophy at the very outset of the novel, comparing himself to Cato when he mentions the possibility of suicide. He further demonstrates knowledge of Hinduism, Zoroastrianism, and indigenous Polynesian religions throughout the text, and he makes a number of references to Christianity, Judaism, and Islam on the one hand and the pre-Christian mythology of the Greco-Roman world on the other. Certainly the most obvious appearance of religious difference in *Moby-Dick* comes with the appearance of Queequeg. What makes Queequeg such a fascinating character is the interaction between his role as a symbolically freighted figure who is an emblem of otherness and his role as an organic intellectual who investigates questions of difference as well as embodying them. Queequeg is, of course, the ultimate multi-religious seeker in this text, far braver and more adventurous in his thinking than is Ishmael. We find out in Queequeg's biography that he is the heir of a royal family, and that he left his own family to seek after the truth. This story, were it to be narrated by an ABCFM missionary, would end with Queequeg finding the Truth in Christianity, but what happens instead is that Queequeg comes to believe that his own upbringing achieved as close an approximation of truth as he can hope for, deciding: "it's a wicked world in all meridians; I'll die a pagan" (*M-D* 56).

Even Queequeg's identification as "George Washington cannibalistically developed" has a great deal of significance for religious readings of *Moby-Dick* (50). Washington was himself frequently described in terms associated with religious veneration, and in the context of American civil religion he functions as a kind of secondary deity. The relationship between Queequeg and predecessors in Melville's fiction like Marnoo and Babbalanja is worth probing. Queequeg resembles Marnoo in his status as a go-between, a figure in whom cultural hybridity and difference is made manifest. He resembles Babbalanja, however, in his status as a philosophical seeker who embraces both Western and Eastern modes of thought. Where he goes beyond both is in his friendship with Ishmael: Marnoo is a kind of living idol on which to gaze, and Babbalanja is the embodiment of philosophic wisdom, but only Queequeg truly can be said to be a fully rounded human character.

Ishmael's decision to worship Yojo with Queequeg is often read as a symptom of Melville's irreverence toward Christianity, but it is something more than that. Ishmael decides to worship Yojo on solidly Christian ethical grounds, and if there is a kind of subversive humor at work in the passage, there is also a strong biblical warrant for his behavior. He reasons that were he a missionary attempting to convert Queegueg, he would wish Queequeg to be converted; therefore, since Queequeg wished to convert him, the only way to follow the ethical logic of the Sermon on the Mount is to become a convert himself. This half-playful, half-serious willingness to mingle religious traditions recurs in Ishmael's interactions with Queequeg, from Ishmael's discussion of Queequeg's fast as a "Ramadan," thus applying an Islamic framework to Queequeg's distinctly non-Abrahamic religious tradition, to Ishmael's attributing sorrow to Queequeg with regard to Ishmael's own unwillingness to embrace "evangelical pagan piety" (*M-D* 86). This tendency toward religious syncretism reaches its climax with Ishmael's declaration to Captain Bildad that Queequeg is "a born member of the First Congregational Church" and "a deacon himself" (*M-D* 88). In the midst of his riddling and joking, Ishmael makes a straightforward statement in favor of a universal human communion, expounding that Queequeg belongs to "that same ancient Catholic Church to which you and I, and Captain Peleg there, and Queequeg here, and all of us, and every mother's son and soul of us; the great and everlasting First Congregation of this whole worshipping world" (*M-D* 88). Ishmael's serious point here is that there is, for Melville, a sense of universal human communion that transcends racial, cultural, and religious difference. The fact that, as Captain Peleg had pointed out a few lines earlier, Queequeg's blue facial tattoos remain, suggests that this communion is one that is defined by the irreducible differences in the communicants, as well as by their shared humanity. Melville thus creates a pair of characters in Ishmael and Queequeg who have found a means of living with difference, without attempting either to deny its existence or to make it grounds for dominance over the other.

Ishmael's conversion to living with religious difference is complete by the time he signs up to ship with the *Pequod*, and, paradoxically, it is precisely this conversion that leads him into a state of contentment with the sort of incompletion and incongruity that the *Pequod*'s very construction represents. Indeed, the *Pequod* is a kind of allegory for Ishmael's own mind. It has been composed out of the fragments of the various physical and cultural components of North American civilization, and its crew consists of an "Anacharsis Clootz deposition from all the isles of the earth" including Queequeg, an American Indian named Tashtego, and an African named Daggoo said to resemble the biblical Persian monarch Ahasuerus (*M-D* 121). The syncretism of its construction and its crew mirror the development of Ishmael's thought, not only over the course of *Moby-Dick*'s narration, but also before and after the experiences narrated in the novel. Ishmael is never done growing, like Melville, because he is constantly absorbing and translating difference, to borrow a turn of phrase from Walt Whitman.[21]

This absorption of difference appears in discursive elements of the text as well as characters and objects. What are we to make of the numerous references to Hinduism in the cetological chapters of *Moby-Dick*? One approach has been to argue that this is largely window dressing, as H. Bruce Franklin did in *The Wake of the Gods*. Another is to make the novel as a whole a fundamentally Hindu document, which H. B. Kulkarni did in his provocative but underappreciated study *Moby Dick: A Hindu Avatar*.[22] For Kulkarni, Ishmael's spiritual and ethical development throughout the novel shows a high level of congruity with Hindu philosophy, and when Ishmael's story reaches its climax, his ability to see through the veil of illusion that he describes in his discussion of both Ahab's and his own understanding of the meaning of Moby-Dick means that he has arrived at a distinctively Hindu sort of religious triumph.

If we turn to some of the specific moments in which Melville represents Hinduism in *Moby-Dick*, we discover something that is perhaps distinct from both Franklin's arguments and Kulkarni's. It is true, as the former suggests, that there is a strong humorous undercurrent in Ishmael's allusions to Hinduism; it is less clear that this truly indicates a purely satirical attitude toward Hinduism on Melville's part.[23] In "Of the Monstrous Pictures of Whales," Melville intentionally or otherwise mangles various facts about the images in the caves of Elephanta, but what is foremost about this discussion of Hinduism is that he places it as chronologically first among efforts at representing the whale, thus suggesting a similar priority in representations of the divine.

Crossing strands with both Indology and Egyptology is Melville's continuing interest in the indigenous religious traditions of the Pacific. As in *Typee*, *Omoo*, and *Mardi*, the indigenous religions of the South Pacific always hover in the background, and Melville tends to explain the South Pacific in terms of Asia and North Africa and vice versa. Even Queequeg's characterization, with its patchwork of Islamic and South Seas indigenous references, serves to create this sense of a linkage between these widely dispersed traditions. Melville puts these differing parts of the world into conversation with each other in several crucial moments in *Moby-Dick*.

"A Bower in the Arsacides," chapter 102 of *Moby-Dick*, illustrates Melville's syncretic method at its best. The chapter is set in the South Seas and purports to unlock the mysteries of the whale's frame while incidentally presenting a portrait of a utopian South Sea island. Ishmael begins with the teasing suggestion that he can "unbutton [the whale] still further, and untagging the points of his hose, unbuckling his garters, and casting loose the hooks and eyes of his innermost bones set before you in his ultimatum, that is to say, his unconditional skeleton" (*M-D* 448). Ishmael here imagines a sort of ontological striptease for the whale: he is undressed (stripped of his flesh) in order to reveal his essence in the form of his skeleton. As is so often the case in *Moby-Dick*, the essence of the whale points further to the meaning and significance of existence itself; the nakedness of the whale's skeleton corresponds to a desired exposure of the deity and a certainty about his intentions. Lest we doubt that the nudity of the whale's skeleton corresponds to the exposure of the Hebrew/Christian deity, the second paragraph of the chapter constitutes a burlesque of the concluding chapters of the book of Job, as Ishmael reproves himself, saying "Explain thyself, Ishmael. Can you land a full-grown whale on your deck for examination, as a cook dishes a roast pig?" (*M-D* 448). The language clearly parallels God's reprimand to Job from the King James Bible: "Canst thou draw out Leviathan with a hook?" In Job, the import of the rebuke is to set limits to human knowledge. Ishmael's translation of the rebuke into the language of whaling serves to render comical this otherwise stark indictment of human capacity for ultimate knowledge. The end of the paragraph shifts from Ishmael as Job to Ishmael as Jonah, identifying Jonah as the one figure who has been said to experience the inside of a living whale, and lightheartedly describing Jonah's experience of the whale as encompassing not only the "joists and beams" of the skeleton, but also the "tallow-vats, dairy rooms, butteries, and cheeseries in his bowels" (*M-D* 448). The effect is to deflate the seriousness of the pursuit of knowledge, all the while allowing the profundity of Job's questioning of God to lurk in the background. Moreover, it transforms the very bowels of the whale to a kind of domestic space: the enormity of unmodified nature being brought down to the human level.

After this humorous beginning, Ishmael reveals that he has come as close as possible to duplicating Jonah's experience of the interior of the whale: thanks to his "late royal friend Tranquo, king of Tranque, one of the Arsacides" (*M-D* 449). He has walked inside the ribs of the whale's skeleton and observed the ways in which it is incorporated into nature itself. The experience seems to change him personally, and it certainly changes the tone of the narrative:

> It was a wondrous sight. The wood was as green as the mosses of the Icy Glen; the trees stood high and haughty, feeling their living sap; the industrious earth beneath was as a weaver's loom, with a gorgeous

> carpet on it, whereof the ground-vine tendrils formed the warp and the woof, and the living flowers the figures. All the trees, with all their laden branches; all the shrubs, and ferns, and grasses; the message-carrying air; all these unceasingly were active. Through the lacings of the leaves, the great sun seemed a flying shuttle weaving the unwearied verdure. Oh busy weaver! unseen weaver! pause!—one word!—whither flows the fabric? what palace may it deck? wherefore all these ceaseless toilings? Speak weaver!—stay thy hand!—but one single word with thee! Nay—the shuttle flies—the figures float forth from the loom; the freshet rushing carpet forever slides away. The weaver-god he weaves, and by that weaving, he is deafened, that he hears no mortal voice; and by that humming, we too, who look upon the loom, are deafened; and only when we escape it shall we hear the thousand voices that speak through it. (*M-D* 449–50)

This passage has generated a number of impressive and subtle readings, and many critics, most notably Christopher Sten in *The Weaver-God, He Weaves* (1996), have rightly acknowledged its centrality to understanding Melville's aesthetics.[24] I want to read it carefully and at length in light of his treatment of religious difference, however, as I regard this specific moment as illuminating most fully how theology, culture, and aesthetics come together for Melville in his greatest novel. First, Melville revises in a thoroughgoing manner the picture of indigenous worship in the Pacific that he had constructed earlier in *Typee*. The gothic imagery and the coy allusions to cannibalism that characterized Melville's description of the scene of worship among the Typees are gone here, and in their place is a setting that resembles a cathedral, but emphasizes light rather than darkness. Here Melville is picking up a trope from his earlier work, but rather than revising mildly a fairly standard view of non-Protestant worship as he does in *Typee*, Melville uses the cathedral metaphor to create a truly visionary scene. The passage moves from an imagined space in the South Pacific world that Melville had dealt with at such length in his earlier work to a reflection on the nature of both reality and divinity. The patterns created by the leaves suggest both the stained-glass windows of a cathedral and the arabesque designs of non-representational Islamic art. The sound of the wind in the trees, which Ishmael compares to a loom, is the expression of the singular voice of God, but all of an immense number of human voices, suggesting the Transcendentalist idea of the Oversoul as the sum of human intellect and expression.[25] The performance of religious difference in this chapter is superb: Melville, through Ishmael, provides a humorously discursive narrative approach to understanding the uncertainties associated with the presence of a multiplicity of faiths and doubts in the world, and then follows it with a lyrically visionary approach, summing up beautifully much of what is at the core of this magnificent novel.

Melville deals with religious difference through his range of characters as well as through Ishmael's narrative voice. Most prominently, Fedallah, the Parsee leader of the shadow crew that Ahab has secreted onto the *Pequod*, possesses numerous elements, both in his physical description and in his character, that connect him to a number of religious traditions. Fedallah's religious status has been the subject of critical controversy, speculation, and uncertainty since the earliest days of *Moby-Dick* criticism. Early on, it was recognized that Fedallah fit only loosely with the Zoroastrian religion that Melville attributed to him. His name, as Dorothee Metlitsky Finkelstein pointed out, seems to associate him more with Islam than with Zoroastrianism, and his appearance has certain affinities with the grooming requirements for Sikh men, who are not permitted to cut their hair and who wear turbans.[26] Moreover, the crew that he commands is composed of Southeast Asian Muslims. So what can we make of Melville's syncretism in this case? Surely on one level we can read it as characteristic of nineteenth-century treatments of the non-Western world. Religions and geographical locations get jumbled together with relatively little concern for verisimilitude in, for example, works such as "Ligiea," by Edgar Allan Poe, Melville's near contemporary. Yet Melville's syncretism seems more intentional and designed than Poe's. The Parsees in India were and are of Iranian origin, and represent the remnants of the ancient Zoroastrian faith of Persia that was displaced by the triumph of Islam. Given Melville's long-term interest in the points of conflict and complementarity between late Greco-Roman religion and early Christianity, it is no surprise that he found the cognate case of Zoroastrianism and Islam to be a powerful source for his thought and art. The aspects of Zoroastrian theology most likely to be of interest to Melville would have included Zoroastrianism's understanding of a dualistic moral universe and of the struggle between good and evil as being fundamentally irreconcilable.[27]

Reading Jonah: Religious Difference and the Bible

Melville's interest in religious difference goes beyond the consideration of world religions and extends to a careful consideration of the nuances of Christianity itself. It would be easy to ignore "Jonah Historically Regarded" in a study like this one because the story of Jonah appears so firmly centered in the Hebrew and Christian religious tradition to many readers. This chapter, however, provides us with a remarkably compressed example of Melville's technique of playing with religious difference, not just for effect or for cheap laughs (though surely also for those purposes), but also for the epistemological insight provided by this sort of inquiry. In this chapter, Ishmael engages in a tongue-in-cheek defense of the historicity of Jonah, one of the first biblical stories to be debunked by means of the historical-critical method of biblical scholarship, and thus one of the points on which nascent fundamentalists took their most vigorous stand. It is worth reminding ourselves at this point that fundamentalism itself did not exist, or at the least had not yet been named, in Melville's time. Indeed, one of Melville's sharpest intuitions about the modern era was that he commented on fundamentalism in religion before it was prepared to comment upon itself, thus resulting in anachronistic references to "fundamentalism" on the part of some of his characters by early Melville critics like William Braswell, whose 1943 study, *Melville's Religious Thought*, remains among the most careful and thoughtful discussions of Melville's treatment of religion.[28]

In "Jonah Historically Regarded," Melville ridicules readings of the Bible that do not attend to the contradictions of the text or that insist on taking passages as scientific rather than poetic truth. Ishmael provides a tongue-in-cheek defense of the historicity of Jonah by remarking upon all the "evidence" for the events in the book. He begins with a parody of logical hairsplitting and question-begging (including an apparent affirmation of belief in the story of Hercules), and by the end of the chapter, he has worked his way into a multi-religious paradox: the two-stranded clincher for his argument for the reasonableness of the Jonah narrative is that, on the one hand a Portuguese Catholic priest has argued that Jonah must have been transported around the Cape of Good Hope in a "magnification of the general miracle"; on the other "to this day, the highly enlightened Turks devoutly believe in the historical story of Jonah" (*M-D* 366). Ishmael thus makes the historicity of a biblical text, a point defended ferociously by conservative Protestants, to depend on extra-biblical testimony from a Catholic priest and a Muslim empire, both of which would have been denigrated by the very Protestants on behalf of whom Ishmael mounts his tongue-in-cheek defense. Here the fact of religious difference, and unlooked-for points of similarity across these differences, again highlights the instability and uncertainty of religious identities.

"Jonah Historically Regarded" becomes a vantage point from which to revisit Father Mapple's sermon in the early pages of the novel. This sermon might seem to be the negation of religious difference: Father Mapple knows exactly, it would seem, who God is, what he expects, and what the responsibilities of human beings, both clerical and lay, are in relation to this God and his expectations. And yet Father Mapple's sermon is oddly parallel to many of the elements of religious difference that work their way through the novel. Father Mapple's "two-stranded lesson" is characteristic of Melville's general narrative method from *Typee* onward, and he achieves the most significant effects in his sermon by playing against each other alternative interpretations of both the world and one's duty (*M-D* 42). For Father Mapple, Jonah's story is a parable of the difficulty of submitting one's human will to the will of God, and he urges his listeners to engage in just such an act of submission as Jonah initially fails to engage in. The allure of such submission, however, is paradoxically the radical freedom that it provides. Mapple closes his sermon with an image of the explosive freedom from constraint experienced by those who submit to God, but whose very submission frees them from more mundane constraints:

> Delight is to him—a far, far upward and inward delight—who against the proud gods and commodores of this earth, ever stands forth his own inexorable self. Delight is to him whose strong arms yet support him, when the ship of this base, treacherous world has gone down beneath him. Delight is to him who gives no quarter in the truth, and kills, burns and destroys all sin, though he pluck it from under the robes of senators and judges. Delight—top-gallant delight is to him who acknowledges no law or lord but the Lord his God and is only patriot to heaven. Delight is to him, whom all the waves of the billows of the seas can never shake from this sure Keell of Ages. And eternal delight and deliciousness will be his, who coming to lay him down, can say with his final breath—O Father!—chiefly known to me by thy rod—mortal or immortal, here I die. I have striven to be thine, more than to be the world's, or mine own. Yet this is nothing; I leave eternity to thee, for what is man that he should live out the lifetime of his God? (*M-D* 48)

Mapple's "two-stranded lesson" relates to two complementary modes of being in relation to the divine: he advocates submission to God, but to God alone, thus entailing a sort of rebelliousness relative to all earthly powers. The instability of such a position is noteworthy: it can lead on the one hand to intellectual timidity, but for the individual convinced that duty toward God has been or is being fulfilled, it can release tremendous intellectual energy and iconoclasm. This sermon is thus a case study in Melville's combination in his prose of heroic, individualistic elements with communal and Christian elements. Furthermore, Father Mapple's blend of intransigence and submission mirrors that of the description of Christ inscribed onto the front pastedown of Melville's copy of *The New Testament and Psalms*: Christian love and romantic heroism are made to coexist, however unstable this compound may be, and however much Father Mapple's two strands may pull against each other.

The second sermon in *Moby-Dick*, Fleece's sermon to the sharks, takes on added significance in this light. Fleece is making a universal ethical appeal based on the morality of the Sermon on the Mount, and he likewise draws upon the sense of human possibility characteristic of liberal Protestantism.[29] If the sharks "gobern" their appetites and behave in a seemly manner, they can live lives compatible with virtue and reason and become angelic; if not, they are condemned to their own brutish nature. Fleece, however, suspects that the sharks will prove unable to control their desire for whale meat, so he concludes his sermon with a spirited condemnation, inviting the sharks to "fill your dam' bellies till they bust—and den die" (*M-D* 295). Fleece's sermon is shorter and more direct than is Father Mapple's, but the argument is much the same: self-denial is crucial for salvation, but rare to the point of being heroic.

This tendency to submerge serious commentary on religious difference into even the coarsest sort of humor is of course most manifest in "The Cassock," the brief chapter in *Moby-Dick* devoted to the uses of the whale's penis. Ishmael approaches the subject of the whale's penis with characteristic indirection:

> Not the wondrous cistern in the whale's head; not the prodigy of his unhinged lower jaw; not the miracle of his symmetrical tale; none of these would so surprise you as half a glimpse of his unaccountable cone—longer than a Kentuckian is tall, nigh a foot in diameter at the base, and jet-black as Yojo, the ebony idol of Queequeg. And an idol indeed it is, or rather, in old times its likeness was. Such an idol as that found in the groves of Queen Maachah in Judea, and for worshipping which, king Asa, her son, did depose her, and destroyed the idol, and burnt it for an abomination at the brook of Kedron, as darkly set forth in the 15th chapter of the first book of Kings. (*M-D* 419)

This moment deserves some unpacking. Ishmael carefully talks his way around the whale's penis, but makes clear through indirection precisely what this "enigmatical object" is. Moreover, he makes this clear specifically by reference to those portions of the Bible that deal most harshly with the matter of religious difference. That the phallus was used as a devotional object in ancient Canaanite religions provided a justification for the absolute contempt in which these religions are held in the Hebrew scriptures. Melville is thus engaged in a discussion of religious difference that parallels in some ways his treatment of Asian religions in other portions of the novel. The passage also is highly suggestive with regard to Ahab's role as captain of the ship and mad Elijah's role as the figure who warns Ishmael and Queequeg against going aboard the *Pequod*. The biblical Ahab is condemned by the Hebrew God and opposed by Elijah precisely because he makes use of Canaanite religious practices.

Ishmael moves from these forbidding religious practices to matters closer to home, with relatively safe gibes toward Catholicism mixed with riskier jabs at Protestant doctrine. The whale's penis is connected in a derisive manner with Catholic vestments, making the whale a "candidate for an archbishoprick," but the mincing that the boy dressed in the skin of the whale's penis was engaged in is producing "Bible leaves," thus including the central sacred object for Protestants in the risqué joke (*M-D* 420). Melville moves quite smoothly from a sacred symbol in a condemned, non-monotheistic religion to sacred symbols within the two major branches of Christianity extant in the nineteenth-century United States, suggesting unlooked-for points of continuity between Christianity and other faiths. Melville is interested here in the ways in which various religious symbols can easily resolve themselves into parody, simply through a small shift in context. The fact that it is Catholicism and Protestantism that are invoked here as the parameters for religious difference is significant, as it points us back to the questions of religious difference within Christianity that hover in the background of Melville's work up through *Moby-Dick* and come to the fore in the later work.

World religions and biblical interpretation both play major roles in Melville's depiction of religious difference in *Moby-Dick*, but his representation of American religious minorities is likewise highly significant. The two religious minorities that loom the largest in *Moby-Dick*, the Quakers and the Shakers, were both idiosyncratic religious movements whose beliefs placed them in one way or another outside the American mainstream. As noted above, sexuality and violence provide an important part of Melville's dialogue with Marquesan culture and religion in *Typee* and *Omoo*, and it is in regard to these two strands that the Quakers and Shakers represent alternatives to American Christianity more generally. The Quakers have opted out of the practice of violence embodied in war-making, and the Shakers have opted out of the practice of sexuality contained within procreative lovemaking. Both represent a kind of withdrawal from the commonsense world of nineteenth-century American Protestantism, and Melville is interested in the difference that these forms of withdrawal make.

In *White-Jacket*, Melville had used the Quakers as a model for a version of Christianity that renounced the violence that the narrator associated with mainstream Christian denominations (the "war-voting Bench of Bishops"), but in *Moby-Dick* he was up to something different. He emphasizes throughout the novel the way in which Quaker nonviolence, which he associates with the most careful adherence to the ethical standards of the Sermon on the Mount, could become a sort of dead letter once profit became a dominant motive. Bildad, Peleg, and Ahab are, each in his own way, "Quakers with a vengeance," violent adherents of a distinctively nonviolent creed (*M-D* 73). The Shakers present a still more curious and nuanced case. This religious group was, unlike the Quakers (or the Dunkers, whom Melville references in *Israel Potter*), a truly made-in-America religious tradition, owing its origins to the religious vision of one American woman, Mother Ann Lee. The role of Gabriel, the Shaker sailor on the *Jereboam* who warns Captain Ahab of his impending doom, in *Moby-Dick* reflects this sense of possibility associated with Shakerism. Gabriel is mad, in one sense, but as with Pip after he is abandoned at sea, it is a divine madness, one that clarifies the character's vision rather than simply rendering him ridiculous. When Gabriel warns Ahab to abandon his blasphemous quest, he is able to speak with such authority because of his status as a figure separated from the world by his religious faith—and the fact of Shaker celibacy makes his separation absolute in a degree to which even Quakers cannot aspire.

A crucial moment with regard to Quaker pacifism is Starbuck's temptation to murder Ahab. Near the climax of the novel, Starbuck finds himself in a position to end Ahab's mad pursuit of the white whale by assassinating him. There are obvious echoes of David's refusal to slay Saul in the Hebrew scriptures, but there is also a crucial tension between the demand in the Sermon on the Mount for followers of Jesus to turn the other cheek, a demand observed with great seriousness by Quakers, and the need to prevent evil from exercising its power in the world. Starbuck is ultimately unable to assassinate Ahab, but he has come up against the crux of Melville's treatment of religious difference: the tension between the resolution of competing imperatives within institutional religious tradition and the personal resolution of these same imperatives on the part of the individual.

Quakers and Shakers play a background role at this stage of Melville's career to the global interreligious elements discussed above, but they also point toward his growing interest in the new developments in religious faith that would help to redefine religious experience in the Americas. These elements predominate in his fiction from the later portions of the 1850s, but they are not absent from *Moby-Dick*, as the Quaker ownership of the *Pequod* and the appearance of Gabriel in the narrative make clear. As the 1850s went on, Melville would make more and wider references to small, distinctive Christian denominations and sects within the United States, and the presence of these elements within the Oriental frames of *Moby-Dick* is a harbinger of things to come.

"I Alone Am Escaped": Religious Difference in the Epilogue

The crisscrossing patterns of difference that emerge in *Moby-Dick*—Eastern and Western, Catholic and Protestant, Presbyterian and Quaker—are brought to a point of brilliant irresolution in the "Epilogue" to the novel. The echoes of Job from the epilogue have been discussed frequently and are quite evident. Ishmael's conclusion also invokes the prophetic books from the Hebrew scriptures, most notably the book of Daniel, when he describes the sharks as having "glided by as if with padlocks on their mouths" (*M-D* 573). It is really only at this moment, when the *Rachel* recovers Ishmael, "another orphan," that the narrator whom we meet at the start of *Moby-Dick* is truly born.

When Ishmael is retrieved by the *Rachel*, then, he has achieved a state which has been described at various times by virtually all of the major religious traditions with which Melville was in dialogue. He is in a state of separation from worldly ambition and desire, having lost all those things after which he has previously striven. Like Pip, the young African American cabin boy who was abandoned at sea before being recovered, he has found himself caught up in the supreme isolation of the sea—indeed for a longer time than Pip himself—and thus the lyrically mournful description of Pip's brief time as a castaway applies even more directly to Ishmael himself. Because Pip's experience as a castaway is framed in terms of madness, and because racism was so evidently a cause for his abandonment, the serious religious significance of Pip's vision, and of the fact that Ishmael was in a position to describe it, can easily be missed. With regard to Pip's abandonment at sea, Ishmael suggests:

> The sea had jeeringly kept his finite body up, but had jeeringly drowned the infinite of his soul. Not drowned entirely though. Rather carried down alive to wondrous depths, where strange shapes

> of the unwarped primal world glided to and fro before his passive eyes; and the miser-merman, Wisdom, revealed his hoarded heaps; and among the joyous, heartless, ever juvenile eternities, Pip saw the multitudinous, God-omnipresent, coral insects, that out of the firmament of waters heaved the colossal orbs. He saw God's foot upon the treadle of the loom, and spoke it; and therefore his shipmates called him mad. So man's insanity is heaven's sense, and wandering from all mortal reason, man comes at last to that celestial thought, which, to reason, is absurd and frantic; and weal or woe, feels then uncompromised, indifferent as his God. (*M-D* 414)

Pip's experience is not unknowable because, as we find out at the end of the novel, Ishmael has experienced it, and the lyrical intensity with which Ishmael describes Pip's situation derives its force from Ishmael's own status as a castaway floating upon the deep after the *Pequod* goes down. Certain aspects of Pip's experience bring the religious undercurrent to the fore: Pip has seen the "hoarded heaps" of the "miser-merman, Wisdom," and Ishmael alone, as he says quoting Job in the epigraph to the epilogue, is escaped to tell us.

Ishmael's and Pip's "indifference" become mutually illuminating here. Both have passed through a transformative experience, and both have been fundamentally altered by it. In neither case is this experience a conventionally religious conversion, but in both it offers a deeper insight into the nature of divinity itself. Pip's uncompromised, indifferent state at the end of chapter 93 suggests the condition of a man who has survived a significant trauma, but also that of a man who has overcome his worldly attachments. Pip has achieved something like enlightenment, and Ishmael's ability to narrate *Moby-Dick* depends on a similar level of non-attachment to the passing world. This quality is curiously connected to Ishmael's relationship with Queequeg as well: the coffin that Ishmael clings to is the coffin Queequeg has made, and Queequeg's decision to make the coffin illustrates his state of awareness of and learned indifference to his own mortality. He is compared directly to medieval Catholic monks who slept in their coffins, and it is clear that like Ishmael by the end of the narrative and Pip after his experience as a castaway, he has achieved what Ahab could only desire, the piercing through of the "pasteboard masks" of illusion.

Ishmael's perspective subsequent to the *Pequod*'s sinking and Pip's perspective subsequent to his time as a castaway come together to electrifying effect in "The Doubloon," a chapter that sums up the use of religious difference in *Moby-Dick* better than any other. In this chapter, characters each gaze upon the doubloon that Ahab has hammered onto the masthead and offer their respective interpretations: Flask from the standpoint of naive materialism, Starbuck from the standpoint of orthodox Christianity, and Ahab from the standpoint of overwhelming individual self-assertion. It is Pip's parsing of the verb "to look" that captures the degree to which the characters' differing perspectives inevitably shape the meaning of the coin for them, just as cultural perspectives have earlier been shown to shape the meaning of the whale. Ishmael's observation of Pip's statements, which he comprehends while Stubb, who is also observing Pip and also observed by Ishmael does not, is enabled by his own achieved indifference: telling the story in retrospect, he shares Pip's unearthly wisdom.

The blending of Ishmael and Pip in their experiences and observations should cause us to remember one vital fact about *Moby-Dick*: not just the epilogue, but the telling of the entire novel occur after the sinking of the *Pequod*. All of Ishmael's reflections are those of a man who has experienced both individual egotism and community at their highest pitch, of a man who has seen through the illusions of life, who has had the most compressed experience of asceticism imaginable in his time floating on Queequeg's coffin at sea. This is in no small part the reason that *Moby-Dick* is not fragmented in the way that *Mardi* is. *Mardi* presents us with the dialogue among a variety of religious, cultural, and artistic impulses; *Moby-Dick* presents us with the way in which one highly active and complex consciousness absorbs all of these impulses and transforms them. The trajectory from *Mardi* to *Moby-Dick*, then, and through the telling of *Moby-Dick* itself, is through dealing with difference through relativistic comparison to dealing with difference through unstable synthesis.

Melville's Own Faith: The View from the Masthead in 1851

Is it possible to discern a point of view from which Melville himself is writing in the midst of the welter of biblical allusions, references to Calvinist, Catholic, Unitarian, and Quaker theology, suggestive linkages with Judaism, Islam, Zoroastrianism, Hinduism, Buddhism, ancient Egyptian religion, and anthropological asides on the indigenous religions of American Indians and South Pacific islanders? Must we regard Melville's stance as an insoluble cipher? I want to suggest that the answer to this last question is an emphatic "No!" It is certainly not possible to fit the Melville of *Moby-Dick* into a neat category with regard to religious belief, but equally certainly, it is possible to discern the broad contours of Melville's stance on religious and ethical questions.

The Melville who wrote the early novels of the Pacific and *Moby-Dick* was in the process of a rapid intellectual and artistic development in a very compressed period of time. In the first two novels, he is a typical anti-authoritarian rebel, railing against the destructive effects of institutions and the hypocrisies that maintain them. Despite his own dismissal of *Redburn* and *White-Jacket* as work for hire, there is discernable moral and intellectual growth in these pieces. While he continues to be appalled and indignant at hypocrisy, there is a genuine sense of compassion and empathy for the poor and for victims of violence. *Mardi*, while it must be regarded as a failure in relation to the grandiose aims that Melville had for it, has the effect of working out a developing relationship between Melville's use of a variety of doctrinal traditions and mythologies to get at the question of the nature of truth, and his efforts at constructing a consistent, knowable ethical norm for human interactions. *Mardi* also begins to capture the sheer intellectual exuberance of Melville's work at this stage in his development, forecasting further the extravagances of *Moby-Dick*, *Pierre*, and *The Confidence-Man*. *Moby-Dick*, finally, shows Melville reaching an artistic and intellectual pinnacle: the play of representations of religious difference and dialogue is so fluid that it moves throughout the entire novel, possible to miss only because it is so ubiquitous.

Melville's correspondence from the months when he was completing *Moby-Dick* verifies the impression that religious difference was at the center of his preoccupations in 1851. His most famous letters to Nathaniel Hawthorne are suffused with religious imagery, and it is used in a way that reflects a specific concern with difference. For example, in Melville's often-quoted letter of November 1851, Melville invokes one of the most sacred and contested figures in Christian devotional and liturgical practice: the Eucharist. Melville writes:

> In me divine magnanimities are spontaneous and instantaneous—catch them while you can. The world goes round and the other side comes up. So now I can't write what I felt. But I felt pantheistic then—your heart beat in my ribs and mine in yours, and both in God's. A sense of unspeakable security is in me at the moment, on account of your having understood the book. I have written a wicked book, and feel spotless as the lamb. Ineffable socialities are in me. I would sit down and dine with you and all the gods in old Rome's Pantheon. It is a strange feeling—no hopefulness is in it, and no

> despair. Content—that is it; and irresponsibility; but without licentious inclination. I speak now of my profoundest sense of being, not of an incidental feeling.
>
> Whence come you, Hawthorne? By what right do you drink from my flagon of life? And when I put it to my lips, lo, they are yours and not mine. I feel that the Godhead is broken up like the bread at the Supper, and that we are its pieces. Hence this infinite fraternity of feeling. (*Corres*. 212)

The images here blend the religious and the erotic perfectly. Hawthorne and Melville themselves become a physical realization of the divine love incarnated in the Eucharist, and thus part of the Godhead. Surely those who identify a homoerotic subtext are correct here; the erotic intensity of the imagery is overwhelming, complete with the implication of a passionate kiss. Melville's use of the term "pantheistic" in this letter also clarifies his repeated use of the term throughout *Moby-Dick*. Pantheism here is the surge of emotion that erases doctrinal distinctions and identities, creating communities of belief and feeling that can transcend membership in a particular church or adherence to a particular creed. Melville frequently treats this term with a kind of ironic detachment through much of *Moby-Dick*, having Ishmael issue the warning "Heed it well, ye Pantheists!" after describing the precarious position of a Platonic dreamer on the masthead of a whale ship (*M-D* 159). Melville's conflicted relationship with "pantheism" contributes both to the humor of the scene and to its uneasy sense that a too eager embrace of possibility can ultimately prove destructive in a world that is all too constrained by solid realities. Here, however, in this intensely personal letter to Hawthorne, Melville uses "pantheism" without his characteristic irony, making the "infinite fraternity of feeling" an earnest expression of the artistic and emotional communion that he and Hawthorne and others who write and think partake in. The vision here is a powerful one: human connectedness creates the grounds for the moment that transcends ordinary human experience, and at least in this one letter, the lonely impulse toward creation and the impulse toward community and self-sacrifice are one.

The relationship among doctrine, ethics, and feeling—what Jonathan Edwards referred to as the "religious affections"—is what brings together the divergent religious aspects of *Moby-Dick*. Doctrine provides a conceptual framework necessary to understand and evaluate both deeds of benevolence and feeling of connectedness and awe. While ethics and emotion are dependent on doctrine to give them shape and focus, they are also constrained and limited by doctrine. Here, Melville's conflicted reading of Emerson and Goethe, whom he regarded as the modern pantheists par excellence, becomes instructive. In a letter to Hawthorne, after citing Goethe's admonition to "live in the All," Melville retorted, "What nonsense! Here is a fellow with a raging toothache. 'My dear boy,' Goethe says to him, 'you are sorely afflicted with that toothache, but you must *live in the all*, and then you will be happy" (*Corres.* 193). Melville concludes, "As with all great genius, there is an immense deal of flummery in Goethe, and in proportion to my own contact with him, a monstrous deal in me" (193–94). The lesson here is clear: however intellectually satisfying and abstractly inspiring a thinker's vision may be, concrete realities, the pains, joys, and sorrows that make up human life, ultimately trump the authority of ideas on their own. If our metaphysics take no account of toothaches, they are sadly lacking, and if our theology takes no account of the actual sensations of human suffering, theodicy becomes hollow at best. Something like this is at work in another of Melville's letters to Hawthorne, from April 1851, when he exclaims "Why is it, Mr. Hawthorne, that in the last stages of metaphysics a fellow always falls to *swearing* so?" (*Corres.* 186–87). Melville's affection for bold intellectual exploration is countered by his sense of the necessity of retaining a clear tie to life as experienced, with all the complexity, uncertainty, and even anger that can be lost in the too great coherence of intellectual systems.

It is in light of these questions of pantheism, syncretism, and interreligious doctrinal disputes that Ishmael's famous discussion of the Catskill eagle and King Solomon becomes most intelligible. In Melville's copy of the *Holy Bible with Apocrypha*, he marked the portions classified as wisdom literature with particular care and attention. This obsession with the wisdom literature of the Old Testament is clearly evident in his extended meditation on Ecclesiastes in the Catskill eagle portion of "The Try-Works" chapter:

> Nevertheless, the sun hides not Virginia's Dismal Swamp, nor Rome's accursed Campagna, nor wide Sahara, nor all the millions of miles of deserts and of griefs beneath the moon. The sun hides not the ocean, which is the dark side of this earth, and which is two thirds of this earth. So, therefore, that mortal man who hath more of joy than of sorrow in him, that mortal man cannot be true—not true, or undeveloped. With books the same. The truest of all men was the Man of Sorrows, and the truest of all books is Solomon's, and Ecclesiastes is the fine hammered steel of woe. "All is vanity." ALL. This willful world hath not got hold of unchristian Solomon's wisdom yet. But he who dodges hospitals and jails, and walks fast crossing graveyards,

> and would rather talk of operas than hell; and calls Cowper, Young, Pascal, Rousseau poor devils all of sick men; and throughout a care-free lifetime swears by Rabelais as passing wise and therefore jolly; not that man is fitted to sit down on tombstones, and break the green damp mould with unfathomably wondrous Solomon. (*M-D* 424)

Melville's range of allusion here is truly stunning. He builds the passage around a reflection on Solomon's acknowledgment of the vanity of human desire and aspiration, and he fuses a series of authors who might seem to fit very curiously with each other indeed as examples of allegedly "sick men" who shared Solomon's insights. What each of these figures shares is a willingness to see past the pleasant surfaces of life—to recognize that, as Ishmael memorably concludes in "The Whiteness of the Whale," "all deified Nature absolutely paints like the harlot, whose allurements cover nothing but the charnel house within" (*M-D* 195). Still more suggestive is Ishmael's use of the term "unchristian Solomon"—on one level this is simply true: Solomon precedes Jesus in time and therefore cannot be logically described as a Christian—but the more resonant aspect of this description is that Solomon here represents an actual alternative to Christianity. If the resurrection ultimately redeems all the vanities of existence within orthodox Christian belief, Solomon's insistence on the vanity of human existence runs counter to this redemptive message. The fact that Jesus himself is evoked specifically as the "Man of Sorrows" here suggests that there is something of "unchristian Solomon" even in the central figure in the Christian religion, and thus of non-Christian religious insight in general within Christianity.

The often-quoted image that follows this virtuoso passage on the wisdom of Solomon becomes much clearer and more luminous in light of the complex set of allusions to Solomon and to the more recent authors whom Melville invokes. Here, the religious import of Melville's imagery is especially rich:

> And there is a Catskill eagle in some souls that can alike dive down into the blackest gorges, and soar out of them again and become invisible in the sunny spaces. And even if he forever flies within the gorge, that gorge is in the mountains; so that even in his lowest swoop the mountain eagle is higher than other birds upon the plain, even though they soar. (*M-D* 415)

The Catskill eagle, and those souls who resemble the Catskill eagle, express a sense of the division of human experience between moments of transcendent power and freedom and moments of constraint and loss. This dual sense of explosive freedom and repressive constraint finds echoes in numerous of Melville's contemporaries. Thoreau acknowledges a similar impulse in the concluding chapter of *Walden*:

> I fear chiefly lest my expression may not be extravagant enough, may not wander far enough beyond the narrow limits of my daily experience, so as to be adequate to the truth of which I have been convinced. Extra vagance! it depends on how you are yarded. The migrating buffalo, which seeks new pastures in another latitude, is not extravagant like the cow which kicks over the pail, leaps the cowyard fence, and runs after her calf, in milking time. I desire to speak somewhere without bounds; like a man in a waking moment, to men in their waking moments; for I am convinced that I cannot exaggerate enough even to lay the foundation of a true expression. Who that has heard a strain of music feared then lest he should speak extravagantly any more forever?[30]

What joins Thoreau with Melville here is a shared interest in the questions of boundaries and the way in which one maintains one's sense of self in relation to them. If they ultimately proceed in different directions—Thoreau toward an unbounded state of freedom and daring, Dickinson toward a fierce oscillation between explosion and restraint, and Melville toward a stance that creates spiritual freedom within material constraints—the fundamental impulse is the same. The expression of this impulse likewise mirrors Melville's allegorical discussion of philosophy and poetry in *Mardi*: like the poet Yoomy, the Catskill eagle soars; like the philosopher Babbalanja, the Catskill eagle dives (*Mardi* 438). Melville's comprehension of difference in this portion of *Moby-Dick* thus encompasses modes of expression as well as matters of doctrine.

Melville's conflicted status as a figure who partakes of both belief and unbelief in a variety of traditions becomes more intelligible when we realize how characteristic of his times Melville was. Indeed, this sort of capacity to serve as a representative figure for one's own time while remaining intensely idiosyncratic is one of the things that Ishmael identifies as being a sign of greatness in Ahab:

> So that there are instances among [the Quakers] of men, who, named with scripture names—a singularly common fashion on the island—and in childhood naturally imbibing the stately dramatic thee and thou of the Quaker idiom; still from the audacious, boundless, and

> daring adventure of their subsequent lives, strangely blend with these unoutgrown peculiarities, a thousand bold dashes of character not unworthy of a Scandinavian sea-king or a poetical pagan Roman. And when these things unite in a man of greatly superior natural force, with a globular brain and a ponderous heart; who has also by the stillness and seclusion of many long night watches in the remotest waters, and beneath constellation never seen here at the north, been led to think untraditionally and independently; receiving all nature's sweet or savage impressions fresh from her own virgin, voluntary, and confiding breast, and thereby chiefly, but with some help from accidental advantages, to learn a bold and nervous lofty language—that man makes one in a whole nation's census—a mighty pageant creature, formed for noble tragedies. (*M-D* 73)

Ahab is a "mighty pageant creature" precisely because he is intimately embedded in his own Quaker community—thus becoming both a solitary representation of godlike genius and a figure intimately conjoined to a collective story. Ahab's "bold and nervous lofty language" comes from himself and from solitary reflection upon nature, but also from his status as a Quaker and a member of a culture immersed in the Hebrew and Christian scriptures. In himself, Ahab embodies Melville's twin poles of solitude and sociability. Indeed, Ahab's very wound seems in part to be most essentially defined, not by a missing limb, but by the inability to make the sorts of human connections that would render the loss of this limb bearable—the fact that he is driven by the need for power and control over his fellow humans as much as over the whale or the hidden, inscrutable divinity that the whale represents means that he is unable to experience the sort of healing through interpersonal connection that Ishmael experiences with Queequeg or when working with the other sailors on the *Pequod*. Simultaneously, it is true that Ahab could not be Ahab apart from the influences of his own Quaker community, however much he strikes against it in this last voyage of his life: his language is drawn, as Ishmael reflects early on in the novel, from the Quaker tradition, and Ahab's voice would not be what it is were he not a Quaker.

Melville's concept of originality is never that of the individual who is completely free from all constraints; rather, it is a conception of an individual who fully realizes the clashes and tensions between individual free will and communal and cosmic necessity. This sense of the pressure that the collective always exerts on the individual, and even of the degree to which the idea of individuality is itself a fiction, is an intuition that would have been equally reinforced for Melville in the Dutch Reformed

Church of his youth and among the indigenous peoples of the Pacific and their religious traditions. The thematic emphasis on uncertainty, then, which we see so widely dispersed in Melville's writing, is connected to these contrary impulses. The individual wishes to be heroic, like the version of Jesus present in the quotation from Goethe on the inside cover of Melville's copy of *The New Testament and Psalms*, but the very impulse toward solitude and creation that characterizes these figures makes them increasingly dependent on the connections that come from community. The community into which one is born inevitably impinges on one's independence, and the community of the living and the dead that one chooses is what enables creative independence in the first place. Melville's profound ambivalence about the questions posed by religious difference is shaped by his insight into the complementary nature of individual creativity and the varieties of community in which the creative individual lives and moves. Among the most overused and frequently abused quotations from any portion of Melville's body of work is his rhetorical flourish in "Hawthorne and His Mosses" that "For genius, all over the world, stands hand in hand, and one shock of recognition runs the whole circle round" (*PT* 249). As hackneyed as this quotation may seem by now, it truly captures something essential about Melville's artistic, ethical, and theological vision: genius is lonely and involves a nearly blasphemous degree of trust in one's own capabilities, but it is also richly interdependent with the efforts of others.

Melville's devotion to questions of difference and uncertainty thus becomes relevant to the reflections that he shares with Hawthorne on the topic of money and the marketplace. One of Melville's most frequently cited remarks from his letters to Hawthorne is the line "Dollars damn me, and the malicious devil is forever grinning in at me with his hand upon the door " (*Corres.* 191). The demonic imagery Melville associates with money here stands in stark contrast to the imagery he draws from the Gospels throughout his letters. Even as Melville seeks to imagine a community based on genuine compassion and shared human dignity, he is forced to acknowledge the divisiveness of financial concerns, and his letters frequently oscillate between assertions that his writings strive to rise to the moral and spiritual level of the Gospels and the ironic rebuttal to these aspirations provided by the fundamental necessity of obtaining cash. Melville's use of Eucharistic imagery ("the Bread from the Supper") stands in tension with the diabolical power of money to divide humans and disrupt their sense of communion.

This use of Eucharistic imagery that appears in his letters to Hawthorne becomes all the more striking when we realize how deeply *Moby-Dick* was invested in the same sort of imagery. In an earlier letter to Hawthorne, Melville had slyly invoked Eucharistic, sacramental imagery quite irreverently, writing that the "secret motto" of *Moby-Dick* was "ego non baptizo, in nomine—but make out the rest yourself" (*Corres.* 196). Melville follows the reference to a parody of Christian baptism with the suggestion that he will share with Hawthorne a portion of the whale's fin, remarking that "the tail is not yet cooked—though the hell-fire in which the whole book is broiled might not unreasonably have cook it all ere this" (196). The whale's fin becomes a sort of ironic Eucharist, even as Ahab creates a sort of anti-Christian communion in the two major chapters of *Moby-Dick*, "The Quarter-Deck" and "The Candles." Meanwhile, a profound sort of interpersonal communion reminiscent of the Sermon on the Mount is achieved in a highly ironized passage from the opening of the chapter entitled "A Squeeze of the Hand." In this passage, alternately affecting and humorous, Ishmael rhapsodizes about the process of "squeezing case":

> Such an abounding, affectionate, friendly, loving feeling did this avocation beget; that at last I was continually squeezing their hands, and looking into their eyes sentimentally; as much as to say—Oh! My dear fellow beings, why should we longer cherish any social acerbities, or know the slightest ill-humor or envy! Come; let us squeeze hands all round; nay let us all squeeze ourselves into each other; let us squeeze ourselves universally into the very milk and sperm of human kindness.
>
> Would that I could keep squeezing that sperm forever! For now, since by many prolonged, repeated experiences, I have perceived that in all cases, man must eventually lower, or at least shift, his conceit of attainable felicity, not placing it anywhere in the intellect or the fancy; but in the wife, the heart, the bed, the table, the saddle, the fire-side, the country; now that I have perceived all this, I am ready to squeeze case eternally. In thoughts of the visions of the night, I saw long rows of angels in paradise, each with his hands in a jar of spermaceti. (*M-D* 416)

"Squeezing case" seems to offer the opportunity for a truly egalitarian alternative human society, and yet the activity is provisional and temporary—no "social acerbities" may be entertained in the act of squeezing case, but the chase with all its violence both enables this moment of communion and looms as its sequel. In order for the moment of transcendent communion among the men to take place, the whale must be killed, and the ultimate reason for this act of violence is not the men's spiritual, or even carnal, uplift, but rather the pursuit of profit. Moreover, the successful chase that obtained this particular whale is the chase that has resulted in Pip's abandonment at sea—an act that is far removed from the apparent interpersonal communion in the following chapter. Likewise, for Melville, Christian communion both models an ideal of human oneness and compassion, and is the product of the violence of the crucifixion and cognate forms of religious persecution. This dual capacity for community and violence is at the core of Melville's understanding of humanity in all its aspects, both the sharkish and the divine. Whether considering the unsettling mismatch between the cooperative Typee community and the cruelties with which the Typees had been charged, or contemplating the violence embedded in martial discipline, or reminding readers of *Moby-Dick* that even those who are Quakers may be so "with a vengeance," Melville always keeps this particular duality in view.

By the end of 1851, then, Melville had completed a body of work that had probed questions of religious difference and global comparative religion to a degree and with a precision that no other American author had achieved. The years that followed would mark a radical departure from Melville's early use of the sea and the islands of the South Pacific as the crucial settings for most of his work (although the sea would continue to feature largely in *Benito Cereno* and *The Encantadas*). If Melville never fully returned to the "landlessness" of his early work, his attentiveness to cultural and religious difference did not diminish, but rather mutated into new forms. If the Melville of the late 1840s and early 1850s found that travel and global cultural exchange allowed him the best opportunity to explore the differing human approaches to meaning and morality, the Melville of the later 1850s found that the Americas provided him with a broad scope for examining the permutations of religious difference; and in Melville's turn to poetry after 1857, Melville's engagement with questions of difference became still more complex.

The shift that Melville's treatment of religion underwent after *Moby-Dick* was about theology as well as geography. Religious difference in Melville's middle period is not so much a matter of a clash of doctrines and mythologies, the effects of which he had described and narrated so superbly in *Moby-Dick*, but rather of the tension between religious aspirations and human capacity, and of the intersection between religious traditions and the secular but quasi-religious movements of nationalism, reform, revolution, and self-culture. These ideas had been introduced in the earlier novels, but they assumed center stage in Melville's work from the 1850s, both the short fiction that he wrote for magazines and the titanically ambitious novels *Pierre* and *The Confidence-Man*. On sea or on land, Melville continued to ask the ultimate questions, and to comment incisively on the widely varying answers that human beings have proposed for these questions.

Chapter 3

"Poor Richard Ain't a Dunker": Mapping American Religious Difference, *Pierre* to *The Confidence-Man*

Upon meeting Benjamin Franklin in Paris, Melville's version of Israel Potter is puzzled by Franklin's worldly sagacity. He takes up a copy of *Poor Richard's Almanac*, and he finds in its pages a series of quotations that he reads with a mixture of admiration and concern. When Potter reads such admonitions as "Industry need not wish, and he that lives upon hope will die fasting, as Poor Richard says. There are no gains without pains. Then help hands, for I have no lands, as Poor Richard says," he responds bitterly, noting that "it's wisdom that's cheap, it's fortune that's dear. That ain't in Poor Richard, but it ought to be" (*IP* 54). This hard-earned cynicism regarding the power of cash would prove to be a central theme throughout the 1850s, as indeed it had become in Melville's letters to Hawthorne in the months surrounding the publication of *Moby-Dick*. Following this expression of frustration, Israel makes an odd remark, referring to an American religious group far more obscure than the Quakers or even the Shakers. Having read with some bemusement Poor Richard's assertion that "God helps them that help themselves," he remarks, "Let's consider that. Poor Richard ain't a Dunker, that's certain, though he has lived in Pennsylvania" (*IP* 54).

Melville's invocation of the Dunkers is a curious one, and it also serves to illuminate his method in treating religious matters in the 1850s. Unlike the Shakers, about whom Melville read in *A Summary View of the Millennial Church* (1848), we do not have a definite source for Melville's reading about the Dunkers. It is worth noting, however, that the Shakers and the Dunkers are dealt with in the same chapter of *Evans' Sketch of the Denominations of the Christian World* (1837), by James Aikman, on the grounds that both groups are entirely American in their composition, even though both Mother Ann Lee of the Shakers and the original leaders of the Dunkers emigrated from England and Germany respectively. We do not have a record of Melville reading *Evans' Sketch of the Denominations*, but it is the sort of reference work that he could have consulted in order to find out more about this group. When Melville invokes the Dunkers, he is invoking a group that is significantly more obscure than the Quakers or even the Shakers, a group with its origins in continental Europe rather than in England (Quakers) or North America (Shakers). Some of the same features that would have made the Quakers and Shakers of interest to Melville would have also piqued his interest in the Dunkers. The Dunkers were a Protestant sect that was heavily shaped by German Pietism, and their beliefs included a democratic approach to church government, a tendency to emphasize the Sermon on the Mount as the crucial ethical element in the Gospels, simplicity of lifestyle, pacifism, and, on one occasion and in one place, a commitment to celibacy in the service of religious reflection and the pursuit of divinity through the arts that was connected economically to a variety of Christian communism. If indeed Melville consulted *Evans' Sketch of the Denominations of the Christian World*, he would have read an allusion to the remarkable experiment that took place in Ephrata, Pennsylvania, in the early eighteenth century. Indeed, *Evans* somewhat misrepresented the severity of the Dunkers, whose faith contained more mainstream proponents, by describing them as if the only Dunkers were the members of the Ephrata community. The Ephrata Brethren instituted a celibate community that shared its possessions completely and that devoted itself to esoteric modes of religious worship and the development of new modes of music that they believed could better bring glory to God than traditional varieties of church music. *Evans* describes the Dunkers (again somewhat misleadingly), as follows:

> The Dunkers (or Tunkers) arose about 1724, and formed themselves into a kind of commonwealth, mostly in Pennsylvania. They baptize by immersion, dress like the Dominican friars, never shave head nor beard, have different apartments for the sexes, live chiefly on roots and vegetables, except at their love-feasts, when they eat only mutton. It is said that no bed is allowed to them but in case of sickness, for in their separate cells they have a bench to lie upon, and a block of wood for their pillow. Their principal tenet is the mortification of the body, and they deny the eternity of future punishment. They are commonly called the *harmless* Dunkers.[1]

This sense of selflessness, asceticism, and devotion to the arts seems far removed from the practicality and shrewdness of Franklin and his creation Poor Richard. So, not to be a "Dunker" becomes a very loaded sort of negation indeed. Poor Richard—and of course Franklin himself—is not celibate, not selfless, not committed to a transcendent and impractical ideal. (Indeed, Melville has quite a bit of fun with Franklin's reputation as a geriatric ladies' man in Paris in *Israel Potter*.) It is not hard to conclude that on some level, Melville saw himself precisely as a Dunker, as a man who in his spiritual and ethical aspirations and his artistic strivings was attempting to arrive at a vision at the truth that can only be arrived at via rigorous discipline.

The element of celibacy that was introduced by the allusions to the Shakers and reinforced by the oblique connection to the Ephrata Commune in *Israel Potter* is highly suggestive of a tendency that would resurface throughout Melville's career. In Melville's markings of 1 Corinthians 7, he calls attention to Paul's discussion of the benefits of celibacy, marking the chapter heavily. Although it is possible to see Melville's interest in these references to celibacy (and to certain potentially misogynistic passages in the Old Testament) as being signs of a hatred of women or of the unhappiness of his marriage, it is possible to take another view. The reason that Paul advocated celibacy, for women as well as men, was that he suggested that family life interfered on a fundamental level with the sort of purity of purpose required of a Christian living in the last days. Melville's reasons for marking this passage may be similar: as an artist determined to tell the truth, he may have found that the demands of family life conflicted with his most fundamental artistic and existential impulses.

Israel Potter's meeting with Benjamin Franklin highlights an important transition in Melville's career. In the works that Melville wrote before 1852, from *Typee* to *Moby-Dick*, his treatment of religious difference is explicit and exuberant: we see a widening circle of global cultural and religious traditions in dialogue with each other, moving from the encounter among the South Seas, Europe, and North America to encounters throughout the Americas, and with Near Eastern and South Asian religious history and practice. This extensiveness of allusion is never absent from Melville's later fiction, but the dominant mode after 1851 is not exuberance but irony.

Melville's most important work of literary criticism, "Hawthorne and His Mosses," likewise shapes and is shaped by his attentiveness to questions of religious difference and what these questions mean for a comprehension of the truth. In "Hawthorne and His Mosses," Melville makes an argument for the efficacy of fiction in the search for truth, and he frames this search for truth in religious terms. Melville identifies the crucial trait in Hawthorne's fiction as being its confrontation with and exemplification of the "power of blackness," and he links this both to a submerged tendency toward Calvinism and the doctrine of Original Sin in Hawthorne's thought and to Hawthorne's unflinching pursuit of truth. If Melville presents Hawthorne as an icon of courage in "Hawthorne and His Mosses," he also links this quality to ambivalence, suggesting that it is the mixture of light and dark, hope and courage in the face of doubt that defines Hawthorne's artistry: "Still more. This black conceit pervades him, through and through. You may be witched by his sunlight—transported by the bright gildings in the skies he builds over you;—but there is the blackness of darkness beyond;—and even his bright gildings but fringe, and play upon the edges of thunder-clouds" (*PT* 243). The chiaroscuro in this image is a superb description of Melville's own religious ambivalence—the predominance of difference as a defining trope for his work means that whatever is true of Melville's religious positioning, its opposite is likewise in no small part true. Characteristically, Melville links this to his sense of the artist as a religious figure: Shakespeare, he writes, "craftily says, or sometimes insinuates, the things, which we feel to be so terrifically true, that it were all but madness, for any good man, in his own proper character, to utter, or even hint of them" (*PT* 244). Melville is also concerned to point to the elusiveness of the truth, however, pointing out that "in this world of lies, Truth is forced to fly like a scared white doe in the woodlands; and only by cunning glimpses will she reveal herself" (*PT* 244). Hawthorne and Shakespeare alike, then, are distinguished by a terrific sense of courage in the pursuit of truth, and a tremendous subtlety in the representation of truth, two traits that Melville valued above all others.

Benjamin Franklin, Plotinus Plinlimmon, and the Church of the Apostles: *Pierre* and *Israel Potter*

Before *Israel Potter*, Melville began probing questions of religious difference within the United States in the novel that followed *Moby-Dick*: *Pierre, or the Ambiguities* (1852). In this at times lurid sentimental gothic novel, Melville represented his narrator as being in consistent dialogue with inherited American Protestant religious traditions, the Bible itself, and the rising schools of thought associated with Transcendentalism and Reformism in antebellum America. Pierre is a young man who is driven by his uncertainty about the character of his father and the possible existence of a sister, to whom he is ambiguously attracted sexually. The question of filial piety thus always looms large in *Pierre*, making this a novel in which Melville works through many of his friend Hawthorne's key obsessions.[2]

Among the most frequently discussed portions of *Pierre* is the pivotal chapter "The Journey and the Pamphlet," and it is clear that in this portion of the novel, Melville is dealing directly with the question of the relationship between Christian ethics and contemporary practice that *Israel Potter* hints at. Plotinus Plinlimmon, the author of the pamphlet, frames his argument in terms of the contrast between secular and sacred time. Plinlimmon, who later appears in person at the Church of the Apostles, argues in his pamphlet that secular and sacred time need not be viewed as being in opposition to each other, but rather are complementary: from the standpoint of heavenly time, "the gratuitous return of good for evil" commanded by Jesus in the Sermon on the Mount must be considered the standard for true virtue; whereas from the standpoint of secular, earthly time, this principle can only be folly. Plinlimmon uses the term "chronometer" to refer to heavenly timekeeping, and "horologe" to refer to earthly timekeeping, and he ultimately argues that chronometrical timekeeping (and thus the commands of the Sermon on the Mount) is falsified in this horological world by "the history of Christendom for the last 1800 years," which after all had been "as full of blood, violence, wrong, and iniquity of every kind, as any other portion of the world's story" (*Pierre* 215). The "virtuous expediency" that Plinlimmon recommends is in fact the reverse of the quest for an elusive but intrinsically desirable truth that Melville endorsed in "Hawthorne and His Mosses": rather than risk suffering and disappointment for an ideal, Plinlimmon enjoins his readers to embrace prudence and renounce idealism altogether.

Melville offers an alternative to Plinlimmon's cynicism in this chapter, however. In the narrator's commentary on the enthusiasm that young men feel when presented with an ideal vision of life and morality like the Sermon on the Mount, the alternative presented to Plinlimmon's callow volubility is silence. Immediately before the beginning of Plinlimmon's pamphlet, the narrator observes that the pamphlet seems "more the excellently illustrated restatement of the problem, than the solution to the problem itself" (*Pierre* 210). The fact that this is the last observation that the narrator makes before sharing the text of the pamphlet may make it seem that the narrator has presented no solution to the problem of the discrepancy between worldly prudence and heavenly love that the pamphlet poses, but of course he has presented a solution at the very outset of the chapter, and repeated it several pages later. In the opening paragraph, the narrator concludes with the observation that "Silence is the only voice of our God," and he revisits this assertion when he says, "That profound Silence, the only voice of our God, which I before spoke of, from that divine thing without a name, those imposter philosophers pretend to have somehow got an answer; which is as absurd, as though they should say that they had got water out of a stone; for how can a man get a Voice out of Silence" (*Pierre* 204, 208). The answer that Melville proposes, then, to the quandary posed by the distance between humanity's spiritual aspiration and the corruption of the world, is that same that Pip and Ishmael discover in their separate experiences of abandonment at sea in *Moby-Dick*: a sort of purified indifference to the passing world, and the ability to live with divine silence and inscrutability. Pierre, with his enthusiasm for the Sermon on the Mount and his commitment to discovering truth, is a would-be Dunker in a world of Benjamin Franklins, and his inability to choose either cynicism or silence is what sets in motion his tragic fall.

On his way to his eventual collapse, Pierre comes to the curiously named Church of the Apostles. It might be well to consider what such a church might stand for metonymically in the religious landscape of nineteenth-century Manhattan. New York had been the site of a great deal of religious ferment during the first half of the nineteenth century, and the leading impulse behind it seems to have been the desire to get things right once and for all in the interpretation of Christianity.[3] This incorporated both a reactionary element and a utopian one. The name "The Church of the Apostles" points both toward a desire to return to the purity of the early Christian church and toward a desire to begin the church anew without the baggage of the past. It also, however, expresses the Transcendentalist and Reformist impulse for newness and originality. Typically, Melville expresses substantial ambivalence about this sort of impulse: when he describes the Church of the Apostles, he emphasizes its curious mix of artists and lawyers' offices, suggesting that a space that at one time was envisioned as an alternative to the quotidian world of moneymaking has become absorbed into it.

Pierre's bloody conclusion also reflects in its own way on the questions of religious difference that shaped the novel from its beginning. The novel reaches its climax with a confrontation between Pierre and Glen in which Pierre signally fails to turn the other cheek, thus confirming Plinlimmon's skepticism. Pierre's opportunity to realize the demands of the Sermon on the Mount in his life has been lost, and with it Pierre's own grounds for considering himself a good person, a good Christian, or a good artist. Small wonder then, that the novel ends with Pierre's suicide as a man who has lost faith in everything that he believes to matter.

The reception of *Pierre* was as bloody as its conclusion, and it bears some pondering here. As Hershel Parker and Brian Higgins have established, *Pierre* received the most ruthlessly negative response from the critics of any of Melville's novels, extending even to a headline, which

Parker unearthed, that magisterially pronounced "Herman Melville Crazy."[4] What was the source of this vitriolic condemnation? One view has been that Melville courted precisely this response by turning on the public during the period when he was completing the novel, and deliberately marring his own work. This argument seems plausible, and is supported by the most formidable of Melville biographers, Hershel Parker, but it perhaps falls short of explaining the full intensity of the dismissal of this work.[5] Nor does the lurid, gothic quality or the use of incest as a plot device fully explain the forcefulness of its censure. Perhaps the most plausible explanation for the vehement rejection which this novel received is that by suggesting that nineteenth-century American respectability ran counter to the very religion that formed its basis—and unlike other expressions of dissent, *Pierre* gave no hope that this situation was resolvable.

When Melville turned from the nihilism of the final scene of *Pierre* to *Israel Potter*, he recalibrated his treatment of religious difference to encompass the development of a secular public square based on the acknowledgment of religious difference in the earliest years of the republic. Indeed, this brief and often ignored novella is among the earliest and most incisive treatments of the idea of civil religion in American literature.[6] Israel, the title character, is based on a historical figure who has participated in the Battle of Bunker Hill only to find himself a captive of the British. He is thus a part of one of the great public sacrifices in American civil religion, the heroism of the American revolutionaries, but he himself has become a castaway relative to the young nation's development.

The most extensive of the historical cameos in the midst of which Israel finds himself is his prolonged visit with Benjamin Franklin in Paris. In Melville's portrayal, Franklin is both an admirable figure and a curiously amoral one, a figure who partakes equally of the sage and the trickster. Franklin is of course one of the winners to emerge from the American Revolution, achieving success through intelligence, cunning, and clever self-promotion. When Israel observes "Poor Richard ain't a Dunker," then, he is commenting on the transformation that has taken place in the movement from an approach to religious belief and practice that is based on uncompromising self-sacrifice to one that makes room for human frailty and desire. He is also commenting on a contrast between the historical winners and losers who emerged from America's revolution: idiosyncratic groups like the Dunkers, who flourished in earlier times, make way for a new and distinctively American persona—all this despite the fact that, as Melville may have known, Franklin himself praised the Dunkers for their industry and tolerance on some occasions. We find ourselves asking again, where does Melville stand in all this? Does he regard himself as Poor Richard, or as a Dunker? In part, the fiction from the remainder of the 1850s is devoted to providing an answer to this question, which is a crucial point of conflict throughout *Israel Potter*.

In the character of John Paul Jones, the defiant captain of the *Bonhomme Richard*, whom Israel meets later in the novel, Melville provides an alternative, though not a solution, to the dichotomy between Dunkers and Poor Richards. Jones is neither an avatar of self-sacrifice nor of expedience, but rather a heroically determined figure who will not submit to the designs of others if they interfere with his own sense of destiny. Jones is like a version of Father Mapple whose rebellion is truly universal, or a purely human version of the inflexible Jesus of the Goethe quotation in the front of Melville's copy of the New Testament. In this way, Jones harks back to Captain Ahab and forward to the Indian-hating Colonel Moredock of *The Confidence-Man*, and his presence sharpens the ethical question that Melville poses: how can one absorb both the heroic and the communal virtues, and become a member of a community without relaxing toward mediocrity or tensing in the direction of intolerance, while still retaining the freedom and aesthetic independence necessary to be an artist? This question would recur in various forms throughout Melville's short fiction.

Failing Faith and Feeble Knees: *The Piazza Tales*

Melville's most wide-ranging treatment of religious difference between *Moby-Dick* and *Clarel* was his collection of short stories and sketches, most of which were originally published in magazines, entitled *The Piazza Tales*. *The Piazza Tales* included the novella *Benito Cereno*, the short stories "The Piazza," "Bartleby, the Scrivener," "The Lightning-Rod Man," and "The Bell Tower," and also the ten-sketch mini-collection *The Encantadas*. From the first piece in *Piazza Tales* Melville makes it clear that the interrogation of religious difference that has shaped his career so far will continue to do so.

The element of irony that predominates in *The Piazza Tales* is evident in abundance in the opening story, "The Piazza," a tale that is noteworthy for the way in which the grand range of allusion in Melville's earlier works is both enlisted and subordinated to the mordant wit of his later fiction.[7] Certainly this tale is nothing if not broadly allusive: Melville repeatedly invokes Shakespeare, Cervantes, Spenser, and Tennyson throughout the story, while including sly commentary on his narrator's (and thus his own) ocean-going past. Despite its allusions to the romance tradition, the story has an eerily contemporary feel to it, taking as it does house-pride and house-envy as the dominant sources of its humor. The allusions, and their religious resonances, are significant, however. Early in the story, Melville's narrator uses the piazza that his narrator is building as a metaphor for a place of worship, saying:

> And beauty is like piety—you cannot run and read it; tranquility and constancy, with, now-a-days, an easy chair, are needed. For though, of old, when reverence was in vogue, and indolence was not, the devotees of Nature, doubtless, used to stand and adore—just as, in the cathedrals of those ages, the worshippers of a higher Power did—yet, in these times of failing faith and feeble knees, we have the piazza and the pew. (*PT* 2)

The tone here varies between the sermonic and the jocular. Melville's narrator brings together art, nature, and religion in his discussion of the mountain and the need for a piazza, and what he says about them takes the form of a comic jeremiad: nineteenth-century men and women need piazzas for the same reason they need pews. In both cases, there has been a falling away from a prior age of faith to a current age of uncertainty, and in churches and on mountainsides alike, modern humans need to sit. There is a shrewd comment here on the nature of modernity. Melville's contemporaries, faced with uncertainty about the meaning of both faith and the natural world, have to maintain a certain ironic distance even from their most cherished beliefs. This use of the religious and the natural and the ambivalence of the modern relation to both appears again when Melville's narrator compares the mountain to Westminster Abbey: "But, if damps abound at times at Westminster Abbey, because it is so old, why not within this monastery of mountains, which is older?" (*PT* 2). This question of relative age is crucial in the story, because Melville finds himself referring persistently back to European masterworks—not just architectural monuments like Westminster Abbey, but also the works of Spenser and Cervantes. Finding an equivalent to Westminster Abbey in the mountains, which are geologically ancient despite being in a young country, becomes the equivalent of finding grounds for artistic confidence in an America that lacks the tradition associated with the long scope of European history. Melville refers to this tradition with a mix of reverence and sarcasm, commenting with biting irony on the fact that in the aftermath of the 1848 revolutions, "these kings, they had the casting vote, and voted for themselves" (*PT* 3). Non-Western religious references likewise proliferate in this very brief story, from the reference to a massive stone quarried from the local hills as the Kaaba (the sacred stone around which Muslim pilgrims to Mecca congregate), to his reference to Marianna, the woman he meets on the mountain, and who resembles "some Tahiti girl, secreted for the sacrifice, first catching sight, through the palms, of Captain Cook" (*PT* 9). The effect of all these widely disparate cultural references coming together is quite jarring: the story is set in New England, but contemporary Europe, and the Europe of legend and folklore, and the Islamic Near East, and the Polynesian islands are all somehow present.

The second story in *Piazza Tales*, "Bartleby, the Scrivener," is both the most famous of the collection and one that is devoted to differing approaches to faith and deeds within the Christian tradition.[8] As with the narrator of "The Piazza," the lawyer who narrates "Bartleby" is caught in the contradiction between a powerful and absolute code of ethics and the modern tendency toward equivocation, and he bridges the gap with self-mocking irony. In the opening paragraphs of "Bartleby," the narrator, who is a lawyer who does "a cozy business among rich men's deeds," speaks with a sort of prideful humility about his work for John Jacob Astor. By the end of the piece, he has gone to the extreme of inviting Bartleby to live with him in order to rescue Bartleby from his own self-neglect. Here again religious difference is defined by the varying responses possible to central ethical questions posed by life in the nineteenth century. The narrator's ethical dilemmas are framed in part by several different understandings of Christianity: on the day when he discovers that Bartleby has taken up residence in his office, he has intended to attend Trinity Church, an already historic Episcopalian church on Wall Street. When he considers the possibility that he may be predestined to provide shelter for Bartleby in perpetuity, he turns to the ultimate American Calvinist theologian, Jonathan Edwards, and the British Deist Joseph Priestly. And, as American as the setting for Bartleby may be, when the narrator reflects on Bartleby's isolation, he turns to the ancient Near Eastern ruins of Petra for his metaphor. In his ruminations on Bartleby's hermit-like state in the office, the narrator invokes the Protestant critique of Catholic monasticism as being too separated from the everyday world. Thus, although it is not often foregrounded, religious difference lurks in the background of Melville's most famous short story.

Benito Cereno extends the emphasis on the ethical dimensions of religious experience from the interpersonal level to the international level, considering the central moral and ethical issue of Melville's age: the enslavement of one group of human beings by another.[9] As a result of its thematic focus on the slave trade, it also extends Melville's treatment of differing approaches to ethics from Wall Street to the wider vista of the Americas as a whole. The narrative method changes, however. The narrators of "The Piazza" and "Bartleby" are both urbane, witty men who define themselves by their verbal acuity. In this story, as in *Israel Potter*, Melville uses a real-life protagonist who has actually written his own account of the events described in the form of the American sea captain Amasa Delano, who interacts with both slavery and Mediterranean Catholicism in the Americas. This novella brings together the ethical and the epistemological in a truly virtuoso performance. With his account of a slave rebellion at sea through the eyes of a narrator who is at once innocent and hypocritical, Amasa Delano, Melville raised his blending of questions of faith and ethics to the highest point it had yet reached. Delano is described at the outset as possessing a "singularly undistrustful good nature" with a dry comment from the narrator about what this may suggest about his intelligence and wisdom (*PT* 47).

As numerous commentators have noted, this is the work in which Melville makes the most extended use of the anti-Catholic tropes that predominated in much nineteenth-century Protestant writing in the United States, but the crux of the story is not so much about the villainy of Catholic Spanish and Portuguese slave traders as the complicity of the seemingly virtuous Delano. The ship is called the *San Dominick* and thus named, as Jenny Franchot has pointed out in *Roads to Rome*,[10] for the religious order most closely associated with the Inquisition, and when Delano notes figures moving about on the ship, he associates them with "Blackfriars" in a "white-washed monastery"—a pun on the fact that the Africans, not the Europeans are really in control of the *San Dominick*, but also a reference to the Dominican order and to Protestant tendencies to associate Catholic clergy with Jesus's critique of the Pharisees as being "white-washed sepulchers" (*PT* 48).

Religious difference also enters this piece through its emphasis on interpretation. Repeatedly, Delano is invited to read the signs in front of him, and repeatedly he fails to do so. When, for example, Babo is shaving Don Benito, in one of the most famous tableaux of the novella, Delano allows his fancy to run free:

> As master and man stood before him, the black upholding the white, Captain Delano could not but bethink him of the beauty of that relationship which could present such a spectacle of fidelity on the one hand and confidence on the other. The scene was heightened by the

> contrast in dress, denoting their relative positions. The Spaniard wore a loose Chili jacket of dark velvet; white small clothes and stockings, with silver buckles at the knee and instep; a high-crowned sombrero, of fine grass; a slender sword, silver-mounted, hung from a knot in his sash; the last being an almost invariable adjunct, more for utility than ornament, of a South American gentleman's dress to this hour. Excepting when his occasional nervous contortions brought about disarray, there was a certain precision in his attire, curiously at variance with the unsightly disorder around; especially in the belittered Ghetto, forward of the main-mast, wholly occupied by the blacks.
>
> The servant wore nothing but wide trousers, apparently, from their coarseness and patches, made out of some old topsail; they were clean, and confined at the waist by some bit of unstranded rope, which with his composed, deprecatory air at times, made him look something like a begging friar of the order of St. Francis. (*PT* 57)

This is a rich passage, and one that encapsulates most of the story's themes and motifs in one image. We see a contrast between Don Benito as the representative of the violent, man-of-war world that Melville has already critiqued in *White-Jacket* bearing all the sartorial signs of power and control, and contrasted with him, Babo as a mendicant Franciscan friar, wearing garments that suggest the renunciation of the world. Don Benito represents power Babo represents powerlessness; and a mutual faith in the justice of the system in which they are enmeshed, "fidelity" on Babo's part, "confidence" on Don Benito's, holds the entire pattern together. Concepts drawn from the "romantic racialism" that obtained even in antislavery American religious cultures contributes its own piece to the mosaic, in that a convention of such works as Harriet Beecher Stowe's *Uncle Tom's Cabin* was to see Africans as more humble than Europeans and therefore closer to God.[11]

The problem, of course, is that none of these appearances are true, and the entire scene is a fabric of increasingly potent ironies. Don Benito appears to be in command; Babo is in command; Don Benito is sartorially sophisticated and Babo simple, but Babo's intellectual powers have triumphed over Don Benito's; the "whitewashed" ship is in the control of "the blacks." Babo's seemingly dutiful service is a performance, and the "confident" Don Benito is in terror for his life even as Babo has no reason to show the least "fidelity" to his enslaver. On a still lower level, however, the paradoxes of the Sermon on the Mount have been acted out completely: if not the earth, the seemingly meek have at least inherited the San Dominick. Religious and cultural difference have here been woven flawlessly with the novella's themes of appearance and reality and its profound undermining of racialized hierarchies.

A formal device that would reappear in *Billy Budd* was Melville's use of official documents associated with Babo's trial as a means of illustrating the vexed relation of official accounts to the truth. Unlike the later ostensible report from a trial in *Billy Budd*, this account does not illustrate in an obvious manner the gap between truth and received opinion (rather fulfilling the function of revealing the facts about the *San Dominick* that Delano had missed), but it does touch suggestively on this matter when Delano is in conversation with Don Benito at the end of the story. When Delano asks Benito Cereno why he is still mournful after he has been rescued from the slave rebellion, saying "you are saved; what has cast a shadow upon you," Don Benito's only reply is "the negro" (*PT* 116). For Don Benito, the report may have explained the matter to the satisfaction of the local bureaucrats, and Babo may have been silenced forever, first by his own choice and then by his execution, but the meaning of the story has escaped the bounds of the narrative. The silence of Don Benito, and of Babo, at the end of the story suggests that here as elsewhere in Melville's fiction, the ultimate truths remain incommunicable.

"The Lightning-Rod Man" continues the collection's focus on the tension between doctrine and ethics. It also revisits one of the earliest sources of conflict and controversy in Melville's career—the missionary impulse within Christianity. In *Typee* and *Omoo* Melville had scandalized devout pro-mission Protestants by satirizing evangelical missionaries in the South Pacific, and this story makes clear that the defects of Christian missions are still very much on Melville's mind. This story is narrated by a man who is bemused by a visit from an earnest salesman peddling lightning rods and armed with the most alarming statistics about the dangers presented by lightning. The narrator's playful references to the salesman as Jupiter Tonans bring to the fore the element of religious difference in the story. The salesman represents himself in strictly Christian terms, threatening what is simultaneously the actual effect of an electrical storm and a metaphor for the wrath of the Almighty. By tying this connection between lightning and the wrath of the monotheistic Christian deity to the ancient pagan tradition of worshipping a sky god, the narrator relativizes the salesman's message in ways that the salesman cannot accept: hence the salesman's violent response to the narrators baiting at the end of the story. That Melville did not believe that the sort of enlightened critique that the narrator offered would dissuade believers in redemption and damnation from their narratives is apparent from the conclusion of the story: the salesman "still dwells in the land, still travels in storm-time, and drives a brave trade with the fears of man" (*PT* 124). One thing that this story should make clear is that a major part of Melville's response to the sort of religious difference represented by nineteenth-century revivalism was a liberal, rationalized Christianity like that implicitly espoused by the narrator of this story when he dismisses the salesman as a "Tetzel" preying on the fears of humanity and suggests that God's compassion should trump this fear. The reference to the salesman as a "Tetzel" is a loaded one: the salesman is a representative of evangelical Protestantism, but he is being compared by the narrator to a Catholic monk infamous for the peddling of indulgences.[12] Both Catholicism and pre-Christian religious traditions thus provide the language for Melville's critique of nineteenth-century revivalism.

In addition to his attempts at making a living as a writer of magazine fiction, in the 1850s Melville turned to the public lecture. Melville's lectures on travel and the South Seas from the later 1850s (as reconstructed by Merton M. Sealts) also served to point his audience to questions of religious and cultural difference.[13] In "Traveling," Melville advocated travel as a means of coming to understand and appreciate cultural difference. Melville argued that the benefit of travel is that it enables people to dispense with their preconceptions, particularly those that cluster around race, culture, and religion, writing: "Travel to a large and generous nature is as a new birth. Its legitimate tendency is to teach a profound personal humility, while it enlarges the sphere of comprehensive benevolence until it includes the whole human race" (*PT* 423). This emphasis on physical travel as both enabling and metaphorically corresponding to the experience of difference makes this essay, brief though it is, a fulcrum of sorts for Melville's career. From *Typee* to *Moby-Dick*, the role of travel by sea in creating cross-cultural and interreligious contact is central to the themes and plots of Melville's novels, and in *The Confidence-Man* the Mississippi River takes on a similar role. In Melville's poetry, this focus on the role of travel in creating and representing encounters with difference only intensifies, so in a sense, "Traveling" shows the continuity that obtains across Melville's career.

Although "Traveling" is the most obviously engaged with questions of religious difference of Melville's lectures, several others shed light on the questions that we have been considering in this chapter. In "Statues in Rome," Melville demonstrates an interest in the interaction between the ancient classical and the Christian worlds that would shape much of his poetry in *Timoleon* quite profoundly.[14] This point is full of meaning, given the degree to which the Christian and the classical provided the poles on which early republican thought in the United States oscillated. Melville seems to prefer the classical to the Christian in some regards; he writes:

> And yet there was about all the Romans a heroic tone peculiar to ancient life. Their virtues were great and noble, and these virtues made them great and noble. They possessed a natural majesty that was not put on and taken off at pleasure, as was that of certain eastern monarchs when they put on or took off their garments of Tyrian dye. It is to be hoped that this is not wholly lost from the world, although the sense of earthly vanity inculcated by Christianity may have swallowed it up in humility. (*PT* 402)

Here, as is so often the case in Melville's commentary on Christianity, there is ambivalence at work. Melville certainly expressed approval at various points in his career for Christianity's inculcation of a "sense of earthly vanity," but he also seems to have had reservations regarding the possibility of art's coexistence with such a realization. Thus art for Melville arises out of a meeting of opposing impulses: the classical virtues on the one hand, and Christian humility on the other.

Melville's remarks on Milton are especially illuminating in this regard. Melville points out the pre-Christian elements embedded in Milton that, in his view, are the very markers of Milton's greatness as a verbal artist, and he compares them with the pre-Christian elements in the Vatican that help to make that locale a great repository of the world's art as well as a strictly Christian and specifically Roman Catholic religious site. Melville argues:

> "Paradise Lost" is but a great Vatican done into verse. Milton must have gleaned from these representations of the great men or the gods of ancient Rome high ideas of the grand in form and bearing. Many of those ideas from heathen personages he afterwards appropriated to his celestials, just as the Pope's artist converted the old heathen Pantheon into a Christian church. Lucifer and his angels cast down from heaven are thus taken from a group at a private palace in Padua, among the most wonderful works of statuary. This was sculptured out of a single block, five feet in height, by one of the later Italian artists. Three-score of the fallen lie wound together writhing and tortured, while, proud and sullen in the midst, is Satan, unbroken and defiant, his whole body breathing revenge and his attitude one never to submit or yield. (*PT* 403)

Melville's commentary on Milton's artistic process here is highly illuminating with regard to his own. By making the Vatican into a poem, Milton has incorporated a religious tradition antithetical to his own Puritanism, that of the Catholic Church, and made it a source of vitality in his own art. Likewise, the Church itself has incorporated the art of pagan Rome into its own Christian architecture. Melville becomes in this view one more in a series of artists who finds a way to incorporate opposing religious stances into a new artistic vision.

In yet another lecture, "The South Seas," Melville makes a connection between his American audience in the 1850s and his early work in *Typee* and *Omoo*. This lecture outlines the lessons Melville had distilled from his time in the Marquesas, Tahiti, and Hawaii. Like "Traveling," this piece provides us with an opportunity to see how Melville's reflections on his experiences in the Marquesas, Tahiti, and Hawaii developed over the years. Melville provides an overview of the history of European imperialism in the Pacific, from Balboa and Magellan to the nineteenth-century British, French, and American presence in the Pacific. He reflects particularly on the way in which the South Pacific comes to be seen as a site for potential utopias, noting the interest of such diverse groups as Protestant missionaries, Mormons, Free Lovers, and utopians of various philosophies. Melville's ultimate plea is for the Pacific Islanders to be spared further encroachment from Western civilization until Europe and North America have themselves matured morally:

> As a philanthropist in general, and a friend to the Polynesians in particular, I hope these Edens of the South Seas, blessed with fertile soils and peopled with happy natives, many being yet uncontaminated by the contact with civilization, will long remain unspoiled in their simplicity, beauty, and purity. And as for annexation, I beg to offer up an earnest prayer—and I entreat all present and all Christians to join me in it—that the banns of union should be forbidden until *we* have found for ourselves a civilization morally, mentally, and physically higher than one which has culminated in almshouses, prisons, and hospitals. (*PT* 420)

Here Melville argues that the claims of difference must be respected, that the Polynesians' own civilization should be honored, and that a critical eye should be turned on the failings of European and North American civilization. As is so often the case for Melville, he suggests that truth will be found in the presence of difference, rather than in its effacement.

When we look at these lectures as a group, we can see one of the reasons for Melville's ambivalence toward Christianity: his admiration for the Sermon on the Mount is mingled with a sense of disappointment in the aesthetic shortcomings of a religious ethic founded on humility. The sort of self-assertion that art requires seems somehow out of keeping with a way of life that denies the self and follows another. Thus the oscillation between the urge toward individual freedom, creation, and charisma and communal charity, support, and affection that characterizes Melville's marginalia and his early accounts of freedom and community in the Marquesas continues to be an obsession in his public life throughout the 1850s. All of these elements would coalesce spectacularly in a novel that would have to wait decades longer than *Moby-Dick* to be recognized as a major work of American literature: *The Confidence-Man.*

"That Multiform Pilgrim Species": The Inter-Religious Riddle of *The Confidence-Man*

With the exception of *Billy Budd* and some brief pieces connected to his poetry, Melville's career as a writer of prose fiction ended with a truly strange novel by the title of *The Confidence-Man, His Masquerade* (1857). This novel is the narrative of a series of shifting disguises adopted by a mid-nineteenth-century confidence man on a Mississippi steamboat. The novel received an intensely negative reaction from contemporary critics when it was first published, and even after the Melville Revival of the 1920s, it continued to be regarded as a minor work of limited interest until it was recovered for modern scholarship by Elizabeth S. Foster at the start of the 1950s, nearly a century after its publication. After Foster, H. Bruce Franklin and Edgar Dryden, both rising young scholars in the 1960s, identified *The Confidence-Man* as belonging to the center rather than the periphery of Melville's artistic development, and ever since, it has been impossible to consider the full scope of Melville's career without recourse to this enigmatic and darkly humorous novel.[15]

Religious difference in its pan-American manifestation appears even before the novel's opening sentence. The dedication is "to the victims of Auto da Fe"—a phrase which calls up Melville's recurring themes on multiple levels. The Portuguese words "Auto da Fe" would be recognizable to most American Protestant readers from tales of the Spanish Inquisition, and would instantly call up associations with religious fanaticism, superstition, and torture, imprisonment, execution, and terror in the name of religion (a connection that, as Jenny Franchot has pointed out, Melville also made in *Benito Cereno*). On this level, the dedication points toward victims specifically of religious intolerance. On a "still lower level," to use Ahab's evocative turn of phrase, the literal translation of the term matters as well. Literally, an Auto da Fe translates to an "act of faith," so the victims to whom Melville refers seem to be not merely victims of the Spanish Inquisition (a meaning congenial to many Protestants and nativists as referring to the iniquities of Roman Catholicism and continental European culture), but rather all those who have been injured by deeds based on faith—their own, or that of others. The concept of faith, then, as a trans-religious, cross-cultural dimension of human experience is what is opened up for sustained questioning here. What follows in the body of the text is an anatomy of faith in its various manifestations and distortions.

There is a curious religious divide in readings of this novel that parallels the religious divides to which Melville's allusion to the "Auto da Fe" refers. The majority tradition in readings of *The Confidence-Man* throughout the history of Melville criticism has been to identify the title character with Satan, while a more persuasive minority position has been to identify him at least partially with Christ. The best, and I believe definitive, resolution to this conflict is that proposed by Jonathan A. Cook in his 1996 study *Satirical Apocalypse*: "For in fact *The Confidence-Man* recreates the Parousia and Apostasy, the Second Coming of Christ and Last Loosening of Satan as a single event; it also synthesizes a dense variety of allusions to the book of Revelation, the New Testament, and the Bible as a whole."[16] As Cook argues, the Confidence Man of the title, in his various guises throughout the text, is both Christ and Antichrist, and the impossibility of drawing a clear line of demarcation between the two is the crucial tension in the text. This is reminiscent of Merlin Bowen's argument that Melville's characteristic philosophical mode is "armed neutrality."[17]

Once we arrive at the first sentence, the pan-American dimension of religious difference is amplified further. When the title character first appears, he does so "suddenly as Manco Capac at Lake Titicaca," indicating his status as a kind of indigenously American deity (*C-M* 1). In Inca religious traditions, Manco Capac is both a god and a son of a god—a clear parallel to the status of Jesus Christ as God the Son within Christianity.[18] Moreover, Manco Capac is credited as the figure in Incan history who ended human sacrifice, thus providing another resonance with the Christian story of redemption. That Melville means to allude to descriptions of Christ in his initial presentation of the Confidence Man is equally apparent. The Confidence Man's first guise is as "a man in cream-colors" whose "cheek was fair, his chin downy, his hair flaxen, his hat a white fur one with a long fleecy nap." The description mirrors both sentimentalized portraits of Jesus and the biblical references to Jesus as the "Lamb of God." Moreover, the emphasis on the whiteness of the Confidence Man's garb and the light color of his hair recalls the description of Christ as a judge in the book of Revelation. The man in the cream-colored suit is thus, as Franklin pointed out, both Jesus Christ and Manco Capac, and the implications for how we understand Melville's sense of the relationship among religious traditions is profound. Melville looks for analogues to Christian religious ideals in a global context, and rather than arguing that they point toward a kind of "anonymous Christianity," as Karl Rahner would in the twentieth century, he sees these instances as pointing toward a wider human consensus on the nature of just behavior.[19]

The importance of this figure for understanding the novel as a whole has long been noted. Franklin, for example, argued that the initial introduction of the Peruvian deity is a key to understanding both the structure of the entire novel and its artistry. The Confidence Man, in Franklin's view, constitutes a series of avatars for the divine—the Confidence Man thus is Christ under a series of guises drawn from a variety of religious traditions. Franklin thus connects *The Confidence-Man* explicitly with the references to Asian cultures and religions in *Moby-Dick*, and argues that Hinduism and Buddhism provide a key of sorts to understanding the novel. This reading of the novel highlights the ways in which Melville subtly weaves together world religions and Christian scripture. Also noteworthy, however, is the fact that while Melville draws upon a variety of religious traditions from around the world, he is most explicitly and consistently engaged with the varieties of religious belief in America: with Methodists and Calvinists, with Mormons and "Come outers" (those who sought to maintain their purity by leaving behind religious institutions altogether), with missionaries to the Indians and "Indian haters." This suggests that more than in any previous text, Melville is concerned to bring the sort of cosmopolitan vision that he describes in his lecture on "Traveling" to bear on America itself. Melville found as much exotic material on the Mississippi as he did in the South Seas, and this novel represents his most sustained attempt to come to terms with the full range of American cultural experience.

Melville comments explicitly on this goal in the conclusion to the second chapter of *The Confidence-Man*, comparing the travelers on a Mississippi steamboat to the medieval Christian pilgrims in *The Canterbury Tales* and to nineteenth-century Muslim pilgrims at Mecca:

> As among Chaucer's Canterbury pilgrims, or those oriental ones crossing the Red Sea toward Mecca in the festival month, there was no lack of variety. Natives of all sorts, and foreigners; men of business and men of pleasure; parlor men and backwoodsmen; farm-hunters

> and fame-hunters; heiress-hunters, gold-hunters, buffalo-hunters, bee-hunters, happiness hunters, truth hunters, and still keener hunters after all these hunters. Fine ladies in slippers, and moccasined squaws; Northern speculators and Eastern philosophers; English, Irish, Germans, Scots, Danes; Santa Fe traders in striped blankets, and Broadway bucks in cravats of cloth of gold; fine looking Kentucky boatsmen, and Japanese-looking Mississippi cotton-planters; Quakers in full drab, and United States soldiers in full regimentals; slaves, black, mulatto, quadroon; modish young Spanish Creoles, and old-fashioned French Jews; Mormons and Papists; Dives and Lazarus; jesters and mourners; teetotalers and convivialists; deacons and blacklegs; hardshell Baptists and clay-eaters; grinning negroes, and Sioux chiefs as solemn as high-priests. In short, a piebald parliament, and Anacharsis Cloots congress of all kinds of that multiform pilgrim species, man. (*C-M* 9)

This catalog is rather astounding in its comprehensiveness, and it is further noteworthy that Melville is concerned to link together a series of pairings that seem to resolve themselves into contradictions, only to reveal themselves upon further reflection to be complementary. The Quakers and the soldiers, for example, form an evident antimony: the Quakers are pacifists, and the soldiers are warriors, but their very attire joins them in a curious manner, in that both are wearing uniforms that call for the suppression of individuality in the name of a communal good. The dialectic between difference and syncretism that we saw to be so essential to Melville's crafting of *Moby-Dick* is on full display here. Even the concluding image of the "piebald parliament" of "that multiform pilgrim species, man" captures this tension: humans are seen to be both startlingly diverse and remarkably similar in their most essential qualities.

Melville's biblical reading and marginalia interact powerfully with the form of *The Confidence-Man.* 1 Corinthians 13 is the central allusion around which the entire narrative is built, and Melville's marginalia to his copy of *The New Testament and Psalms* is highly illuminating in relation to this chapter. In his copy of the volume, Melville marks 1 Corinthians 13 carefully, pointing out the verses that make salvation depend upon the exercise of love in particular. *The Confidence-Man* has long been recognized as a vital text for understanding Melville's relationship to religious belief. Elizabeth Foster made an early argument for viewing the novel as a critical allegory on unsatisfactory varieties of Christianity, a viewpoint that Hershel Parker has reinforced across his long and productive career. In 1962 H. Bruce Franklin broadened this reading by calling particular attention to the role of comparative mythology in shaping the text. Both the allegorical elements that Foster noted and the mythological elements that Franklin explored were used in the service of Melville's representation and critique of the varieties of religious difference that flourished on the antebellum American frontier.[20] Using a device that he had used previously to great effect in *Moby-Dick*, Melville catalogs the variety of nationalities and faiths aboard the *Fidele* using Anacharsis Clootz's deputation to the Parliament of Man as a trope.

The question of Christian love and its desirability and practicability recur throughout the text. Indeed, on one level the novel is a kind of extended meditation on what it means to love one's neighbor as oneself. More than in any of Melville's earlier novels, this novel poses this question in specifically financial terms. At the core of Melville's challenge to the claim to Christianity and civilization made by his culture is a very simple query: what cost are you willing to bear as the price of your convictions? We might compare this to William James's concept of the "cash value of an idea" developed half a century later.[21] This expression is frequently misread as the expression of crass materialism on James's part, but in reality, it makes belief correspond to something concrete by asserting that belief must do something in the world rather than simply hover above it. In this respect, it corresponds to the passages in the Epistle of James and the thirteenth chapter of 1 Corinthians that Melville had marked with such attentive care in his copy of *The New Testament and Psalms*: faith without works is dead, and faith that refuses to act upon its own assurance to give aid to those in distress can hardly be considered a vital element in modern life. Both James the Apostle and William James the philosopher make the willingness to put action in the service of faith the central test for any belief system, so the passengers on the *Fidele* are confronted with a choice that bridges the gap of nineteen centuries in bringing together biblical injunctions to charity with the emerging ideas of nineteenth-century American pragmatism. Thus the question of whether one will offer the sum of $100 to the person who asks for it carries a great deal of weight indeed in relation to the question of faith.

This very question, whether to give $100 to someone who asks for it simply because the person has asked for it, in keeping with Jesus's commands in the Sermon on the Mount, is raised directly in *The Confidence-Man* when the man in the traveling cap asks the miser for help. After having been given a cup of water, the miser says that he will give his "confidence" to the man who has helped him (with "confidence," both linguistically and in the context of the novel standing in for faith), and immediately meets with the reply, "Very good. Now give me a hundred dollars" (*C-M*

74). The miser's dismay at this request reveals the limits of his faith as well as of his charity.

In keeping with this theme of the relative merits of faith, hope, and charity in the nineteenth century, one of the most hotly debated chapters in this novel is "The Metaphysics of Indian-Hating." Hershel Parker, for example, has argued vigorously for an allegorical reading of this chapter, in which the "Indian-hater" has little to do with actual indigenous peoples, and much to do with the allegorical purity of purpose that Melville is alleged to ascribe to "true" Christianity.[22] Parker's case is formidable, particularly given his status as Melville's most authoritative biographer to date. It seems more likely, however, that Melville, a writer perennially concerned with ethical matters, especially in relation to theological ideas, is concerned with the ethical content of "Indian-hating" as well as its form. Melville commented explicitly on these matters in the late 1840s in his review of Francis Parkman's *The California and Oregon Trails*, "Mr. Parkman's Tour." In this review, Melville makes a specifically anti-racist argument, and he bases this argument on religious imperatives. Melville argues that:

> it is too often the case, that civilized beings sojourning among savages soon come to regard them with disdain and contempt. But though in many cases this feeling is almost natural, it is not defensible; and it is wholly wrong. Why should we contemn them? Because we are better than they? Assuredly not; for herein we are rebuked by the story of the Publican and the Pharisee. Because, then, that in many things we are happier? But this should be ground for commiseration, not disdain. Xavier and Elliot despised not the savages; and had Newton or Milton dwelt among them they would not have done so. When we affect to contemn savages, we should remember that by so doing we asperse our own progenitors; for they were savages also. Who can swear, that among the naked British barbarians sent to Rome to be stared at more than 1500 years ago, the ancestor of Bacon might not have been found? Why, among the very Thugs of India, or the bloody Dyaks of Borneo, exists the germ of all that is intellectually elevated and grand. We are all of us—Anglo-Saxons, Dyaks, and Indians—sprung from one head, and made in one image. And if we regret this brotherhood now, we shall be forced to join hands hereafter. A misfortune is not a fault; and good luck is not meritorious. The savage is born a savage; and the civilized being but inherits his civilization, nothing more. Let us not disdain, then, but pity. And wherever we recognise the image of God, let us reverence it, though it swing from the gallows. (*PT* 231–32)

This extended quote provides a substantial statement of Melville's views on the relationship between "savagery" and "civilization" at the time that he was writing his early novels; in the absence of any evidence that his views on the subject changed (and given the presence of significant evidence in his poetry that they did not), we should presumably see this as the authorial viewpoint behind the discussion of Indian-hating in *The Confidence-Man*. The content of the passage is both clear and powerful: all humans are brothers and sisters, and a denial of this fraternity represents a failure of both charity and understanding.

Moreover, as the discussion of *Pierre* and "Bartleby" above indicates, Melville found the Sermon on the Mount to be central to his understanding of Christianity. The "Indian-hating" discussed in this chapter could not be further removed from the ethics of the Sermon on the Mount, and it is hard to imagine that Melville chose to bracket out these concerns altogether. Colonel Moredock, the "Indian-hater" who is the titular character of the chapter, could instead be seen as a limit case for the values of the Sermon on the Mount: he has experienced extreme violation, and his choice has been to reject utterly the principle of love for one's enemy in favor of unalloyed vengefulness. The "Indian-hater," then, may be as Parker suggests, a model Christian in his purity of purpose, but he is also presented by Melville as antithetical to Christianity in his rejection of what Melville consistently identifies as the faith's most central tenet. For example: the "Indian-hater" is described as an ascetic comparable to a Catholic monk. What is Melville up to here? One rather straightforward reading is that this is an expression of praise for the Indian-hater's unmixed devotion to his cause, and it is this reading that Parker has defended. A celibate Catholic monk, after all, has given up most of what the outside world might regard as desirable in life—sex, family, possessions, personal autonomy—in order to obtain what he regards as a higher goal. If the monk's asceticism translates into violence against others (a scenario with extensive precedent in the history of Christianity), it is by no means clear that the monk's asceticism is adequate to allow him to be described as a representative of Christianity. Whether this is the case depends, in fact, on one's definition of what Christianity is: if it is simply an inflexible asceticism, then the monk, and by extension the Indian-hater, does indeed serve as a model of Christian purity of purpose and determination. If, however, Christianity is defined as in *Pierre* as encompassing "the gratuitous return of good for evil," then the Indian-hater is nothing more nor less than an Antichrist who parodies but does not correspond to the Christ of the Gospels (*Pierre* 215). This dubious state of affairs, in which Christ and Antichrist can become so easily confused, is precisely what is at stake in

The Confidence-Man, as can be seen particularly in the complex roles played by numerous characters throughout the text.

This uncertainty frames Melville's representations of the various religious types who appear in his last full-length novel. When the sophomore has the opportunity to buy lots in the "New Jerusalem" as part of a speculative scheme proposed to him by the man in the traveling-cap, he expresses various doubts about the validity of the scheme and ultimately declines to buy. He makes the correct choice to refrain from having confidence in a fraudulent salesman, but he also affects an undue confidence in himself that the narrator seems ironically to suggest may involve him in later follies. The miser refuses to give money for a sham charity, but finds himself taken in by his own greed when the opportunity for financial speculation arises. The Missourian, a character from a slave state, turns out to be both antislavery and anti-abolitionist. Examples could be multiplied, but it is the common denominator that matters the most here: in each case, the internal dynamics of a character are shown to be various and unstable.

In each of the above cases, a simple understanding of a character is undermined by a further alteration in his behavior. The discussion of Transcendentalism that is introduced with the character of Mark Winsome also cuts through conventional categories of religious belief. By the standards of, say, the sober Methodist minister introduced early in *The Confidence-Man*, Winsome is clearly heretical, but he is at the same time deeply concerned with questions of mortality, immortality, and the nature and destiny of humanity. Winsome presents an uncompromising argument for a way of viewing humanity that compliments human nature with a vision of its perfectibility, but also makes demands of human nature that seem wildly out of keeping with its frailties.

The character of Egbert has often been identified with Henry David Thoreau, but the fit is not exact. One possibility worth exploring is that Winsome and Egbert are both palimpsests—certainly Winsome suggests Emerson on some levels, but he also recalls Melville's discussions of Goethe. If we read Winsome not simply as "Emerson," but as "Emerson/Goethe," Egbert's role becomes clarified. If Egbert is only marginally like Emerson's disciple Thoreau (certainly his commercial interests seem to distance him from Thoreau), he is very much like Goethe's disciple (and Emerson's sometime model) Thomas Carlyle. In this reading, Egbert becomes "Carlyle/Thoreau," which helps to account for Egbert's hardheaded devotion to work and practicality—characteristics with which Thoreau is at most ambivalently associated. The satire on Transcendentalism presented by Mark Winsome likewise works if we imagine him as an amalgam of Emerson and Goethe, each of whom Melville admired but also criticized sharply for excessive intellectualism, abstraction, and pomposity.

Melville's relation to both Carlyle and Thoreau is a complex one. Carlyle, as noted in earlier chapters, was the source for Melville's inscriptions on the front and rear pastedowns of his copy of *The New Testament and Psalms* in his capacity as Goethe's translator. In these passages Goethe presents a heroic reading of Christianity that imagines Jesus as an individual who practices self-trust. This melds nicely with Carlyle's own devotion to heroic models as those which best realize human possibility, and fits as well with Melville's ambivalent attraction to monomaniacal creations of his own like Captain Ahab. Carlyle's insistence on (and indeed creation of) the normative Victorian work ethic is likewise a point of both repulsion and attraction for Melville, who both celebrates and decries the work ethic at various points in his writing.[23]

Thoreau, meanwhile, resonates with Melville quite profoundly on some points: as noted in the previous chapter, he shares an impulse toward explosive freedom from constraint. Melville's fierce critique of the attitudes and policies of many American individuals and institutions toward indigenous peoples in the Americas and the Pacific Islands is another substantial point of resonance with Thoreau: it is easy to forget that Thoreau's nineteenth-century reputation was as a kind of white Indian, a man who was culturally indigenous as well as ethnically European in his heritage. Melville's own status in his youth as an ersatz "Typee" in New England corresponds to this view of Thoreau.

Reading Thoreau's work in relation to Melville's work is still more suggestive. Thematically, Thoreau emphasizes elements that are quite similar to Melville's most consistent obsessions. Understanding the congruity between Melville's religious vision and Thoreau's can shed substantial light on one of the major mysteries of Melville scholarship: why did Melville react so violently to the verse at the end of the book of Revelation that condemned anyone who took away from the words of the Christian scriptures? Thoreau provides us with a way into an answer for this question. With a hint of sacrilege relative to conventional understandings of scripture in nineteenth-century American Protestantism, Thoreau calls in *Walden* for wider attention to the "Bibles of mankind."[24] For Thoreau, then, the Hebrew and Christian scriptures represent merely a portion of humanity's sacred texts, a point of view which perhaps explains Melville's decision to strike out the very passage in the book of Revelation that condemns anyone who adulterates the sufficiency of the biblical canon. Melville's interest in the Mormon faith, indicated by his mentions of Mormons at several points in *The Confidence-Man*, is perhaps also explainable through this particular tendency in Melville's religious thought. The introduction of the *Book of Mormon* as a divinely revealed extension of the biblical canon by Joseph Smith has the effect of expanding the ancient Christian canon and suggesting that inspiration is a component of the present as well as of the distant past. From the opposite side of the religious spectrum, meanwhile, the presence of works deemed non-canonical by Protestants in Roman Catholic bibles has the effect of opening up the possibilities of revelation and divine inspiration beyond the bounds of Melville's youthful Calvinism and his mature Unitarianism.[25]

Apocrypha and Apocalypse: Revelation as Difference

Perhaps the most telling of all the aspects of *The Confidence-Man* that touch on religious difference is the discussion of the Apocrypha from the concluding pages of the novel. These pages are clearly focused on questions of interpretation and authority, and the tortured and torturous language that Melville has his narrators employ in the course of discussing the Apocrypha serves to reinforce the leading idea of the elusiveness of an authoritative account of truth that recurs throughout the novel. The Cosmopolitan draws the old man into conversation by quoting a particularly misanthropic passage from Ecclesiasticus, a book from the Apocrypha that Melville marked carefully in his personal copy of the Bible. The Cosmopolitan remarks that in this passage, faith in humanity and love for humanity are undermined by such remarks as "he will smile upon thee and speak thee fair, and say, What wantest thou? If thou be for his profit he will use thee . . ." (*C-M* 242). As the conversation continues, he asserts, "What an ugly thing wisdom must be! Give me folly that dimples the cheek, say I, rather than wisdom that curdles the blood. . . . For how can that be trustworthy that teaches distrust" (*C-M* 243). The Cosmopolitan has made trust itself its own criterion, regardless of that in which trust is reposed, and the old man agrees that trust is the one fundamental necessity of a virtuous life.

The old man is, of course, deceived both as to his own character and that of the Cosmopolitan. He believes himself to be a man of faith, but his every action shows him to be a man of prudent doubt, from his purchase of the money-belt to his desire for a life preserver. His doubts do not, however, extend to the Cosmopolitan himself, who may be the person that the old man should most fear. If we read the Confidence Man as a non-supernatural figure—a literal "confidence man" relieving steamboat travelers of their worldly goods—then the old man is likely to have been robbed more thoroughly than he would have been by any pickpocket now that he has reposed trust in the Cosmopolitan. If we read the Confidence Man as an allegorical representation of Satan, the implication becomes grimmer still—perhaps the old man is being defrauded of his very soul. If we read the Confidence Man as a series of avatars of Christ, as H. Bruce Franklin and Edgar Dryden suggest, we find that the case becomes very complex, so much so as to merit extended unpacking.

The old man is described in terms drawn from the biblical book of Revelation that seem to establish his identity as a Christian witness and martyr. He is a "man in a robe" like those given to martyred saints in Revelation, and the Drummond light by which he reads illuminates a "horned altar" (*C-M* 240). He has committed himself from childhood to a reading of the sacred scriptures of Christianity. Is the Confidence Man Christ claiming his own, or is he an Antichrist deceiving even the elect? The answer, as Jonathan A. Cook has suggested, is both, and neither.[26] If the Cosmopolitan is Christ, the old man is an imperfect but faithful saint being called home to heaven, and what will follow of this masquerade is eternal life. If the Cosmopolitan is Antichrist, the man is being deprived of his soul in the very moment of his death—a cruel confirmation of the depravity not only of humanity, but of God. If the Cosmopolitan is a merely human thief, the old man is about to be robbed, and all that will follow of the masquerade is a scene of shame, anguish, and pathos. If the Cosmopolitan is truly a "frank, good man" as his name suggests, he is performing a fundamental act of natural piety by honoring his elders through the person of the old man. This is one of those points at which criticism cannot help but become biography. Do we imagine Melville as embittered and possibly insane when he finishes his last full-length novel? Do we imagine him as preserving an exalted moral vision of potential human goodness while he simultaneously acknowledges human evil? Is he at this point a sage or an alcoholic failure? Must his writing at this stage be construed as an expression of cynicism or hope? I want to suggest that where Melville has brought us at the end of *The Confidence-Man* is to an agnostic stance in its strongest and richest sense, and he has used models of religious difference from at home and abroad, from biblical interpretation and world religions, in order to do so. I understand agnosticism here as that state of mind that Ishmael describes in *Moby-Dick* as "doubts of all things earthly, intuitions of some things heavenly" (*M-D* 374). It is emphatically not a state of disengagement from the ultimate questions, but rather an especially bold and consistent probing of those questions, leading to a suspended state that is not belief, not unbelief, nor yet something in between, but rather a continuing and impassioned inquiry.

There is a visual pun that is easy to miss in the dialogue between the old man and the Cosmopolitan. The old man holds up the portion of the Bible that is "apocrypha" and thus untrustworthy and then declares that whatever falls to either side of this segment must be solid biblical truth. What is noteworthy here is that according to the old man's definition, then, the center, the very heart, of the Bible is misanthropic and potentially misleading—even as the old man is ostensibly denouncing misanthropy. The infallible words of God, in this reading, cluster about a delusive and dangerous center, thus undermining the truth claims of both the New and Old Testaments. Lest we miss this point, one of the passengers who is trying to sleep while the old man and the Cosmopolitan talk draws our attention to it by conflating the Apocrypha with the Apocalypse. The old man reassures the Cosmopolitan that he need not pay any attention to the misanthropic language of Ecclesiasticus because it is apocryphal: "The word [apocrypha] itself, I've heard from the pulpit, implies something of uncertain credit. So if your disturbance be raised from aught in this apocrypha . . . in that case, think no more of it, for it's apocrypha" (*C-M* 243). No sooner has the old man said the word "apocrypha" than the passenger who is playing the role of a chorus in the background says "What's that about the Apocalypse?" (*C-M* 243). This play on the similarity of the two words takes us to the heart of the matter: things hidden are conflated with things revealed, the word of God is conflated with the words of human beings, and a fundamental uncertainty about the status of religious knowledge is encapsulated in the pun of a sleepy and perhaps drunken passenger. The antimonies and paradoxical correspondences that shape *The Confidence-Man* in its entirety are brought into sharp relief: faith versus works, doubt versus trust, scripture versus forgery, misanthropy versus philanthropy, the Confidence Man as Christ versus the Confidence Man as Antichrist, America as dream and America as cheat: all are compressed into these few evocative moments at the close of the novel.

Even the tension between the old man and his fellow passengers bears the impress of religious difference: the old man's most vigorous critic is identifiably Irish because of his brogue, and thus presumably Catholic as well. His outrage at the conversation between the Cosmopolitan and the old man is that of a man who needs his rest, but it is also that of man whose faith is being declared invalid in passing, as if the Catholic faith, which acknowledges the authority of such books as Sirach, could enter into a religious discussion only as an error to be dismissed, not as a standpoint to be contemplated. The Irish man's vituperation against the Cosmopolitan and the old man is based on their lack of precisely that which Sirach as the author and Ecclesiasticus as the book are meant to provide, wisdom: "Arrah, and is it wisdom the two geese are gabbling about all this while? To bed with ye, ye divils, and don't be after burning your fingers with the likes of wisdom" (*C-M* 243). The Irish man's casual cursing here ("ye divils") calls attention to the dubious relation between the divine and the diabolic that provides the frame for so much of *The Confidence-Man*'s irony.

If *The Confidence-Man* resembles an ironized nineteenth-century *Pilgrim's Progess*, Melville is careful to remind us that Bunyan's is not the only form of Christianity, nor the only vision of a Christian's pilgrimage through life. This is the point not only of Melville's invocations of Catholicism in *The Confidence-Man*, but also of his numerous invocations of varieties of Protestantism and of Mormonism. Indeed, it is precisely this sense of divergent paths that can be reasonably labeled as "Christian" that provides the grounds for uncertainty in *The Confidence-Man.*

The Apocrypha/Apocalypse distinction thus highlights the centrality of religious difference to the meaning of *The Confidence-Man.* Shifting the terms of interpretation slightly can make a divine figure into a diabolical one, and another small shift can restore the apparent divinity. Catholicism, which recognizes the Apocrypha as scriptural, and evangelical Protestantism, which does not, are committed to different views of what constitutes the full text of the Christian scripture—views sufficiently different as to make the import of the passage from the final chapter of the book of Revelation that Melville crossed out and then annotated with a comment that was later excised mean very different things depending on one's creed. Calvinism and Unitarianism are committed to fundamentally different views about what constitutes the truth about human nature, sufficiently so that the divine and the diabolical can easily become transposed in terms of the two kindred faiths' theological formulations. All these variants of Christianity, and the numerous others alluded to in the text express reverence for the teachings of Jesus Christ, which Melville saw as being most definitively expressed in the Sermon on the Mount. Meanwhile, religious figures from locales as diverse as India and Peru seem to chime on some level with the commands of Christ as expressed in the Sermon on the Mount. What Melville does is to show that it is impossible to discount either the real congruities among a range of Christian and non-Christian faiths or to fail to acknowledge the substantial disagreements. Moreover, doctrine seems quite flimsy when it is confronted by so basic a demand as the request for $100. Transcendentalists, Unitarians,

Calvinists, and the religiously indifferent seem to be brought together by a fundamental suspicion of their neighbors, which serves to justify their unwillingness to give to those in need. This is perhaps the most vital example of Melville's ability to reconfigure the religious landscape of his time. If $100 is too high a price to pay for one's soul, however defined, it hardly seems to matter whether one subscribes to either the total depravity or the ultimate perfectibility of human beings, or to the special divinity of Christ or the general divinity of humankind.

In a sense, the story that Melville was reaching toward throughout the 1850s and told in an extended form in *The Confidence-Man* is much like the story that Charles Taylor told in *A Secular Age*, a magisterial study published in 2007, 150 years after the publication of *The Confidence-Man*. Taylor narrates the movement from a society in which religious belief is an inevitable background for social interaction of all sorts to one in which religious belief is a choice, one which may be held all the more fervently because of this status as a choice, but nonetheless separable from one's imagined social existence.[27] Time and again in *The Confidence-Man*, characters affirm religious and philosophical identities that they have adopted, but the world in which they live and move is one in which the choice of whether or not to lend $100 to the person who requests it is one that transcends any sort of religious commitments. Faith in cash, and for that matter in benevolent human associations that at times may altruistically dispense cash, not faith in a benign or malignant deity, is the most fundamental background for *The Confidence-Man*, and this, for the multi-religious passengers of the *Fidele* and their American contemporaries, Melville included, has made all the difference. The relationship between *The Confidence-Man* and *Clarel* is in part defined by the fact that *Clarel* extended this pattern of secularization to the wider world, showing how far-flung localities around the globe shared in the fate of the *Fidele*.

From *Pierre* to *The Confidence-Man*, then, Melville examined the range of religious practices prevalent in America from a distinctively cosmopolitan vantage point. As in his earlier novels, Melville makes extensive use of non-Western, non-monotheistic religious traditions in order to understand the variety of faiths in his own homeland, and the varieties of faith and doubt that made up his own uneasy relationship to religious belief. At the same time, Melville demonstrates a keen eye for the theological disputes that divided Americans in the 1850s, and for the ways in which non-theological divisions could become more important than doctrine in determining the nature of religious experience. For the Melville of 1857, both faith and doubt are fundamentally unsatisfactory options: faith leads one into the destructive enthusiasm of Pierre or the vulnerability to manipulation that is suggested in various scenes in *The Confidence-Man*. Doubt taken to its extreme, meanwhile, deprives the self of its very substance, leaving an ambivalent believer and doubter like Melville caught between illusion and annihilation. As we know from Nathaniel Hawthorne's meeting with Melville in Liverpool, by the mid-1850s an admired friend could quote Melville as saying that he had "pretty much made his mind up to be annihilated" (*Journals* 628). If this was Melville's resting place in 1857, did it remain so? As we will see in the chapters that follow, Melville continued to enrich his range of faiths and doubts throughout the second half of his life. If the materialism and pluralism of the 1850s bred doubt and confusion, calling forth an astonishingly complex artistic response in Melville's last full-length prose work, these uncertainties would be magnified tremendously by the events of the American Civil War, which loomed in the years immediately following Melville's publication of *The Confidence-Man* and would shape decisively Melville's career as a poet.

Chapter 4

"Conflict of Convictions": Remapping Religious Difference in *Battle-Pieces*

The American Civil War was the defining crisis of Melville's lifetime, and its implications were religious as well as political, social, economic, and racial. As Abraham Lincoln noted in his Second Inaugural Address, Americans on both sides of the conflict "read the same Bible and pray[ed] to the same God," but arrived at radically different moral conclusions regarding the war.[1] Melville's response to the war is cataloged in his 1866 collection of Civil War poems, *Battle-Pieces, and Aspects of the War*, in which he sought to analyze the causes and effects of the war, and to suggest the moral and ethical conclusions that could be drawn from the carnage. Melville's treatment of religious difference was significantly altered in these poems: rather than representing the points of division between or among faiths and denominations, Melville was concerned with the conflicting ways in which his fellow Northerners and their Southern counterparts addressed the central moral questions of their time, and the ways in which the times themselves called for a reinvestigation of critical moral questions. Regional difference and religiously influenced political difference replaced doctrinal difference, and the ethical strand that had always been important in Melville's work became exceptionally so in his Civil War poetry. *Pierre* and *The Confidence-Man* had represented the beginning of a major crisis of artistic conviction for Melville, but it was in *Battle-Pieces* that this crisis reached its fruition in a distinct mode of writing that would shape the remainder of Melville's career.[2]

If Melville's move to poetry represented a rupture with the prose forms that characterized his career in the 1840s and 1850s, the theme of religious difference, conflict, and cooperation remained central, and important continuities remained as well in Melville's modes of representing these matters. In *Battle-Pieces*, as in Melville's fiction from *Typee* to *The Confidence-Man*, Melville made use of both the diversity within Christianity and the diverse relationships among world religions to frame the political tension between North and South as well as the racial and cultural tensions that the war highlighted and that were often willfully overlooked in the postwar period. As is most centrally evident in "Lee in the Capitol," a poem which, despite its length, is often ignored or downplayed in discussions of *Battle-Pieces*, Melville continued to use both religious conflict and the syncretic analogies that he found among varying religious traditions to structure his work, as well as to use these conflicts and coincidences as a fertile source of metaphors and images.

Melville was not, we now know, an apprentice poet when he was writing *Battle-Pieces*. As Hershel Parker has shown, first in the second volume of his biography of Melville and later in *Melville: The Making of the Poet* (2008), he was prepared to publish a volume of poetry as early as 1860, and many of the works that he did publish later on were completed or at least begun at this stage of his career. Parker has demonstrated that even by 1860, Melville had already been engaged in a wide-ranging study of poetic techniques and theories, and by 1866, we are dealing with the work of a mature poet who has reflected extensively on his craft.[3] It should come as no surprise, then, that *Battle-Pieces* is a carefully constructed work of art on both the level of the individual poems and the level of the collection as a whole. Melville's careful artistic construction of the poems, and his attempt to create an organic form for writing about the war, which Stanton Garner has discussed at length in *The Civil War World of Herman Melville*, is paralleled by Melville's concern to use modes of thought consistent with the massive changes wrought by the war.[4] For Melville, *Battle-Pieces* is clearly meant to represent new wine in new wineskins, both artistically and in terms of philosophy, theology, and politics.

Battle-Pieces is the most directly occasional of Melville's works, with a dedication "to the memory of the three hundred thousand who in the war for the maintenance of the Union fell devotedly under the flags of their fathers," and Melville's prefatory note identifies the fall of Richmond as the inspiration for the writing of most of the poems. Indeed, Melville seemed to regard himself more as a mouthpiece for the times in this collection of poems than as a willing human subject, perhaps explaining the lack of a powerful narrative voice as an organizing principle. At the end of his prefatory note, Melville remarks that "I seem, in most of these verses, to have but placed a harp in the window, and noted the contrasted airs which the wayward winds have played upon the strings" (*PP* 3). The powerful sense of self that both Melville's characters and his narrators revealed in his novels and short stories is oddly muted in this collection of poems, perhaps suggesting a learned and not entirely feigned humility in the face of world-altering events. This humility allowed Melville to probe the uncertainties spawned by the war in ways that seem to have caused some discomfort for his earlier critics, but which have resonated powerfully in recent decades.

Reading Martyrdom in "The Portent"

The nature of the engagement with religious difference that emerges in *Battle-Pieces* is forecast by the first poem in the collection: "The Portent." This brief poem, inspired by the execution of John Brown after his unsuccessful raid on Harper's Ferry, illustrates both the depth of Melville's engagement with religion in the collection and his reticence about the sort of religious posturing that appeared in his earlier works. The poem brackets the living John Brown and the content of his moral and religious crusade against slavery out of its text entirely, but his story was well enough known (and to a large degree remains so) that we can assume knowledge of Brown on the part of not only Melville's contemporaries, but also in varying degrees most subsequent generations of readers. Brown had attacked Harper's Ferry hoping to trigger a large-scale slave revolt, but instead was executed along with his sons who had participated in the raid.[5] Historians have disagreed about Brown's wisdom and even his sanity, but there is a broad consensus that Brown in his death helped to heighten North-South tensions to a point at which war became inevitable. Melville's Brown, however, is already executed, a defeated corpse on display in front of his enemies. The very rhythm of the poem captures the ominous sense of rupture suggested by Brown's execution: the meter is trochaic, with an added syllable at the end of most lines. Only in the fifth and fourteenth lines does the more conventional iambic foot predominate. The opening stanza begins with the macabre suggestion of a dead man's body "Hanging from a beam, / Slowly swaying" (lines 1–2). Here the trochaic rhythm, which emphasizes the back and forth motion of the line, mimics the slow, rocking motion that John Brown's corpse makes immediately after his execution has been completed. The parenthetical "such the law" that concludes the second line counters the graphic image with legal abstraction: Brown must be destroyed because of the law, but his condemnation seems to lack an independent moral force. The third line underscores Brown's status as a sign and symbol of the coming war: "Gaunt the shadow on your green." The duality that we have seen here as a perennial hallmark of Melville's work appears in the contrast of Brown's black shadow against the green of the grass below.

The next line, consisting of the single word "Shenandoah!" deserves more comment than it is usually given. The place name is the source of Melville's trochees, as the emphasis falls on the first and third syllables. By making "Shenandoah" itself the defining formal device in his poem, Melville emphasizes the shaping force of brute facts—of events and places themselves—upon poetry. At the same time, the use of "Shenandoah" as the name of the place described illustrates the power of the imagination in shaping events. Brown's raid took place in the Shenandoah Valley, but other place names (Harper's Ferry, for example) would be more apt in relation to Brown himself. The name "Shenandoah" becomes so resonant in part because of events that Brown's execution foretold: from the years 1862 to 1864, multiple battles were fought in the Shenandoah Valley, and these battles were both decisive in relation to the outcome of the war and representative of the war's ferocity. Thus, Melville's choice of a place name with which to associate Brown's "portent" is shaped by memory, and the scene that is described in the poem is a retrospective colored by the events of the Civil War themselves.

The only iambic line in the first stanza follows the very moment at which the reason for Melville's choice of a generally trochaic form becomes clear: if "Shenandoah!" confirms the trochaic rhythm and teaches us to expect more trochees, "The cut is on the crown" defeats our expectations by using the more conventional iambic foot. It has become a commonplace to note the Christ imagery in this line, with its suggestion of a wounded head and a crown of thorns. It is also worth noting that this is the point in the poem at which Brown seems ready to be incorporated into a prearranged religious narrative: if Brown is Christ, as he was described by Melville's contemporaries Emerson and Thoreau, then the Civil War becomes a kind of holy war, not on behalf of doctrinal purity, but rather on behalf of human freedom and dignity. Melville acknowledges this view, and does not contradict it, in this line, but the break in the rhythmic pattern of the stanza as a whole embodies wavering and doubt. The sonorous spondees of the following line recall the tolling of a bell, and they refrain from making a positive or negative comment on Brown's vision of a society purified from injustice through violence. The trochaic rhythm returns in the final line "And the stabs shall heal no more"—leaving us with a complex image of Brown's wounds and the nation's that ambiguously affirms Brown's Christlikeness and casts doubt upon it. The unhealed wounds suggest the Catholic Christ of crucifix and stigmata, but they also seem to call into question the possibility of resurrection, both personal and national. The two readings are radically inconsistent with each other, but they coexist uneasily in this line.

The second stanza provides a structural mirror for the first. If the motion of the corpse is suggested in the first line of the first stanza, the hidden, tormented face is suggested in the first line of the second stanza, suggesting a contrast with the public agony of Christ's crucifixion. With the lines "Hidden in the cap / Is an anguish none can draw / So your future veils its face / Shenandoah!" Melville implies that Brown can stand in for his tormented nation, both as a crucial actor in the launching of the war, and in the suffering of his last moments. Here the trochaic rhythm has reasserted itself, and it even carries into the fifth line "But the streaming beard is shown," before being broken by a less sonorous series of spondees than in the first stanza "(Weird John Brown)," and a final, disconcertingly iambic, line, "The meteor of the war." The religious resonances are subtle but significant: Brown can either be, as in the first stanza, a wounded figure of Christ who transforms history, or he can be an icon of fate (Weird John Brown), who suggests a sort of pre-Christian resistance to transformation. Here Melville takes the questions obsessing his contemporaries: Could the violence of the Civil War be considered redemptive? Would Emancipation mean a new and more just racial order in the United States, or would the inequality associated with slavery continue under another guise? Was history a story with a trajectory? Or was it cyclical and tragic, to be associated with the appearance, departure, and return of meteors? Was the swaying of John Brown's corpse, gradually lapsing into stillness, the best metaphor left for the American enterprise, or did Brown's death and that of 300,000 Union soldiers betoken some sort of resurrection? "The Portent" is an eloquent non-answer to these questions, which nonetheless frames the debate that will be developed throughout *Battle-Pieces*. As Melville's readers knew, John Brown could serve as an icon both of racial justice and of divinely sanctioned violence. Melville, who desired the one and feared the other, could only present Brown to his readers, not as a hero or villain, but as the crisis of the Civil War made flesh, and suffering death among them.

Writing Reconstruction: The "Prose Supplement"

If Melville's meditation on John Brown provides the opening portion of the frame for *Battle-Pieces* and suggests the significance of religious difference and multiple perspectives on moral and ethical questions for Melville's poetics, the "Prose Supplement" with which *Battle-Pieces* ends confirms the importance of uncertainty, ambivalence, and religious and cultural difference for understanding Melville's first published collections of poems. The supplement has often been justly criticized for the ways in which it advocates compromise with the defeated Confederacy and perhaps even walks back Melville's more uncompromising critiques of racism and injustice from his earlier works. It is noteworthy, however, that what Melville does in the "Prose Supplement" is not to endorse the Southern cause nor to abandon the egalitarian views that shaped much of his earlier work, including his explicit critiques of slavery in *Mardi* and *The Confidence-Man* and his running critique of racism throughout his fiction. The Melville that we see in the "Prose Supplement," rather, is a man who has been profoundly shaken by the great cataclysm of his age, and is seeking to find a moral vocabulary with which to discuss events which he could not have imagined through most of his life and his career as a writer of fiction. He has noted in the prefatory remarks that the number of Northern soldiers killed was an astonishing 300,000, and while he pointedly declines to dedicate the book to the Confederate dead as well (as Stanton Garner demonstrates, Melville's commitment to the Union was firm throughout the war), it becomes obvious throughout the collection that the young men who died on behalf of the Southern side of the war also were consistently on Melville's mind.[6]

The "Prose Supplement" argues for a gracious policy on the part of the victorious North toward the defeated South. It does not, as we might wish, place matters of racial justice and egalitarianism at the center of its policy recommendations, but neither does it exclude them. Melville's emphasis here is on a cautiousness born of doubt: he invokes the "sacred uncertainty that impends over men and nations" as the guiding principle for Reconstruction. I have chosen this phrase—"sacred uncertainty"—to provide the title of this study with no small amount of deliberation. On the one hand, the moment at which he uses this term is hardly Melville at his best, from our twenty-first-century perspective. We know that arguments for accommodation to Southern whites resulted in a truncated Reconstruction and the grave injustices of segregation and the Southern Jim Crow regime for generations. Certainly, if Melville's use of "sacred uncertainty" here is in the service of this outcome, it is hard to see this as anything but a sad renunciation of much of what makes Melville's earlier fiction so resonant today. We might remember, however, that Melville composed the "Prose Supplement" in 1866, not 1876. The betrayal of the possibilities of Reconstruction that afterward took place were not yet a part of American history, and to read Jim Crow and segregation back into Melville's anguished reflections at the end of an unprecedentedly bloody war seems to fail to consider Melville's own historical moment adequately. In fact, the invocation of "sacred uncertainty" here seems to cut in a different direction entirely: the generosity of the North will be a demonstration of its unwillingness to match Southern fanaticism with equal fanaticism, and to model what a just victory might look like.

Indeed, to assume that Melville's conciliatory gestures arise out of sympathy for the Southern cause requires a reader to ignore Melville's succinct statement of the true goal of the battle for secession: the Confederate cause's "implied end was the erecting in our advanced century of an Anglo-American empire based on the systematic degradation of man" (*PP* 182). This is not the remark of either a moral relativist or a sentimentalist who wishes to excuse the racism and oppression that stood behind the Confederate cause. Rather, it is the observation of a man perplexed by the subordination of admirable impulses to ignoble ends: what had "entrapped" many Southerners of good will into this ultimately reprehensible cause was not only "the arts of the conspirators" who carried out secession, but also "the most sensitive love of liberty" (*PP* 182). Much of the moral force of *Battle-Pieces* is devoted simultaneously to the necessity of condemning the immorality of the Southern cause and the urgency of finding a shared humanity between the two sides which could allow for the possibility of healing. It is precisely this dual necessity that was ignored a decade later in the end of Reconstruction, when reconciliation among white Americans was judged to be more significant than justice for all Americans. The failures of 1876 and beyond were not, however, what Melville endorsed in his collection of poetry in 1866.

An instructive point of contrast in this regard is Nathaniel Hawthorne's essay, "Chiefly about War Matters, by a Peaceable Man," a piece from 1862 that might initially seem to parallel the conciliatory views expressed in the "Prose Supplement." Hawthorne, however, is sympathetic toward the South in ways that Melville is not. In "Chiefly about War Matters," Hawthorne seems to view the war as simply a matter of regional, sectarian folly, without the genuine potential for moral transformation that Melville consistently suggested was part of the story of the war.[7]

Garry Wills's treatment of Abraham Lincoln's Gettysburg Address also provides useful parallels here. Wills noted that Lincoln followed classical Greek modes of oratory in his use of antithesis in his most memorable speech,[8] and this is paralleled by the same element in Melville's "Prose Supplement" and throughout *Battle-Pieces*. Melville had, as we have seen, adopted a similar mode in *Mardi* and *Moby-Dick* through his use of Renaissance rhetorical models, but here the use of antithesis is both more pervasive and qualitatively different. In the "Prose Supplement" Melville employs antithesis to highlight the sense of being caught between unacceptable alternatives.

War and Doubt

With this framing in mind, the pieces of Melville's puzzle in *Battle-Pieces* start to fall into place. Each poem is defined by a complex perspective that neither dissolves into relativism nor dispenses with valid objections to the implied point of view. William Dean Howells's famous dismissal of *Battle-Pieces* as being "like no poetry you have ever read and no life you have ever known," becomes particularly pertinent here.[9] Elizabeth Renker has recently, and persuasively, argued that the Melville of the poetry is fundamentally realist in his modes of expression, but Melville's realism is not that of Howells, the dean (pun intended) of American realists.[10] Melville incorporates a level of epistemological doubt that is ultimately corrosive of realism, at the same time that he undermines the souring rhetoric of his earlier romanticism. As Rosanna Warren and Helen Vendler, two of the most perceptive readers of the aesthetic properties of *Battle-Pieces* have noted, the form of the collection is determined in no small part by both Melville's quest for truth and his idiosyncratic sense of what precisely the concept "truth" might mean.[11] What Melville labors to do in *Battle-Pieces*, then, is to produce a truthful picture of the war in an era when perspective is anything but transparent. If Melville's poetry seems detached from the "blood" of the war, as Howells argued, it is in service of a nuanced understanding of events that are bloody and traumatic and well-remembered enough in themselves not to require gritty details.

"Misgivings" expresses Melville's mature dualism in a particularly elegant form. Like "The Portent," this poem embodies a Melvillean divided perspective in its very form, but (again like "The Portent") it avoids resolving its perspectival possibilities in a straightforward debate. Melville uses natural imagery in this poem to highlight the sense of rupture and vertigo that the war caused, and that in retrospect it seemed everyone should have felt as the war's approach became inevitable. Melville's speaker begins with a long introductory clause that ties the looming conflict to the natural world, then turns to an explicit discussion of the crisis:

> When ocean clouds over inland hills
> Sweep storming in late autumn brown,
> And horror the sodden valley fills,
> And the spire falls crashing in the town,
> I muse upon my country's ills—
> And the tempest bursting from the waste of Time,
> On the world's fairest hope linked with man's foulest crime. (lines 1–7)

The pattern here is largely iambic, with some exceptions. Melville appears here to have used Edgar Allan Poe's theory of meter from "The Rationale of Verse," using two very weak syllables at times in place of one weakly stressed syllable, and he uses anapests to start several predominantly iambic lines, perhaps contributing an unsettling rhythm to correspond to unsettling images of storms and distress.[12] The imagery coalesces around suggestions of both gradual decay (autumn) and sudden destruction (building decimated by storm). The final couplet has been the subject of some debate: Is "man's foulest crime" slavery, or secession? The most prolific critic of Melville's Civil War poetry and scholar of Melville's Civil War years, Stanton Garner, has suggested that it was the latter, but many other Melville scholars have disagreed.[13] The "Prose Supplement" suggests that this is a false choice. Secession for Melville was the culmination of the rejection of equality embodied in slavery, so there was no reason to distinguish between the two in the description of "man's foulest crime." In the same vein, "the world's fairest hope" is clearly the American experiment, but it is this precisely insofar as it provides for equality. The tension between Melville's Unionism and his anti-racism is a modern one, and not an inherent part of this poem. For Melville, the possibility of equality is what makes America a significant moral and even cosmic experiment, and he develops this theme throughout the collection. The second stanza goes on to associate "Nature's dark side" with the coming war, and to end with a reference to the sea and seafaring that will be characteristic of many of the poems from *Battle-Pieces*, as Melville continues to draw many of his most telling images and allusions from the sea: "The hemlock shakes in the rafter, the oak in the driving keel" (*PP* 16). Melville moves in this line from using nature as his grounds for premonitions of disaster to using the effects of nature on natural objects adapted for human use: both houses and vessels will be destroyed in this war, and the literal storms of 1861 give warning of the destruction to come.

"The Conflict of Convictions," the third poem in *Battle-Pieces*, offers a more expansive view of the possibilities announced by the first two poems. Here Melville is at his most explicit about the connections among cosmic struggles between good and evil, the natural world, and the political dimensions of the Civil War. In his note to the poem, Melville wrote that "the gloomy lull of the early part of the winter of 1860–1, seeming big with final disaster for our institutions, affected some minds that believed them to constitute one of the great hopes of mankind, much as the eclipse which came over the promise of the French Revolution affected kindred natures, throwing them for the time into doubts and misgivings universal" (*PP* 173). These "doubts and misgivings universal" are played out on a grand stage in "The Conflict of Convictions." Melville begins the poem with a concrete sensory impression from battle, "On starry heights / The bugle wails the long recall" (lines 1–2), that quickly is absorbed into a cosmic (and Miltonic—perhaps even Blakean) battle between the powers of heaven and hell:

> Derision stirs the deep abyss,
> Heaven's ominous silence over all.
> Return, return O eager Hope,
> And face man's latter fall.
> Events, they make the dreamers quail;
> Satan's old age is strong and hale,
> A disciplined captain, gray in skill,
> And Raphael a white enthusiast still;
> Dashed aims, at which Christ's martyrs pale,
> Shall Mammon's slaves fulfill? (lines 3–12)

The slipperiness of Melville's wordplay is remarkable here. Some things are clear: America, it seems, represents a hope comparable to the creation of the world, and the failure of American institutions implied by the Civil War is comparable in magnitude and severity to the fall of humanity in the persons of Adam and Eve in the book of Genesis, or even to the earlier cosmic fall of Satan. The American dream has turned to terror ("events they make the dreamers quail"), and those who believed that the American Revolution betokened a bright future for humanity, both in America and outside, have been thrown into disarray. Other meanings, become more elusive, however. How do Satan and Raphael map onto the divisions of the Civil War, and how are they to be viewed? The colors invoked provide conflicted hypotheses. Satan is "gray" because of his age, but he also is associated through this color with the uniforms of the Confederacy. Raphael is a "white enthusiast"—is this because his enthusiasm is "white-hot"? This seems the most likely suggestion, but Raphael's whiteness also suggests the racial dimension of the conflict. Indeed, even if we conclude that Raphael is a Northerner and Satan is a Southerner, what can we conclude about the stance that this implies regarding the war, since Satan can be viewed as a romantic hero despite being a theological villain?

Even Melville's concluding rhetorical question here seems endlessly productive of other questions. What are the "dashed aims" the speaker mentions, or who in this poem are "Christ's martyrs" and "Mammon's slaves"? To suggest a couple of possibilities: perhaps Christ's martyrs, understood as the religious underpinnings of European thought, have failed to redeem the world in a temporal sense, and so "Mammon's slaves" have taken up the task, or perhaps Christ's martyrs wisely refrain from attempting temporal redemption, preferring to die in hope of otherworldly glory. In either case, the identity of "Mammon's slaves" remains ambiguous. The most obvious hypothesis regarding their identity is that they are the enslaved African Americans of the antebellum South. In this reading, those who have been forcibly and physically enslaved by Mammon, or crass economic materialism, are accomplishing via the war that was caused by their enslavement a destruction of evil that Christian virtue is powerless to effect. Alternatively, the slaves of Mammon could be those who are morally and psychologically enslaved by greed and materialism—not the slaves, but their masters. In fact, "Mammon's slaves" can be read as referring to nineteenth-century Americans in general in this sense. This generation is enslaved to Mammon through a kind of universal avarice, but may paradoxically prove to be the very generation that will overturn a system of slavery founded on the very worst sort of avarice. Melville's effect, in this opening stanza, is to suggest a sense of disorientation so profound as to remove the very possibility of coherence.

As the poem continues, the reasons for this disorientation are developed. Melville alternates stanzas in a normal typeface with stanzas in italics, and the alternating stanzas indicate a moral clash that is distinct from the clash between the opposing sides in the Civil War. The italicized stanzas give voice to pacifism initially, asserting boldly in the first italicized stanza "Battle no more shall be!" (line 16). The third stanza (and second in non-italic typeface) provides an oblique answer to the previous stanza's pacifism: "The terrors of truth and dart of death / To faith alike are vain" (lines 18–19). If stanza 2 shifted the conflict from North versus South to war versus peace, the third stanza uses the cosmic orientation of the first stanza to shift the discussion to one on the subject of faith and doubt. The italicized lines take up from this point on the personification of doubt, while the non-italicized lines take up the cause of faith. Faith and doubt in this case are morally complex positions: faith argues that violence is sometimes necessary, whereas doubt has taken the position of non- or even anti-violence. As in so many other places in Melville's work, we understand the nuances of this poem if we keep in mind Melville's ambivalent annotations on the Sermon on the Mount and his ambivalent dialogue with pacifist religions in his early work.

Faith and doubt are also complicated in this poem by another ambiguity. In "The Conflict of Convictions," as Melville's own note to the poem discussed above suggests, Melville examines Christian faith in a benevolent deity and a cosmic direction to history in relation to Americans' belief in their nation and its institutions and ideals. This becomes clear, for example, when the non-italicized stanza 5 compares Americans who hold faith in the Union to Christ himself: "Kings wag their heads—Now save thyself / Who wouldst rebuild the world in bloom" (lines 38–39). Melville refers to the taunting of Christ on the cross, and Americans who believe in the future and destiny of their republic are portrayed as being crucified and mocked by disbelievers in democracy. The response in italics ridicules the cosmic and religious pretensions of the lines that precede them, mocking the idea that American democracy could be "the last advance of life" and claiming to see "the rust on the Iron Dome" (lines 43–44). This is a reference to the colloquial nickname given by many Americans to the new Capitol building in Washington, and it playfully and cruelly suggests that the young and powerful republic has already begun to decay. These cynical lines provide echoes of Melville's earlier tendency to describe America in eschatological terms in *Mardi* and *White-Jacket*, but in this case the irony is much more directly evident.

The "Dome" itself becomes a powerful metaphor for Melville's changing approach to religious difference. Structurally, a dome is a useful representation for union that builds comity out of dissonance, as it holds together as the result of the interaction of its structural contraries. It is also, however, a chilling metaphor for a diverse and democratic nation, implying a kind of unity that absorbs and weakens difference, ultimately creating a national homogeneity that would run counter to Melville's cherished pluralistic instincts. Melville acknowledges as much near the end of the poem, foreseeing a day when "the Iron Dome, / Stronger for the stress and strain, / Fling her huge shadow across the main / But the Founders dream shall flee / Age after age shall be / As age after age has been" (lines 77–80). The triumph of the Union is necessary and ardently to be desired, but the Union preserved would be one transformed, and Melville is without illusion about the costs associated with that transformation. The "iron dome" is a symbol of the strength of the Union, but the need for such strength is truly a tragic necessity. If Melville so often seems to be listening to himself and questioning and modifying his own assertions throughout *Battle-Pieces*, it is because of the magnitude of the task of reimagining what democracy might look like in a post–Civil War America and the profound challenge of finding ways in which "Dominion (unsought by the free)" might still nourish freedom (line 76).

Also captured by this poem is Melville's ambivalence about pacifism. It seems fair to say that Melville was powerfully drawn to the ideal of pacifism throughout his career: in works as different as *Typee*, *White-Jacket*, and *Pierre*, Melville explicitly places the command to "turn the other cheek" at the center of Christian doctrine and ethics. And yet, in this poem, the pacifism that Melville so frequently admires becomes united to a kind of world-weary cynicism. Peace and justice, freedom and power, unity and diversity all become convictions that may conflict with each other in an irreconcilable manner for the Melville of *Battle-Pieces*.

The conclusion to the poem takes us back to the numerous contraries that have shaped "The Conflict of Convictions" throughout. All in capital letters, in order to represent a different voice from either of the debating sides, the last stanza reads: "YEA AND NAY— / EACH HATH HIS SAY; BUT GOD HE KEEPS THE MIDDLE WAY. / NONE WAS BY / WHEN HE SPREAD THE SKY; / WISDOM IS VAIN, AND PROPHESY" (lines 85–90). These lines suggest yet another aspect to the role of religious difference in understanding the war: the North and South may have their own versions of God and Satan, but there is also something, whether divinity or fate, that maintains the inscrutability of coming events, and frustrates human designs. Given the intensely American focus of this poem, it is noteworthy that Melville's conceptual structure for the last few lines, affirmation, negation, and indifference, owes a substantial transatlantic debt to Thomas Carlyle, who was a substantial influence on Melville as well as on the Transcendentalist movement with which Melville had a vexed relationship.[14]

What these early poems in *Battle-Pieces* make clear is that Melville's method at this stage in his career was to connect political and historical events with cosmic resonances, suggesting that the precarious state of the Union mirrored the precarious state of the cosmos during the 1860s. In "The Portent" John Brown's head becomes a corollary to the supposed predictive power of comets. In "Misgivings" a physical storm becomes conflated with the spiritual and political storms associated with the Civil War, and in "The Conflict of Convictions," the war between the North and the South becomes conflated with a Miltonic battle between God and Satan before resolving itself into an abstract conflict between faith and doubt.

The "House-Top" is one of Melville's most hotly debated and frequently misread poems. Although it has been read by one of the most distinguished critics of Melville's Civil War poetry, Stanton Garner, as a dramatic monologue, I want to suggest that it can be best read in relation to the uncertainties that inform the collection as a whole.[15] The speaker is, like the Melville of his letters to Hawthorne in the early 1850s, torn between a belief in democracy and a fear of human depravity and destructiveness. The bitter ironies in the lines of the poem grow out of this conflict, and are especially intensified by the conflict of race with class that the 1863 draft riots, providing the context for this poem, exemplified. Melville tended to sympathize, as we saw in many of his earlier novels, with the working class and immigrants as well as with enslaved African Americans, and the draft riots described in this poem pitted one marginalized group against the other, with typically marginalized working-class Irish Catholics turning viciously against New York City's African American population.[16] Small wonder that the dominant mode here is a bitter sort of ambivalence. The poem begins by foregrounding the insomnia created by the riot that both reflects and increases the speaker's sense of disorientation:

> No sleep. The sultriness pervades the air
> And binds the brain—a dense oppression such
> As tawny tigers feel in matted shades,
> Vexing their blood and making them apt for ravage.
> Beneath the stars the roofy desert spreads
> Vacant as Libya. (lines 1–6)

The mixture of images here has the effect of making New York, Melville's longtime home, seem strangely unfamiliar, with the sights of home taking on the topographical characteristics of North Africa. Indeed, the events that followed this eerie moment proved to be terribly unfamiliar and estranging for many New Yorkers: the violence and disorder throughout the city, and especially the brutal attacks on the African American population, might have seemed to undercut the righteousness of the war itself. Melville's speaker appears to have a point when he refers to the federal response by invoking "wise Draco"—these riots were violent, destructive, and motivated in no small part by racism, and had they not been suppressed with force, their destructiveness could have been much more substantial. Melville, characteristically anti-authoritarian in his views, is able in the poem both to mourn what is lost when authority imposes itself violently as in the case of the draft riots and to recognize the necessity of this sort of assertion of authority. Again, Melville invokes theological debates and teases out their political implications.

Race in *Battle-Pieces*

The sheer anguish entailed by what Melville describes as "sacred uncertainty" in the "Prose Supplement" is nowhere more evident than in the small number of poems in which the African American experience is central. Most strikingly, Melville presents African American allusions in "The Swamp Angel" and "Formerly a Slave." "The Swamp Angel," more than perhaps any other poem in *Battle-Pieces*, merits far more attention than it has received. In this poem, the Swamp Angel itself is, as Melville's own note makes clear, not a human being, but a weapon—"The great Parrott gun, planted in the marshes of James Island, and employed in the prolonged, although at times intermitted bombardment of Charleston" (*PP* 175). This weapon is, however, described in terms that make it a stand-in for the slaves who have escaped into the swamp, on their way either to freedom or to death. The Swamp Angel is described in the second line as having "a thick Afric lip," and the image of the cannon is specifically designed to call up the history of slaves who escaped in the swamp and were pursued in the swamp. Charleston, like the biblical city of Babylon, also invoked in the poem, is seen as suffering a grave judgment for its sins at the hands of the Swamp Angel. What is noteworthy here is how thoroughly Melville's discussion of a piece of weaponry is informed by his reflections on religious conflict. Charleston is an antitype of both Babylon and Jerusalem in this poem: it is a city to be condemned, like Babylon, but also a city to be wept over, like Jerusalem. This hearkens to another of Melville's New Testament annotations. Melville marked heavily the passage where Jesus weeps over Jerusalem in the Gospel of Matthew, and the conclusion to "The Swamp Angel," with its prayer to "Christ the Forgiver" (line 47) points toward both the fundamental immorality, in Melville's view, of the Southern cause and its continuity with a historic catalog of humans' wrongs, all of which requires a kind of forgiveness that transcends ordinary human behavior.

Unlike "The Swamp Angel," the African American presence in "Formerly a Slave" is literal rather than metaphorical. Here we have an example of what Douglas Robillard and Hsuan Hsu have discussed as a tendency toward ekphrasis in Melville's poetry—the tendency to write descriptively about objects drawn from the visual arts.[17] The inspiration for the poem is a portrait of an African American woman by Elihu Vedder, and her physical description makes her an icon of the joyful and tragic uncertainties associated with the war. This brief lyric is worth quoting in full:

> The sufferance of her race is shown
> And retrospect of life,
> Which now too late deliverance dawns upon;
> Yet she is not at strife.

Her children's children they shall know
The good withheld from her;
And so her reverie takes prophetic cheer—
In spirit she sees the stir

Far down the depth of thousand years,
And marks the revel shine;
Her dusky face is lit with sober light,
Sibylline, yet benign.

This poem has the potential to be read in retrospect (and indeed has been so read) as a gradualist and condescending approach to the African American experience at the end of the Civil War. After all, the woman here seems content to wait for "the depth of thousand years" for her descendants to obtain justice, and it is taken for granted that this woman will not experience justice in her lifetime. Also present here is the romantic racialism that George Frederickson identified in a great deal of Northern discourse about African Americans and that appears prominently even in Harriet Beecher Stowe's great antislavery novel *Uncle Tom's Cabin*: the woman shows "the sufferance of her race," suggesting that African Americans are uniquely patient and Christlike—a compliment, on the one hand, but one which has the potential to minimize the seriousness of African American suffering and the necessity for redressing the injustices of slavery.[18] And yet, I believe there is something more here than is acknowledged by readings that dwell on the facts mentioned above. If we understand this woman, not as an archetype, but as a human being, we begin to draw some different conclusions. She has suffered greatly—in ways that the expression "the sufferance of her race" can only begin to hint at. She will die without the chance to experience freedom substantially, yet she rejoices in the prospects of her "children's children." This is particularly poignant, given that, as virtually every antislavery novel, story, or oration from the period emphasized, an elderly African American woman who had been a slave might well have lost all contact with her children (not to mention her children's children) because they were sold away from her.[19]

The "prophetic cheer" she takes from her reverie is derived from possibilities that she will never experience, and that will likely be denied her even vicariously because of the division of her family by slavery. To return to typology and to use a trope common to African American preaching and spirituals, she is a kind of Moses, granted a Pisgah view of the Promised Land, but denied its fulfillment. The description of her as "sibylline" is also full of meaning, drawing upon a model for prophecy that is both pre-Christian and distinctly feminine. In the midst of the uncertainty, bafflement, and storms of the postwar era, this woman, formerly a slave, is the icon of the only kind of faith that matters.[20]

The suffering of this elderly woman links her inevitably to the suffering of the combatants in the war. The section entitled "Verses Inscriptive and Memorial" marks a turning point in *Battle-Pieces*. The poems become shorter, more reflective, and less concerned with creating a dramatic situation. The majority of pieces represent the sort of concentrated expression of mourning and loss that one might expect on a tombstone, or on a monument commemorating a terrible event. The dimension of difference and pluralism does not depart even here, however. In one particularly resonant piece, difference becomes the test of the Union's strength, as Melville celebrates soldiers from Maine who were buried in Louisiana after being killed fighting Confederate forces at Baton Rouge:

> Afar they fell. It was the zone
> Of fig and orange, cane and lime
> (A land how all unlike their own,
> With the cold pine-grove overgrown),
> But still their country's clime.
> And there in youth they died for her—
> The Volunteers.
> For her went up their dying prayers:
> So vast the Nation, yet so strong the tie.
> What doubt shall come, then, to deter,
> The Republic's earnest faith and courage high. (lines 1–11)

Melville's position here is not that the distance between Maine and Louisiana renders national unity an illusion, but rather that this distance confirms the power of the Union as a concept. (It is worth noting that this in itself represents a kind of transformation in attitudes toward the cohesiveness of the nation from Thoreau's *Walden*, in which Thoreau expresses doubts about whether "Maine and Texas" have anything substantial in common.)[21] Diversity becomes a condition for unity, and difference in all of its forms serves to affirm rather than deny the presence of bonds that transcend difference. Even geographical distance is made paradoxically to correspond to intimacy. The Union persists, and doubt and uncertainty are ultimately contained by that assurance.

The larger thrust of the inscriptions, indeed, is to mediate between doubt and assurance, which are the poles in relation to which each of these poems is situated. This tendency appears in poem after poem: in "An Epitaph," we are provided with the picture of a grieving widow who gives strength to the other mourners in her town: the widow "Felt deep at heart her faith content / And priest and people borrowed of her cheer" (lines 7–8). "On the Slain at Chickamauga" meditates on one of the most horrifyingly bloody battles of the war, concluding that for those who have suffered and died in the battle "And yet mischance is honorable too— / Seeming defeat in conflict justified / Whose end to closing eyes is hid from view / The will, that never can relent— / The aim, survivor of the bafflement, / Make this memorial due" (lines 10–15). The battle of Chickamauga provided a particularly apt instance for Melville because of the fact that it was a major Union defeat. The soldiers at Chickamauga are validated despite their defeat because they fought "in conflict justified," and here at least, Melville seems ready to renounce uncertainty—"bafflement"—in favor of a definite faith in the Union "aim." What is again apparent is that Melville's uncertainty is never allowed to lapse into mere relativism, and that Melville, unlike some twentieth-century historians, was never in doubt either about the cause of the war or about the moral superiority of the Union. The Union cause was worth dying for because it was the cause of human brotherhood and equality, according to Melville, and his uncertainty never extends to that fundamental fact.

Melville does persist in his uncertainty regarding some of the largest questions about the meaning of the war. In "America," the last of the longer poems before the start of "Verses Inscriptive and Memorial," Melville imagines the nation as a mother, using the imagery of domesticity and sentiment to reflect upon the affective impact of the war. In its movement from a state of harmony and health to disharmony and violence, the structure of the poem is reminiscent of Poe's "The Haunted Palace," which appears in the middle of "The Fall of the House of Usher" and presents an allegory of the human mind.[22] In the first stanza of the poem, Melville considers America as a loving young mother with a happy family, in which "The children in their glee / Were folded to the exulting heart / Of young maternity" (lines 10–12). In the second stanza the national mother's offspring have become torn by a war pitting the best qualities of each side with the other, and by the third stanza, the maternal nation has had a glimpse of the ultimate abyss, imagined as either a dream or a Lazarus-like death and resurrection:

> A watcher looked upon her low, and said—
> She sleeps, but sleeps, she is not dead.
> But in that sleep contortion showed

The terror of the vision there—
A silent vision unavowed,
Revealing earth's foundation bare
And Gorgon in her hidden place. (lines 24–30)

The description of the nation as sleeping mirrors Jesus's words about Lazarus directly before he raised him from the dead in the Gospel account. The nation's vision of terror mirrors both the vision that Pip had in *Moby-Dick* when he was abandoned at sea and the vision that is suggested by another poem from *Battle-Pieces*, "The Apparition," in which the eruption of a bombshell that tears up the earth itself reveals that "Solidity's a crust" (line 12). The nation has learned a terrible lesson about the instability of human existence, but the fourth stanza makes clear that this lesson ultimately has allowed her to emerge purified and strengthened. Conflict, uncertainty, and the terror of instability here become a source ultimately of wisdom and power—a vision toward which Melville struggled throughout *Battle-Pieces*.

The longer poems that conclude the poetic portions of *Battle-Pieces* point toward the poetic practices in which Melville would engage over the next decade while drafting his hyper-ambitious poem *Clarel, A Poem and Pilgrimage in the Holy Land*. Here Melville was particularly concerned with the development of character, examining Robert E. Lee in "Lee in the Capitol." This poem conveys a sense of the ongoing questions raised by the war, and both poems—"Lee in the Capitol" and *Clarel*—suggest that these questions are likely to remain unresolved in the foreseeable future.

The South, Islam, and Reconstruction as Religious Conversion

Of particular interest in the case of "Lee in the Capitol" is Melville's concern with the relationship between a moral man and an unjust cause—and between immoral men and just causes. Lee is portrayed at the start of the poem in his postwar retirement, most actively concerned with forgetting the carnage of which he had been a principal part. He is summoned out of this solitude, however, by members of the United States Senate looking to investigate his role as a leader in the rebellion.

Notably, Melville uses a rather unusual metrical scheme to open the poem: in a curious reversal of the tetrameter/trimeter alternation that we so often expect in narrative poetry, Melville opens with tetrameter and alternates the tetrameter with pentameter. The result can be initially jarring in that the swiftly moving narrative that the tetrameter promises to establish is slowed down by the stately lines of pentameter. As the opening proceeds, the logic of the meter blends almost imperceptibly with the logic of the language, and the poem is throughout a curious amalgam of realistic narrative verse of the sort he would employ at great length in *Clarel* and the epic poetic conventions he admired in *Paradise Lost*. Lee is described as a "soldier-chief" (line 2), echoing the compound form of many Homeric epithets, and he first appears in the poem in a state of pastoral retirement as "a quiet seminary's head" (line 6). Once Lee begins his journey toward the Capitol, the lines smooth out into a more consistent tetrameter, interrupted at times with pentameter when he speaks in more characteristically epic modes, as when he delivers a vaunting speech reminiscent of a Homeric warrior or Milton's Satan directed toward the Capitol itself:

> "So be it! They await me now
> Who wrought this stinging overthrow;
> They wait me; not as on the day
> Of Pope's impelled retreat in disarray—
> By me impelled—when toward yon Dome
> The clouds of war came rolling home." (lines 34–39)

The first three lines from this passage are tetrameter, with a caesura disrupting lines 34 and 36. Line 37 is in pentameter, and lines 38 and 39 resume tetrameter, with a caesura in line 38. The defeated Lee's defiant boast is centered on the line in pentameter, and it recalls similar boasts made by Satan in *Paradise Lost* regarding temporary successes in arms against the overwhelming power of the Almighty. Lee as the speaker in the later oration before the Senate is thus presented as a character at once heroic and morally ambiguous, through both the content and the formal allusions in his speech.

What follows these moments of resentment and rage on Lee's part is a curious verse paragraph that frames its meditation largely in terms of the subjunctive:

> Intrepid soldier! Had his blade been drawn
> For yon starr'd flag, never as now
> Bid to the Senate house had he gone,
> But freely, and in pageant borne,
> As when brave numbers, without number, massed,
> Plumed the broad way, and pouring, passed—

Bannered, beflowered—between the shores
Of faces, and the dinn'd huzzas,
And balconies kindling at the sabre-flash,
'Mid roar of drums and guns, and cymbal-crash,
While Grant and Sherman shone in blue—
Close of the war, and victory's long review. (lines 50–62)

The passage captures something important about Lee as the speaker later in the poem: he is marked by numerous admirable qualities that are rendered fit material for grief and loss by his failure to embrace a just and victorious cause (resembling, perhaps, his fellow Confederates' "sensitive love of liberty entrapped" into the service of "systematic degradation of man" as described in the "Prose Supplement"). Formally, the passage extends Melville's metrical experiments: it begins with a line of pentameter, moves into tetrameter for the next three lines (the middle of which is catalectic, approximating pentameter), returns to pentameter in the fifth line, and then approximates the pattern in the second portion of the stanza. Again, Melville moves between narrative modes via his use of pentameter and tetrameter, suggesting the gap between Lee's epic possibilities and the grim reality of his role as a defeated general in an unjust cause.

Melville is interested both in Lee's dignity and in the severity of the crime of which he is unquestionably guilty. Lee stands before the assembled congressmen and senators as an acknowledged and unsuccessful rebel—the sort of person, Melville well knew, who in earlier generations would have certainly met a public and gruesome end. At the same time, Melville's narrator asserts, it must be remembered that Lee is a criminal because he has been defeated, something that would have been true for George Washington, for whom the capital city has been named, had he been vanquished by the British in the American Revolution. The fact that Lee is pleading his case rather than suffering for his crimes is in fact a demonstration of the difference between the Union and previous victors in similar circumstances. And yet Lee's plea is for understanding for a defeated and culpable South.

Lee acknowledges that his judges are both victorious and justified by the outcome of the war, but suggests "Where various hazards meet the eyes, / To elect in magnanimity is wise" (lines 142–43). Lee makes the (self-interested) argument that the uncertainties that face the Union make a generous policy toward the South desirable. The point of view ascribed here to Lee is one that points toward a reconciliation between the North and the South that downplays the role of slavery in the war, echoing some of the more troubling sentiments from the "Prose Supplement." Melville's position with regard to Lee is unstable here: on the one hand, Lee is treated throughout as a tragic and admirable figure by the frame narrator, but on the other, his status as the leader of a morally reprehensible rebellion is acknowledged. One question that the poem poses, then, is how to deal responsibly with the brute reality of the Civil War—the fact that potentially admirable men have betrayed the Union in defense of a principle that is abhorrent to Melville as both a Union supporter and a moral critic of slavery means that the position of Northerners attempting to understand how to respond to the end of the war is fraught with alternatives that are both unacceptable and unavoidable.

One of the most striking moments in "Lee in the Capitol" demonstrates how thoroughly the model of religious difference defines Melville's approach to the Civil War: Melville puts into Lee's mouth a long anecdote about a Muslim girl in medieval Palestine who is ordered to convert to Christianity by her captors, and finds it necessary to justify to them her refusal to do so:

> A story here may be applied:
> "In Moorish lands there lived a maid
> Brought to confess by vow the creed
> Of Christians. Fain would priests persuade
> That now she must approve by deed
> The faith she kept." (lines 234–38)

Although she has been willing to renounce her faith in the abstract, the Muslim maid is unwilling to accede to the demand that follows: that she forsake her father. She is willing to exchange one abstract creed for another, but the concrete act of denying family ties is unthinkable. She ultimately declares her willingness to be burned at the stake rather than renounce her devotion to her family.

The Muslim maid here is a carefully chosen example, both for Melville as the author and for the character of Lee in the poem. By using her for his example, Lee is cautiously acknowledging the rectitude of the North's cause: just as Christianity is the true religion for both Lee and his interlocutors, the Union represents the political truth for America. Again, both Lee and his interlocutors would regard Islam as falling short of the truth of Christianity, which suggests that the South has been in the wrong relative to the North. This does not mean, however, that the consensus that Lee is invoking means that the maid's Christian inquisitors are right to persecute her. Instead, the maid's intransigence is presented as both morally admirable and psychologically understandable, and Lee's case is that Southerners may be mistaken in their beliefs, but their refusal to abandon them is psychologically inescapable. This also resurrects a motif that ran through much of Melville's earlier work: the sense of admiration that moral inflexibility can produce. The extended quote from Goethe on the inside cover of Melville's copy of *The New Testament and Psalms* imputes moral inflexibility to Christ himself; in a paradoxical sense, then, the Muslim maid's refusal to convert to Christianity if such conversion means renouncing filial piety becomes itself a Christlike act. The Muslim maid imitates Christ by refusing to worship him if that worship entails a violation of her moral compass. Her intransigence likewise points back to earlier Melvillean heroes and villains that include Captain Ahab, Bartleby, John Paul Jones, and Babo, and forward to numerous figures in *Clarel*, *Timoleon*, and *John Marr and Other Sailors*. It is also worth noting that the maid's identity as "Moorish" potentially suggests African heritage as well as Islamic faith. In a delicious paradox, Lee is forced to justify Southern white feelings with reference to an African model—a rhetorical choice that brings home the decisiveness of the North's moral victory at the same time that Lee cautions the North not to lose the moral high ground. Lee is able to make a case for the South in this poem only by accepting the North's moral narrative for the war. Given Lee's personal distaste for slavery, which antedated the war, he is perhaps better positioned than most Southerners to make this sort of admission. Also noteworthy here is that the strength and physical and moral courage of women provide an essential component of Melville's understanding of morality in the wake of the Civil War. The "Moorish maid," like the sibylline ex-slave and the Union widow, provide models for what it means to live with dignity and trans-religious faith amid the fraught uncertainties of war. This attraction to feminine modes of belief was not new to Melville's work, as anyone who has read "The Chola Widow" in *The Encantadas* can attest, but it is in the process of gathering an urgency that will express itself most fully in *Clarel* and the works that follow.

The potential sources for the story of the Moorish maid also shed some light on Lee's choice of her anecdote. In a poem with which Melville would likely have been familiar (at the very least, we know from Merton M. Sealts's *Melville's Reading* that Melville consulted other works by this author), Robert Southey's 1798 poem "The Lover's Rock," a "Moorish maid" appears in a familial and interreligious context that is largely reversed in Lee's oration. Southey's "Moorish maid," a young woman named Laila, runs away with a Christian youth named Manuel, in defiance of her father's wishes. Her outraged father pursues and captures her and condemns her and her lover to death for her disobedience. Just as her father's archers are about to shoot her and Manuel down, both of them leap over a cliff together, thus ending their lives in a mutual suicide.[23] In another possible source, "The Legend of the Three Beautiful Princesses" in Washington Irving's *The Alhambra*—which we know from Sealts that Melville owned in the form of a copy of *The Works of Washington Irving*—Irving raises the ante and narrates the story of three princesses who were born to a Moorish monarch and a European Christian woman that he had abducted and who ultimately fall in love and elope with Christian captives of their Muslim father. As in the poem by Southey, Irving's is a story of Muslim women who prefer Christian lovers to fathers who are tyrannical and cruel and are racialized as non-European.[24] When Melville puts the tale of a "Moorish maid" who chooses her "Moorish" father over his European, Christian persecutors into Lee's mouth, he is thus reversing the expected narrative utterly. Lee's tale is a substantial inversion of the stories told by Irving and Southey. Rather than telling the story of a cruel non-European, non-Christian father and a daughter who is drawn to Europe and Christianity despite her upbringing, the story that Melville gives Lee is that of a young woman who is loyal to a father who is both Islamic in faith and associated with Africa in race and ethnicity, implicitly arguing that bonds within the human family are limited neither to Europe nor to Christianity.

Lee's implication is that interpersonal connections are essential, and to whatever degree faith, whether spiritual or political, attempts to deny these connections, that faith must prove unsuccessful. The narrator's frame that surrounds Lee's narrative suggests that Lee's eloquence and the example of the Muslim maid will not be heeded: "Instinct disowns each darkening prophecy: / Faith in America never dies; / Heaven shall the ordained end fulfill, / We march with Providence cheery still" (lines 256–59). If Lee's speech is both an admission of Southern guilt and the rightness of the Union cause and a warning of the danger of abstract and uncomplicated faith, the narrator suspects that only the first element will be heeded. The line "Faith in America never dies" gives a rich sense of Melville's ambivalence in the aftermath of the war: does this mean that *faith* never dies in America, or does it mean that *faith in America* is immortal? The ambiguity here is deeply significant, as Melville connects the religiosity of his nation with a bent toward civil religion and American exceptionalism. The cheery faith in a Providence that favors those in the right may, Melville suggests, lead his compatriots astray. At this point as at so many others in *Battle-Pieces*, however, it is necessary to note that Melville's call for uncertainty is not the expression of a relativistic justification of slavery or secession, both of which Melville abhorred, but rather a call for self-knowledge and self-doubt even among those who are in the right. Melville's Lee is not the Lee of Confederate nostalgia but a vanquished foe whose merits could be acknowledged even as his role in a crime was remembered. The "sacred uncertainty" expressed in "Lee in the Capitol" is that which emerges when moral earnestness meets up with a bewildering moral complexity that can neither be resolved into certainty or dismissed via relativism, but must be retained with a profound sense of anguish at its unsatisfactory resolution.

The frame narrator for Lee's speech is not given the last word in *Battle-Pieces*, however. The final poem in the collection gives voice to "A Meditation: Attributed to a Northerner after attending the last of two funerals from the same homestead—those of a national and a confederate officer (brothers), his kinsmen, who had died from the effects of the wounds received in the closing battles." The full title reveals a close connection to Lee's story of the Muslim maid in "Lee in the Capitol." The Northerner who meditates on the death of the two soldiers is contemplating the tragic rending of kinship bonds, but he is not conducting this meditation from a vantage point of detachment. He is himself a kinsman of both soldiers, and thus is thoroughly implicated in the fratricide on which he ponders. The Northerner begins the poem by imagining a scene that he knows must have been repeated often throughout the war, and perhaps at times between his own kinsmen:

> How often in the years that close,
> When truce had stilled the sieging gun,
> The soldiers, mounting on their works,
> With mutual curious glance have run
> From face to face along the fronting show,
> And kinsman spy, or friend—even in a foe,
>
> What thoughts conflicting then were shared,
> While sacred tenderness perforce
> Welled from the heart and wet the eye,
> Rebelled against the sanctioned sin of blood,
> And Christian Wars of natural brotherhood. (lines 1–12)

Melville's language here brings the military and the domestic into unsettling contact: soldiers in the midst of military operations find themselves acknowledging family ties, and their response is a form of "sacred tenderness" for their enemies. Melville's use of "sacred" here to modify "tenderness" calls to mind his extensive annotation of the Sermon on the

Mount in his copy of *The New Testament and Psalms*, where he seems particularly concerned with Jesus's command to love one's enemies. It also recalls "The Journey and the Pamphlet" in *Pierre*, in which Melville's narrator refers to the Sermon on the Mount in particular and the command to love one's enemies in particular as "the greatest real miracle" to come out of any of the world's religions. The adversaries in this case are not bound by Christlike love and forgiveness to express "tenderness" but by natural, biological bonds. The phrase "Christian Wars of natural brotherhood" is more striking still—presumably if one takes the Sermon on the Mount seriously, Christians ought to forsake warring against all other humans, and especially other Christians, whereas the Civil War featured literal, biological, brothers warring against each other with Christianity serving as a source of inspiration for both sides. The irony of the phrase is thus rich and multifaceted. The following lines, "Then stirred the god within the breast / The witness that is man's at birth; / A deep misgiving undermined / Each plea and subterfuge of earth" (lines 13–16), demonstrate that conscience can cut both ways. The "plea[s] and subterfuge[s] of earth" may be either the natural ties of flesh and blood that must be overcome by adherence to a higher law, or the rationalizations for war that make it permissible to slaughter even one's own kin. The irony here is brutal, and the sense of mixed reverent tenderness and anguish for one's estranged kin is palpable. The use of "misgiving" takes us back to the uncertainties that frame the beginning of *Battle-Pieces*, in poems like "The Portent," "The Conflict of Convictions," and indeed, the poem "Misgivings" itself.

Melville's attentiveness to personal ties and to the savage ironies of war is surely worthy of being admired here, but there is a less admirable side to the Northerner's rhetoric of kinship. After acknowledging the cruelty of a fratricidal war, he seems to shift blame onto the victims of slavery, musing: "Can Africa pay back this blood / Spilled on Potomac's shore" (lines 21–22). The logic here seems morally repellent, to say the least—the Northerner seems to assume that the victims of slavery owe white Americans for the carnage of the Civil War, a position that both trivializes slavery and ignores the sacrifices that black soldiers made on behalf of the Union in the Civil War. What then are we to make of this disconcerting moment in the final poem of *Battle-Pieces*? Two points are worth recalling here: first, as callous as the Northerner's words are, his position was shared by many white Northerners who were ardent opponents of slavery and supporters of African American liberty. Second, there are some reasons for concluding that Melville's views were not identical with those of the hypothetical Northerner in "A Meditation." Recall, for example, the story of the Moorish maid. What is noteworthy about this story is the way in which the Christians' persecution of the maid is presented as a violation of natural piety: not only is the maid devoted to her family, but Lee's anecdote makes it clear that the maid and those trying to convert her are part of one common human family. There is a substantial irony here, in that Lee fought to defend precisely the sort of denial of the existence of a common human family that the story of the Moorish maid emphasizes, which serves to heighten the sense that Melville, in *Battle-Pieces*, is sorting his way through issues for which there are no apparent and satisfactory resolutions. Melville's careful crafting of both "Lee in the Capitol" and "A Meditation" suggests that Melville is both acknowledging and critiquing the impulse for national reconciliation that would fail so signally in providing for racial justice. The emphasis on the kinship of all humans across racial lines has deep roots in Melville's writing. As early as 1847 he wrote that humans of different races were brothers who would have to "join hands hereafter," if they failed to do so in the present life (*PT* 231). Once again, Melville's anti-racism and commitment to seeing the human race as both a universal family and a universal church becomes an essential element in framing his work, even as his conclusions are not always precisely those we would wish him to draw in light of a subsequent history that is available to us but was not to him.

This familial model is also available in another strand of nineteenth-century writing: antislavery novels before and pro-Reconstruction novels after the end of the Civil War. If the model of brothers divided by war and by conscience obsessed many early chroniclers of the war, in fiction, poetry, and nonfiction alike, this tendency finds a striking parallel in the abolitionist model of slave families divided by the war upon those of African descent represented by slavery, in the work of writers ranging from Harriet Beecher Stowe and Lydia Maria Child to William Wells Brown and Frances E. W. Harper.[25] Reconstruction and the debates surrounding it thus become very intimate indeed: the underlying question, persistently, is about who counts as family, in both individual and national terms. If Melville does not visualize the national family in precisely the way that those of us who admire him now would wish, he at least calls attention to the fractured, unstable nature of the familial metaphors that were being applied to the American nation in the immediate aftermath of the Civil War.

When Lee invokes the "Moorish maid" in Melville's poem, the nature of the metaphor calls attention to both sides of this representation of the familial aspect of civil conflict. On the one hand, it reinforces the idea that the North and South are required by natural piety to reunite and that white Northerners share a bond with white Southerners; on the other, it reminds the perceptive reader that the unreconstructed South has denied precisely these demands of natural piety in its rejection of liberty and equality for its African American population. From now on, Melville seems to suggest, even the pleas for clemency mustered by the defeated South will need to take on something of the flavor of the opposing side. There is a premonition here of later debates (including some at the present time) in which apparently egalitarian or populist arguments are used when inegalitarian results are sought. Even in its attempts to be reconciled to the Union without abandoning its racial caste system, the South's rhetoric as expressed by Lee must take on something of the ecumenical, ethical quality that we now associate with the abolitionist movement and other progressive religious movements of the nineteenth century.

What, then, is the import of "Lee in the Capitol" for twenty-first-century scholars trying to assess Melville's treatment of race and religious difference—for those who are attempting to reconstruct Melville on Reconstruction? My suggestion is that the "Moorish maid" is crucial for understanding the racial and religious politics of this poem, and indeed of *Battle-Pieces* more broadly. By using the "Moorish maid"—a potentially African (or at least racially ambiguous) woman, and a member of a persecuted religious minority—as Lee's rhetorical device for asking for clemency, Melville refuses to erase the lingering questions surrounding race and broadly divergent interpretations of religious and ethical imperatives in the service of social consensus. Indeed, he calls attention to precisely those remaining conflicts that his pacific "Prose Supplement" cannot erase. In Melville's writing of Reconstruction, if Lee is allowed to request forgiveness for the South, Melville's readers, in the Reconstruction period and after, are still not permitted to forget.

To return to Melville's treatment of John Brown at the beginning of *Battle-Pieces*: one element of Brown's story that could well have been especially resonant for Melville was Brown's testimony at his trial for treason. Confronted with the case against him, Brown memorably replied:

> This court acknowledges too, as I suppose, the validity of the law of God. I see a book kissed, which I suppose to be the Bible, or at least the New Testament, which teaches me that all things whatsoever I would have men do unto me, I should do so even to them. It teaches me further to remember them that are in bonds as bound with them. I endeavored to act up to that instruction.[26]

For Herman Melville, a man who had a long history of reflection on the command to love one's neighbor as oneself, both in his published work and his letters and marginalia, this would have summarized the crucial issue in the war that was to come. How *am* I to love my neighbor as myself? At many points in Melville's career, a form of pacifism reminiscent of the readings of the Sermon on the Mount produced by the Radical Reformation (the phase of the Protestant Reformation associated with Anabaptism and pacifism) appears to be the most desirable answer to this question, but the confluence of war and emancipation in the Civil War raised challenges that would have anguished even the most unambivalent pacifist. The abolitionist movement had for long been connected closely to pacifism, most notably in the person of William Lloyd Garrison, and John Brown's invocation of love of neighbor as the central justification for his violence touched on a crucial contradiction that would only be intensified by the onset of the war. In the case of *Battle-Pieces*, religious difference is neither a matter of competing world religions, as in Melville's early novels, nor of varying denominational and charismatic models of Christianity as in his work from the mid-1850s. Rather, here the fault lines are between contraries that are internal to any individual faith tradition: pacifism versus just war, racial equality versus racial hierarchy, justice versus injustice, mercy versus wrath. Determining the proper stance in relation to these alternatives is the crux of Melville's internal dialogues in *Battle-Pieces*.

Melville's faith in the ability of art to probe these contraries is evident in a piece that brings together the ekphrastic and the literary: "'The Coming Storm': A Picture by S. R. Gifford Owned by E.B. Included in the N.A. Exhibition, April, 1865." In this frequently quoted poem near the end of the main portion of *Battle-Pieces*, Melville comments on Gifford's painting in terms that strongly defend the capacity of literature to engage with violence. Identifying the owner, actor Edwin Booth, brother to Lincoln's assassin, as a spiritual child of Shakespeare, Melville writes:

> The Hamlet in his heart was 'ware:
> Such hearts can antedate.
>
> No utter surprise can come to him
> Who reaches Shakespeare's core
> That which we seek and shun is there—
> Man's final lore. (lines 11–16)

Melville here suggests that literature can reflect meaningfully on the sorts of large-scale political conflicts which were played out in the Civil War, and that it can do so precisely because of its ability to examine the contraries of the human heart. If Shakespeare can reveal to us "that which we seek and shun," literature can offer a conceptual basis for understanding the bewildering moral and theological complexities even of an event so cataclysmic and seemingly unprecedented as the Civil War. Melville's reflections in this poem on Shakespeare as an interpreter of tragedy on a cosmic scale indicate the direction of his future poetry and prose—toward dramatic dialogues that explored with nuance and detail the great religious, philosophical, and moral crises of the later nineteenth century.

Even as Melville proposed that literature could speak to the uncertainties that were spawned by the Civil War, he meditated on both the power and the potential danger of a religious understanding of the conflict. In "The Martyr," Melville considered the meaning of Lincoln's assassination for the coming Reconstruction. As many Americans had noted, Lincoln was assassinated on Good Friday, with the result that he came to be viewed by supporters of the Union as a martyr at the least, and perhaps even a nineteenth-century version of Christ. Melville acknowledges the mythic power of this representation in the lines:

> Good Friday was the day
> Of the prodigy and crime
> When they killed him in his pity
> When they killed him in his prime
> Of clemency and calm—
> When with yearning he was filled,
> To redeem the evil-willed,
> And though conqueror, be kind; (lines 1–8)

The Lincoln in these lines resembles Christ in his offer of mercy for the wicked, and he appears as a redeemer who "yearn[s]" to "redeem" the conquered South in a manner reminiscent of Christ weeping over Jerusalem, a moment in the Gospels, which as we have seen, had a great effect upon Melville. The following lines point out that, also like Christ, Lincoln was killed by treachery: "But they killed him in his kindness, / In their madness and their blindness, /And they killed him from behind" (lines 9–11). Lincoln's assassination becomes a crucifixion, and the South becomes both betrayer and executioner in this reading of the Lincoln assassination. Melville's interest in religious difference, and in the dangers of importing contemporary events into the contexts of foundational religious narratives, appears in the refrain, however. Good Friday has historically been a day of mourning and repentance across (nearly) the full gamut of Christian religious traditions and denominations, but it has also been a day marked and marred historically by Christian violence against the Jewish people as a result of the libel, now (in our time) renounced by most Christian churches, that the Jewish people were uniquely responsible for the death of Jesus. The five-line refrain, repeated twice in the poem, meditates on the dangers of this sort of religiously sanctioned violence associated with mourning when Melville's speaker warns, "There is a sobbing of the strong, And a pall upon the land; / But the people in their weeping / Bare the iron hand / Beware the people weeping / When they bare the iron hand" (lines 12–17; 29–34). Communal mourning can turn all too easily into communal violence, as Melville knows, and while there seems to be a certain vengeful satisfaction in the poem on one level, there is also the anguished realization that "the people weeping" can be guilty of their own crimes.

Battle-Pieces is ultimately neither the apprentice work that the early readers of Melville's poetry presumed nor the sterile reflections of a man detached from the reality of war that Howells criticized. Instead, the collection represents the reflections of a fully engaged civilian who attempts to write about the conflicts of the war in a way that transcends the passions of the moment. This effort toward transcendence means that *Battle-Pieces* could not escape from an engagement with questions of pluralism, ethics, and religious doubt and uncertainty. The "sacred uncertainty" that Melville makes the pivot of his "Prose Supplement" to *Battle-Pieces* thus becomes crucial to an understanding of his entire career. Before *Battle-Pieces*, Melville would feed his uncertainties into exuberant expressions of a variety of faiths and doubts, expressing each of his contradictions with almost equal fervor—although, to be sure, irony and doubt come to predominate by the time of *The Confidence-Man*. From *Battle-Pieces* on, Melville did not abandon the contraries that shape his earlier work, but instead, to use his own coinage from *Moby-Dick*, "subtilized" them, keeping contradictory and complementary views associated with a variety of doctrines and their negations in a precarious balance. As with Melville's support of the Union, however, this balance is never without an ultimate point of view. Melville's faiths (plural) do not dissolve into cynicism in his later work, but rather, like his nationalisms (also plural), remain wary of the dangers and contradictions inherent in themselves.

In retrospect, *Battle-Pieces* marked a major, perhaps the major, turning point in Melville's career. With this collection, Melville moved from extravagant prose to careful poetry, from expansive religious pluralism to the intricate outlining of subtle ethical distinctions across religious traditions, and from a kind of moral bravado to something not unlike what he described in *Moby-Dick* as “manhood’s pondering repose of If” (*M-D* 492). This mature repose would form itself into a detailed interrogation of religious difference that was more systematic than anything else Melville ever wrote in *Clarel*, and into the “short quick probings at the very axis of reality” (*PT* 244) that characterized his later lyrics in *John Marr and Other Sailors* and *Timoleon*. Finally, this tendency would translate itself back into prose, with *Billy Budd*’s purposeful religious ambivalence and artistic skepticism.

Chapter 5

All Souls: *Clarel*, Religious Pluralism, and Unitarianism

When Melville completed *Battle-Pieces*, he had ten more years of experiences, reading, thought, and writing ahead of him before his 18,000-line poem *Clarel, A Poem and Pilgrimage in the Holy Land* would see publication in 1876. Melville had traveled to Rome, Constantinople, Egypt, and Syria (including Palestine) in 1856–57, and he began acquiring books in earnest with a view to writing an ambitious poem on the subject of Holy Land pilgrimage at the start of the 1870s.[1] *Clarel* represents Melville's most direct and sustained engagement with questions of religious difference, including as it does substantial discussions of the monotheistic religions of Christianity, Judaism, and Islam from the perspective of a diverse array of characters and references to Buddhism, Hinduism, and animism. Melville completed his major poetic publications with *John Marr and Other Sailors* and *Timoleon* near the end of his life. Some of the pieces from *Timoleon* were almost certainly from his earliest efforts at poetry in the late 1850s, but others comprised some of his final poetic efforts. Remaining unpublished at Melville's death were the poems of *Weeds and Wildings*, which are suggestive of the final movements of Melville's aesthetic development and religious thought. The later poetry will be discussed in the final chapter in combination with *Billy Budd*; *Clarel* is sufficiently massive and ambitious that it must be considered on its own.[2]

As we have seen, Melville's earlier work reflected, first, the influence of travel, trade, and the cultural exchanges associated with travel and trade, and second, Melville's voluminous and impassioned engagement with what Emerson called "the mind of the past" through his reading.[3] Melville's shorter fiction and *The Confidence-Man* reflected his specifically American engagements with the history, politics, religion, and philosophy of the Western Hemisphere. In *Battle-Pieces*, Melville found his way to visual representations of the moral, ethical, and religious quandaries posed by modern, mechanized warfare and by industrialized society more broadly. All of these elements are emphatically present in *Clarel*, but what is perhaps most striking about the poem is the way in which Melville creates a text replete with analogues to the more ambitious efforts to create meaningful mythologies, cosmogonies, and revised theologies among his contemporaries. *Clarel* has frequently been judged the most idiosyncratic of Melville's work, but what is less frequently acknowledged is its abundant points of contact with other authors of Melville's day and their obsessions; indeed, the point about *Clarel* that has contributed the most to its history of misunderstanding and neglect has been our failure to acknowledge the ways in which it is not idiosyncratic at all.

Liberal Christianity and Comparative Religion: The Examples of Henry Whitney Bellows and Lydia Maria Child

A first elision of *Clarel*'s rich interaction with vital elements in Melville's own culture appears in the tendency of critics to underestimate the importance of liberal Christianity for Melville's project. One of the conventions of Melville scholarship has been to assume that Melville's literary efforts in these years were largely unrelated to the church that Elizabeth Shaw Melville attended in Manhattan, All Soul's Unitarian Church, which Melville himself joined in the 1880s.[4] And yet, an attentive reading of *Clarel* and the later poetry reveals an uncomfortable accommodation between the unorthodox Melville and the theological liberalism associated with All Soul's, especially if we attend to analogies between Bellows's sermons and Melville's poetry. When Bellows has been invoked in relation to Melville scholarship, his significance has been seen as largely biographical: Bellows's conspiracy with Elizabeth Shaw Melville's brothers to rescue her from a possibly mad, possibly abusive, likely alcoholic Herman during the late 1850s has become an important part of recent debates over whether Herman Melville was guilty of physical violence against his wife.[5] The brand of religious liberalism represented by Bellows, however, is much more a part of Melville's body of work than previous analyses have shown.

Henry Whitney Bellows was among the most influential intellectuals of the mid-nineteenth century, and he preached to a congregation that constituted an intellectual and social elite in the postbellum period.[6] Melville clearly was not actively engaged with All Soul's while Bellows was pastor there. The immense biographical labors of Jay Leyda in the mid-twentieth century and of Hershel Parker over the past five decades leave little doubt of this fact.[7] If, however, we turn to internal evidence from *Clarel* and from Bellows's own writings, we begin to see that Bellows may have been a fruitful interlocutor for Melville as a writer nonetheless, and Bellows's status as a figure with whom Melville could be engaged is reinforced by the fact that Elizabeth Shaw Melville was a part of Bellows's congregation. In Bellows's collection of sermons from 1860 entitled *Restatements of Christian Doctrine, in Twenty-Five Sermons*, Bellows argues for a form of Unitarianism that transcends the boundaries of Protestantism. Bellows argues that in order to thrive in the nineteenth century, Unitarianism must attend to precisely that impulse that makes Catholicism attractive, because this impulse is an essential part of all religion:

> How have we sighed for the pilotage of an authorized church; for the chart of an established creed; for the methods and discipline of a fixed and defined religious life. Our sighs and longings, my brethren, are the honest groans of a nature made to find repose in a loving and settled faith; and they unquestionably are the very pangs by which Providence is seeking to bring forth a *new* catholic church—a *new* orthodoxy—that is to say a creed and a ritual which shall have the honest consent of the great bulk of the people—shall express its new or fresh conceptions of Christianity and of Christian faith, discipline, and worship in a way to match the experience, the wisdom, and the wants of a new era and so to secure the uncompromised, the unfeigned, and the hearty confidence of Christendom.[8]

What Bellows argues here is that Unitarianism, which is in some ways an extreme form of Protestantism (indeed so extreme as to be disavowed by many Protestants as irremediably heterodox), must take on aspects of Catholicism and Orthodoxy in order to provide a church in keeping with the spiritual, social, and intellectual aspirations of the nineteenth century. Bellows can be seen as a source (or at least an analogue) for a number of the attitudes expressed in *Clarel*, where as we shall see, numerous characters argue for understandings of Christianity that are outside conventionally Protestant models.

This sheds a great deal of light on the fact that Melville, in *Clarel* and in his later poetry, showed significantly more sympathy for Catholicism than he had earlier in his career. In *Mardi*, for example, Melville had satirized the Catholic Church, and particularly the monarchical role of the pope, in a thinly disguised parody of the church, and in *Moby-Dick*, he compares the skin of the whale's penis to Catholic vestments. In *Clarel*, on the other hand, Catholicism is taken much more seriously as an alternative means of religious organization, and through the character of the Dominican monk, Melville hints at the possibility that Catholicism has a role to play in his view of the modern world.

What is noteworthy about Bellows's brand of Unitarianism is that his views cannot simply be defined as theologically liberal. Rather, as the material quoted above suggests, Bellows was trying to understand how Unitarianism, and liberal Christianity more broadly, could incorporate a connection to the wider stream of Christian history that might add to its vitality. Indeed, Bellows argued for a theology based in an ethical humanism explicitly in a passage that is worth quoting at length:

> By a true Theology, I mean one which regards God as a Father and man as a brother, and which looks upon this life as a preparation for a higher; which believes that God gives us freedom, inspires our reason, and is the author of whatever is generous, self-forgetting, and noble. I find something of this Theology in all sects and churches; from the Roman Catholic at one extreme, to the Universalists and Unitarians, the Spiritualists and Come-Outers at the other. And the opposite, the false Theology, dishonorable to God and degrading to man, I find in all sects, and accompanying all creeds.[9]

It is noteworthy that a passage like this parallels both Melville's explicit statements in his novels and poetry and the markings in his marginalia, not only to the Bible, but to Milton and Shelley, Goethe and Emerson. Melville's engagement with religious difference was thus on a continuum with a broad cultural interest in such matters on the part of his contemporaries, including those who belonged to Elizabeth's (and ultimately his own) church.

Another significant vantage point from which to view *Clarel* is provided by Lydia Maria Child's monumental multivolume work of comparative religious history *The Progress of Religious Ideas: Through Successive Ages* (1855). Child surveyed a wide range of religious traditions, with the goal of providing a comprehensive account of religion around the world, the relationship of Christianity to various world religions, and the implications of these things for Christian belief. Child's approach is no example of smug Protestant Christian chauvinism: she attempted consistently to use the historical method to arrive at a factually accurate account of the genesis of religious ideas, even if they ran counter to her own preconceptions.

Child's method was to proceed through one religious tradition after another, beginning with what she believed to be the earliest and proceeding through the range of religious traditions with which she was familiar. She thus began with a consideration of the ancient Hindu scriptures of India, to which she granted chronological priority over those scriptures that she herself believed to be divinely inspired. In the opening of her first volume, Child made clear the liberalism of her religious project:

> I would candidly advise persons who are conscious of bigoted attachment to any creed, or theory, not to purchase this book. Whether they are bigoted Christians, or bigoted infidels, its tone will be likely to displease them.
>
> My motive in writing has been a very simple one. I wished to show that theology is not religion; with the hope that I might help to break down partition walls; to ameliorate what the eloquent Bushnell calls "the baptized hatreds of the human race." In order to do this, I have endeavored to give a concise and comprehensive account of religions, in the liberal spirit of the motto on my title page.[10]

The motto to which Child refers is drawn from the poetry of James Russell Lowell, and argues that there is some good in all belief systems so long as they are characterized by reverence.[11] We thus see that Melville's interest in a broad range of faiths in *Clarel* is very much in keeping with the more intellectually ambitious liberal Christians of his time.

Child and Bellows both gave evidence of the gathering willingness to learn from religious traditions other than Protestantism, and by looking at their approach to religious difference, we can see how thoroughly the religious pluralism of Transcendentalists like Emerson, Thoreau, and Margaret Fuller was enmeshed in the liberal Christianity of the nineteenth century. Emerson, of course, invoked Hinduism, Buddhism, Islam, and Zoroastrianism frequently in his essays and his poetry (most notably, essays like "Fate" and poems like "Brahma"), and Thoreau built these faiths into his work in a still more substantial way. In *Walden*, to cite one example, Thoreau opened with a catalog of the penances carried out by Hindu ascetics, and he referred to Hinduism and to ancient Egyptian religion in the opening of the chapter entitled "Reading." Margaret Fuller's editorship of *The Dial*, meanwhile, saw the publication of a translation of *The Laws of Menu* [*sic*] as part of the wider Transcendentalist project of engaging with the religions of the non-Western world. When Melville engaged with world religions in *Clarel*, and when he took a broadly ecumenical approach to discussions of Christianity, he was very much in dialogue with a major strand in both liberal Christianity and the secular cultures that were closely connected to it.[12]

Even less obvious contemporaries like Edgar Allan Poe and Nathaniel Hawthorne could demonstrate an ambivalent fascination with the significance of religious and theological difference. In such texts as "Mesmeric Revelation" and *Eureka*, Poe dealt directly with the wide range of religious possibilities available in the nineteenth century, and Hawthorne expressed considerable anxiety about the range of religious possibilities available in the nineteenth century in "The Celestial Railroad" and *The Blithedale Romance*.

In "Mesmeric Revelation," for example, Poe employs a religious seeker who, like Clarel three and half decades later, is seeking for faith in the midst of a crowded religious marketplace and in the midst of a personal spiritual and epistemological crisis. He turns for reassurance to, among other texts, the novel *Charles Elwood, or the Infidel Converted*, by Orestes Brownson.[13] We recognize the significance of this choice when we consider that perhaps no figure in nineteenth-century America embodied religious pluralism to as great a degree as Orestes Brownson. Brownson went through a dizzying range of religious conversions. He began as a fairly traditional Congregationalist, and converted to such disparate religious traditions as Presbyterianism, Universalism, Deism, Unitarianism, Transcendentalism, anticlerical socialism, back to Deism, and finally, in 1844, four years after the publication of *Charles Elwood* but the same year as the initial publication of "Mesmeric Revelation," to Roman Catholicism. The choice of Brownson's novel thus implies that the patient's metaphysical and spiritual crises have something to do with the range of possible sources of truth available to nineteenth-century Americans.[14]

The patient expresses his dissatisfaction with *Charles Elwood*, arguing that the protagonist's attempts to prove the immortality of the soul had "not even succeeded in convincing himself."[15] Because of this inability to resolve his doubts about immortality with reference to the range of religious visions available at the time, the patient has turned to the pseudo-science of mesmerism endorsed by the narrator as the road to truth. The "Mesmeric Revelation" of the title, then, becomes an attempt to realize an alternative approach to truth that can somehow transcend the messy pluralism to which novels like *Charles Elwood* contribute. The revelation that the mesmerized patient brings achieves this transcendence by asserting that all matter in its plurality is part of an "unparticled" oneness of "God" or "Mind":

> Motion is the action of *mind*—not of *thinking*. The unparticled matter, or God, in its quiescence, is (as nearly as we can conceive it) what men call mind. And the power of self-movement (equivalent in effect to human volition) is, in the unparticled matter, the result of its unity

> and omniprevalence; *how* I know not, and now clearly I see that I shall never know. But the unparticled matter, set in motion by a law, or quality, existing within itself, is thinking.[16]

Despite the convoluted prose, what becomes clear in this passage is Poe's desire to create a transcendent unity of a discordant diversity. The heavily ironic framing of the story as a whole suggests that this unity cannot be easily achieved. The struggle to reconcile plurality and unity becomes intensified in Poe's long prose poem *Eureka*.

In *Eureka* Poe reproduces many aspects of the earlier "Mesmeric Revelation," including its tendency toward parody, but he also attempts to suggest a kind of resolution to the challenge of reconciling unity and diversity in human experience. At the end of *Eureka*, Poe writes:

> These creatures are all, too, more or less, and more or less obviously, conscious Intelligences; conscious, first, of a proper identity; conscious second, and by faint and indeterminate glances, of an identity with the divine being of whom we speak—of an identity with God. . . . Think that the sense of individual identity will be gradually merged in the general consciousness—that Man, for example, ceasing imperceptibly to feel himself Man, will at length attain that awfully triumphant epoch when he shall recognize his existence as that of Jehovah.[17]

This passage merits some unpacking. First, any reader familiar with Emerson's concept of the Oversoul will recognize that Poe's idea of Man becoming Jehovah is not as far from Transcendentalism as Poe's occasional ridicule of the Transcendentalists might suggest. Second, Poe subtly mixes very different religious discourses in this passage. The idea of the Godhead functioning as an expression of the unity of the cosmos resembles the Hindu conception of Brahma, but Poe chooses to express this concept using the term "Jehovah," which is specifically drawn from the Western monotheistic tradition. In this way, Poe draws upon alternative religious traditions to envision a new understanding of Christianity that is more consistent with the scientific discoveries of recent centuries. At the end of *Eureka*, religious pluralism and scientific speculation meet to create a sense of possibility and hope.

The other pole of the American engagement with religious difference with which Melville interacts in *Clarel* is anxiety about religious diversity, and this anxiety appears with special intensity in Nathaniel Hawthorne's "The Celestial Railroad," which highlights Hawthorne's anxiety about the kind of frenetic religious marketplace that Nathan Hatch, among others, identifies in nineteenth-century American culture.[18] Hawthorne's framework is, of course, John Bunyan's allegory *Pilgrim's Progress*, the fictional work that most exemplifies the thought-world of early American Protestants. Hawthorne's story is laced with nostalgia for Bunyan's clear theological, moral, and ethical distinctions. Hawthorne's narrator decides to take a ride on a railroad that travels from the City of Destruction to the Celestial City within Bunyan's allegorical representation of the Christian life. He discovers along the way that the very distinctions that make Bunyan's allegory function—between Protestants and Catholics, between Christian and non-Christian, between religion and commerce—seem to have become blurred. Hawthorne, through his narrator, identifies Transcendentalism as the source of much of this blurring. The narrator's guide, Mr. Smooth-It-Away, frequently read as a stand-in for Emerson, reveals in the early portion of the journey that the Slough of Despond has been filled in by:

> throwing into the slough some editions of books of morality, volumes of French philosophy and German Rationalism, tracts, sermons, and essays of modern clergymen, extracts from Plato, Confucius, and various Hindoo sages, together with a few ingenious commentaries upon texts of Scripture—all of which, by some scientific process have been converted into a mass like granite.[19]

This compendium of various philosophical and religious ideas is easily recognizable as the intellectual baggage of Transcendentalism, and indeed, this passage is generally read as an anti-Transcendentalist satire. This reading is no doubt correct, but it is also worth noting that this catalog represents a fairly comprehensive listing of the religious options available to those in nineteenth-century America who wished to preserve a sense of the numinous but did not wish to fall into one of the accepted sectarian religious categories for nineteenth-century Protestants. Hawthorne himself has as much in common with the writers of the treatises that fill up the Slough of Despond as he does with the author of *Pilgrim's Progress*.

Throughout "The Celestial Railroad," Hawthorne undercuts the idea of pluralism as a source of expanded possibility. The "Giant Transcendentalist" who has replaced Pope and Pagan may be less threatening than his predecessors, but he certainly offers no comfort to the would-be pilgrim. Moreover, the ministers that the narrator finds assembled in Vanity Fair offer nothing but illusion:

> The labors of these eminent divines are aided by those of innumerable lecturers, who diffuse such a various profundity, in all manners of human or celestial science, that a man may acquire an omnigenous erudition without the trouble of even learning to read.[20]

In Vanity Fair, the would-be pilgrim is surrounded not by persecutors, but by those who would adulterate belief with whatever notions are most pleasing to the consumer. Hawthorne's complaint here most directly combines a critique of commercialism with a critique of theological liberalism, but it also indicates the exhaustion experienced by those who face a variety of spiritual choices without an adequate epistemological ground for distinguishing among them. For Hawthorne, then, the seductive possibility that religious pluralism offers a means of reaching a higher religious synthesis is undercut by the frightening possibility that pluralism rules out the possibility of a satisfying synthesis altogether. In *Clarel*, Melville moves in and out of the speculative and visionary modes developed by Poe and the skepticism about the possibility of a satisfying synthesis suggested by Hawthorne.

Religious Difference in *Clarel*: Abrahamic Faiths and Asian Saviors

Melville's poetry offers literary scholars an outstanding opportunity to view one of the most vigorous and original intellects of the nineteenth century grappling with the problems raised by both secularization and the nascent fundamentalist reaction against secularization, the relation of personal religious identity to national self-fashioning, and the tension between the revolutionary and reactionary possibilities inherent in any system of belief. Melville's embrace of "sacred uncertainty" as described in the previous chapters in the face of religious and epistemological quandaries provides both a model for understanding the intersection of American literary and religious cultures in the nineteenth century and an exemplum of rigorous wrestling with ultimate questions that is still relevant in the twenty-first century.

Clarel represents Melville's most sustained effort to address in poetic form the major theological and epistemological problems with which he wrestled throughout his career. Melville uses a dialogic poetics that explores the sacred spaces of the "Holy Land" of Ottoman Palestine through multiple competing religious perspectives. *Clarel's* profound intertextuality with earlier attempts to interpret the sacred landscape of Ottoman Palestine is the source of much of the profundity and complexity of the poem's theological insights. Other writers of Holy Land travel narratives, from Bayard Taylor to Mark Twain, emphasize the constructedness of their predecessors' descriptions of the Holy Land and promote their own texts as sources of unbiased insight into the reality of the land. In *Clarel*, however, Melville seeks to reveal the truth about the land not by debunking all other representations of it, but rather by multiplying its representations in his own text. Recognizing the inherent artificiality of literary representations of any landscape, let alone a landscape redolent of powerful sacred associations, Melville seeks to explore the significance of sacred sites by allowing each site to be interpreted from a variety of perspectives by characters with varying theological, philosophical, and political orientations. In this way, as Malini Johar Schueller argues, *Clarel* engages in "a productive critical dialogue with the textual palimpsest that the Near Eastern Orient had become."[21] Melville's reading of an enormous range of texts about the Near East and his ability to represent those texts through his characters in *Clarel* are the qualities that make Melville's writing on the Holy Land, in both its topographical and theological aspects, so distinctive.

The structure of *Clarel* is spatial, with the four parts of the poem set in Jerusalem, the Wilderness, the Mar Saba monastery, and Bethlehem respectively. The Jerusalem cantos bring together the majority of the characters who will interact throughout the poem and begin the poem's pattern of contrapuntal debate. The Wilderness cantos show the pilgrims in motion, traveling out from Jerusalem into the desert. Here the text turns increasingly from the visual to the rhetorical, with intellectually robust debates among the characters providing the substance of the text. In Mar Saba, the pilgrims come into contact with faith as represented by Eastern Orthodox Christian monks, and find natural images that correspond to the images of art and architecture that they have viewed in Jerusalem. In the Bethlehem cantos, the pilgrims return to more characteristic sacred sites. The poem is also a love story, in which the Protestant Christian theology student Clarel seeks to complete himself spiritually as well as relationally through a marriage to Ruth, the daughter of an American Protestant convert to Judaism and his Jewish wife. That the romance ends with Ruth's death implies a certain pessimism on Melville's part regarding the possibility of a final resolution to the issues debated in *Clarel*.

The poem begins with Clarel's arrival in Jerusalem and his reflections regarding his voyage thus far, across the Atlantic and the Mediterranean and overland from Jaffa. The initial form that religious difference takes in the poem is a fairly conventional opposition between East and West.

For example, Clarel reflects early on "Yes, I am young, but Asia old, / The books, the books not all have told" (*Clarel* 1.1.82–83). The treatment of religious difference becomes rapidly and increasingly complex as the Jerusalem cantos continue. The characters who plainly interest Melville most are those who cross conventional religious and cultural boundaries in some startling way, or who represent a certain religious tendency to the fullest, and the first two named characters he meets each embodies one of these characteristics. Abdon, the Jewish Indian living in Jerusalem after having been brought up in Cochin, home to one of India's most ancient Jewish communities (*Clarel* 1.2), provides us with an early example of the first type of character. Nehemiah, an American missionary who is evangelical and millennialist in his theology, represents the second. Both are worthy of some consideration. Abdon has come to Palestine from India in search of an ancient homeland. Nehemiah has come in search of the ancient roots of Christianity, but he is also a representative of the modern world who is seeking to convert the inhabitants of the Holy Land, not just to Christ, but in a very significant way to the nineteenth century as experienced in Europe and North America. Indeed, these two figures are in some ways mirror images of each other; both have abandoned their homes and the comforts and consolations of home in their old age, and they have each done so for reasons that are radically incommensurate with the other's. The fact that Abdon has been willing to leave his ancient Jewish community in tropical India to relocate to arid Palestine indicates the devotion of the Jewish people of the Levant to Judaism, while Nehemiah, philo-Semitic though he may be in his attitudes toward the Jewish people, is attempting to absorb Judaism into Christianity, and thus effectually destroy it as an independent religious tradition. Clarel admires both figures, but it is eminently clear that both of these men cannot get what they want at the same time.

Worth noting here is the degree to which Melville has revisited his earlier critiques of missionaries from *Typee* and *Omoo*. Nehemiah may be naive, even foolish, but he is assuredly not insufficiently evangelized. Even those who reject his creed (as virtually everyone he meets in Palestine does) admire his purity of purpose and his evident charity and virtue. Muslims in Jerusalem who are suspicious of his sanity nonetheless regard him as a holy fool, and when he dies, the pilgrims as a group are genuinely touched by his loss.

In these early cantos, place looms as large as character, and the Jerusalem portion of the text is replete with meditations on sacred spaces, nearly all of which call attention to the complexities of religious difference that come into play in some way for pilgrims to these sites. Most notably, the

Church of the Holy Sepulchre, a site of paramount importance for Catholic and Orthodox pilgrims, is discussed in relation to the ambivalence that it occasions for Protestant travelers in Jerusalem. Melville's lyrical description of the play of light and shadow in the Church of the Holy Sepulchre is one of the finest moments in *Clarel* from both an aesthetic and an epistemological standpoint. The Church of the Holy Sepulchre has been a locus that attracted a great deal of Protestant anger and derision: both a devoutly evangelical biblical archaeologist like Edward Robinson and a genteel travel writer like Bayard Taylor could express contempt for what they saw as the squalor and hypocrisy embodied by the church, and Melville could refer to it in his own journal from the 1850s as "a sickening cheat" (*Journals* 88).[22] Nonetheless, in *Clarel*, he takes this landmark as an opportunity to reflect upon religious difference in a manner reminiscent of Ishmael's description of the space for worship formed by the whale's skeleton in "A Bower in the Arsacides." The reflections of the narrator on the Church of the Holy Sepulchre and the way in which it architecturally embraces the sites of the crucifixion, embalming, and burial and resurrection of Christ, along with the oddly multi-religious associations that the narrator establishes for it, are worth quoting at length:

> What altars old in cluster rare
> And grotto-shrines engird the Tomb:
> Caves, and a crag, and more is there;
> And halls monastic join their gloom.
> To sum in comprehensive bounds
> The Passion's drama in its grounds,
> Immense the temple winds and strays,
> Finding each storied precinct out—
> Absorbs the sites all round about—
> Omnivorous and a world of maze.
> And yet time was when all here stood,
> Separate, and from rood to rood,
> Chapel to shrine, or tent to tent,
> Unsheltered still the pilgrim went
> Where now enroofed the whole coheres—
> Where now through influence of years
> And spells by many a legend lent,
> A sort of nature reappears,
> Somber or sad, and much in tone
> Perhaps with that which here was known,
> Of yore, when from this Salem height,

> Then sylvan in primeval plight,
> Down to Shaveh's dale with wine,
> And bread, after the Four Kings check,
> The Druid priest Melchizedek,
> Abram to bless with rites divine. (*Clarel* 1.3.17–42)

This is a virtuoso performance of religious difference in poetry, and likewise a virtuoso performance in the blending of the architectural and the metaphysical. Melville connects the range of Christian sacred sites contained in the church with the range of religious traditions that went into making up the church's own heritage and claims: he invokes Abraham's blessing by Melchizedek, thus pointing out Christianity's enmeshment with its fellow Abrahamic religions of Judaism and Islam. Moreover, although the historicity of the claim of the Church of the Holy Sepulcher to be the site of the resurrection and crucifixion was contested by Protestants, the events themselves were not, thus making this a site with tremendous ecumenical resonance within Christianity. Most boldly of all, the reference to the biblical Melchizedek as a "Druid priest" points to the existence of faiths that antedate the Abrahamic faiths of Christianity, Judaism, and Islam. The Church of the Holy Sepulcher thus becomes an icon, not just of faith and doubt, but of religious difference writ large.

Melville's delight in frustrating preconceived notions of religious identity is particularly evident in a similar architectural commentary in cantos 16 and 17 of part 4. In canto 16, "The Convent Roof," we are led through a veritable maze of identity. We begin with a description of the ambiguities of place:

> To branching grottoes next they fare,
> Old caves of penitence and prayer,
> Where Paula kneeled—her urn is there—
> Paula the Widow, Scipio's heir
> But Christ's adopted. Well her tomb
> Adjoins her friend's, renowned Jerome. (*Clarel* 4.16.1–5)

The site is associated with the greatest of all ancient biblical translators, Saint Jerome, but Melville's narrator chooses to focus on Saint Paula, and the multiple dimensions of her identity. She is "Scipio's widow" and thus associated with the post-pagan Stoic traditions of pre-Christian Rome, but "Christ's adopted." The expression "Christ's adopted" both plays on her transformed family relationships as a result of her conversion—she will now be remembered as a Christian saint, not a Stoic widow—and on the tenth and eleventh chapters of the Epistle to the Romans, in which Paul suggests that all Gentile Christians are adopted children of God who have been "grafted in" to the Jewish people. The ambivalence expressed here constitutes an echo of Melville's discussion of the relationship between Christianity and the classical world in his lectures from the 1850s: always when considering the relationship between Christian and classical civilizations, Melville is concerned with what it lost as well as what is gained.

Along with its obsession with moral and ethical ambiguities, *Clarel* deals obsessively with the interreligious debates among various branches of Christianity, and as William Potter has shown, with the emerging field of comparative religion.[23] Melville's broadest survey of the implications of global religious pluralism appears early in *Clarel* in the eponymous part 1 canto 5. In this portion of the poem, Clarel begins by observing characters representative of the divisions within Christianity:

> A friar he marked, in robe of blue
> And round Greek cap of sable hue:
> Poor men he led; much haste he made,
> Nor sequence kept, but dragged them so
> Hither and thither, to and fro,
> To random places. Might it be
> That Clarel, who recoil did here,
> Shared but that shock of novelty
> Which makes some Protestants unglad,
> First viewing the mysterious cheer
> Of Peter's fane? (*Clarel* 1.5.48–58)

Clarel's initial reaction to religious difference is one of revulsion, conditioned by Protestant distrust of Greek Orthodox and Roman Catholic traditions of pilgrimage. Melville employs a telling irony at Clarel's expense in these lines, referring to Clarel's experience as a "shock of novelty," when of course the traditions represented by the Greek priest were far more ancient than Clarel's own theological tradition.

From this encounter with non-Protestant Christians, Clarel is led to reflect upon the scope of religious difference around the globe. He begins with scenes relatively close at hand, imagining Muslim pilgrims beginning their journey toward Mecca:

> In gliding turns of dreams which mate
> He saw from forth Damascus' gate
> Tall Islam in her Mahmal go—

Elected Camel, king of all
In mystic housings draped in flow,
Silk-fringed, with many a silver ball,
Worked ciphers on the Koran's car
And sultan's cloth. (*Clarel* 1.5.131–38)

Although Clarel's reverie has been started by an encounter with non-Protestant Christians, he has quickly moved to a consideration of religious difference on a larger scale. He is surrounded by Muslims in the Levant; as a result, his thoughts naturally turn to the tradition of pilgrimage within Islam. Notably, Clarel begins by seeing the sumptuousness of the decorations on the camels, and for a moment, he seems entranced by this vibrant display of difference from American cultural expectations. Clarel's thoughts again turn toward disappointment and doubt, however, when he considers the journey that these pilgrims must make:

In long, long line, their way to tell,
The bones of camels bleaching dwell,
With skeletons but part interred—
Relics of men which friendless fell,
Whose own hands, in last office scooped
Over their limbs the sand. (*Clarel* 1.5.170–75)

The terrors that the pilgrims face seem to overwhelm the splendor of their aspirations. From pilgrims to Mecca from Syria, Clarel's vision moves to "the tawny peasants / the human wave / Which rolls over India, year by year / India, the spawning place and grave" (*Clarel* 1.5.186–88). These Hindu pilgrims as well express the duality of Clarel's vision: there is a magnificence to the "human wave" that moves toward the Ganges, but Clarel cannot help but contemplate the number of pilgrims who will die of plague along the way. Finally, Clarel contemplates the phenomenon of pilgrimage through the widest possible lens:

From eras gone he caught the sound
Of hordes from China's furthest moat,
Crossing the Himalayan mound
To kneel at shrine or relic so,
Of Buddha, the Mongolian Fo,
Or Indian Saviour. What profound
Impulsion makes these tribes to range?
Stable in time's incessant change

> Now first he marks, now awed he heeds
> The intersympathy of creeds,
> Alien or hostile tho' they seem,
> Exalted thought or groveling dream. (*Clarel* 1.5.198–209)

Clarel has an almost mystical experience of the reality of religious pluralism in these lines, and his response is profoundly ambivalent. He senses a deeper unity beneath the variety of the world's religious creeds, but when he considers their fruits, he is not sure whether to embrace them for their "exalted thought" or despise them as deceptive "groveling dream[s]."

Clarel encounters one of the few major world religions not mentioned in part 1, canto 5, when he encounters a young Jewish woman named Ruth and her parents Nathan and Agar. Nathan and Agar are immigrants from the United States. Nathan is modeled on the real-life figure Warder Cresson, who went through a series of conversions that matched even Orestes Brownson's before settling on Judaism and moving to Palestine.[24] Nathan becomes a representative of the incredible diversity of religious opinions that one American could have in the nineteenth century. He also becomes a representative of one specific religious identity, Judaism, within the context of nineteenth-century Palestine, and he is ultimately a victim of the passions that religious difference arouses, both in himself and in others, when he is assassinated by his Arab neighbors as a result of his quarrels with them. Clarel falls in love with Ruth, Nathan's daughter, but is tragically kept apart from her, first by Nathan's death and then by her own. In this strand of *Clarel*'s plot, Melville suggests that reconciliation between divergent religious traditions is more easily contemplated than achieved. This suggestion is highlighted as well by the inflexibility of Nehemiah, a saintly but foolish American Protestant missionary who persists to the end of his life in the belief that he will be able to convert his Jewish and Muslim neighbors in Palestine.

Throughout *Clarel*, then, there is a tension between the universalizing possibilities of an "intersympathy of creeds," Melville's apt description of the ways in which apparent religious variety can be seen to conceal an underlying unity, and the very particular faiths that the multitude of characters that Melville presents in *Clarel* actually profess. For every character like Derwent, the liberal, Broad Church, Anglican clergyman who proposes peace between and among religions and between the various religions and science, there is a character like Ungar, a Catholic of Cherokee ancestry who once fought for the Confederacy and now fights for the Turkish army, and who reasserts the sword of religious particularism vigorously. Like the debates among a spectrum of faiths and the debate between faith and science, Melville leaves the confrontation between religious pluralism as a source of hope and as a source of anxiety and doubt unresolved at the end of *Clarel.*

Frequently, discussions of Melville's representations of religion in his later poetry begin and end with *Clarel.* Melville continued to refine this theme within his work throughout his later career, however. Perhaps the most astonishingly compressed instance of Melville's engagement with religious pluralism appears in his later poem "Buddha." Melville uses a quotation from James 4:14 as an epigraph to this poem, thus creating a comparative frame by means of which to understand the relationship of Christianity and Buddhism. The passage from James reads, "For what is your life? It is even a vapor that appeareth for a little time and then vanisheth away." The poem itself reveals that Melville has spent some time studying Buddhist thought:

> Swooning swim to less and less
> Aspirant to nothingness!
> Sobs of the worlds, and dole of kinds
> That dumb endurers be—
> Nirvana! Absorb us in your skies,
> Annul us into thee.

It is significant that Melville juxtaposes a biblical text with his exposition of Buddhism here. The verse from James calls attention to the brevity of human life and in its context, urges both humility and attention to the afterlife of its readers. The lines that make up the poem itself take the Buddhist doctrine of nirvana, or the cessation of desire achieved by the thoroughly enlightened, to mean an absolute destruction of consciousness. By using the verse from James to frame the austere statement of Buddhist doctrine, Melville offers a practical illustration of the "intersympathy of creeds" that he asserts early in *Clarel.* It is noteworthy, however, that the intersympathy of Christianity and Buddhism in this poem does not imply an absolute convergence. James's reflections on the evanescence of life do not, as Melville's nineteenth-century readers would certainly be aware, lead to a call for the extinction of desire, but rather for an intensified program of good works undergirded by Christian doctrine. The Buddha's parallel call for good works as a means to the cessation of desire does not negate the fact that the two religions ultimately take different approaches to the human problems of desire, evanescence, and failure. As with the thwarted romance of Ruth and Clarel, Melville suggests obliquely in this poem that no easy reconciliation of two different approaches to religious truth is possible.

The complementary and contradictory urges toward reconciliation of differences and acknowledgment of difference are profoundly apparent in Melville's consideration of Roman Catholicism in *Clarel.*

"Remember Hospitable Rome": The Allure of Democratic Catholicism

Melville's specific engagement with Catholicism in *Clarel* is highly indicative of the ways in which both he and his broader culture had changed since the 1840s. If for the early Puritans Catholicism was unambiguously the Antichrist and for most antebellum American Protestants Catholicism was associated with sinister "Popish" plots and subversion from abroad, by the later nineteenth century the American Protestant encounter with Catholicism (to borrow Jenny Franchot's felicitous phrase), had become considerably more ambivalent.[25] As early as the 1840s the prominent Transcendentalist intellectual Orestes Brownson could find a permanent home in the Roman Catholic Church after navigating the full range of American Protestant and post-Protestant religious currents. By the 1860s Emily Dickinson could imagine herself to be a nun invoking Mary's intercession in poems that stood alongside others that skewered the Calvinism of Dickinson's forebears.[26] By the late nineteenth century, Catholicism exercised a profound fascination for American Protestant intellectuals, but this fascination was heavily tinged with anxiety. In Harold Frederic's 1896 novel *The Damnation of Theron Ware*, the title character's initial fascination with Catholicism leads to the loss of his faith, and the novel ultimately suggests that too much curiosity about Catholicism on the part of a Protestant would result, not in conversion or in a revivified Protestantism, but in simple cynicism.[27] Ware is initially captivated by the beauty of the Catholic liturgical tradition and the arguments of a theologically progressive Catholic priest, but in the end he finds no place for himself within the Catholic tradition. *Clarel* suggests an alternative approach to Catholicism by American Protestants, an approach that sees Catholicism less as the menacing, if potentially seductive, religious Other to Protestantism, and more as a source of wisdom that American Protestants and post-Protestants could scorn only at their peril. Like Frederic's novel, *Clarel* deals with a crisis of faith on the part of a sensitive young Protestant theology student, but for Melville's protagonist, the Catholic characters that he meets in Palestine become unexpected sources of alternatives to the debate between scripturally determined faith and scientifically informed doubt in which Clarel is enmeshed. In the course of Melville's

18,000-line poem, Clarel meets a cerebral Dominican priest (described by others as "this intellectual man / Half monk, half tribune, partisan," and by himself as a "staunch Catholic Democrat" (*Clarel* 2.26.52–53; 2.25.82) who advocates Catholicism as an indispensable support for reason and democracy, a Catholic Cherokee from Maryland named Ungar who delivers a blistering attack on nineteenth-century Anglo-American imperialism while embracing the continuity of the Catholic Church, and various other minor characters who flesh out Melville's complex understanding of Catholicism's role in American society and the world.

Melville's representations of Catholicism in *Clarel* are particularly telling in the light of both the nineteenth-century American Protestant representation of the Catholic Church as anti-democratic, spiritually moribund, and intellectually repressive and the corresponding fascination that the church's liturgy and philosophy elicited from American Protestant intellectuals from Theodore Parker to Henry Adams.[28] Understanding the complexity of Melville's engagement with Catholicism in his later poetry can be a significant first step to understanding the role of Catholicism in late nineteenth-century American spiritual and religious diversity.

Melville's engagement with Catholicism in *Clarel* takes three dominant forms: first, Catholicism provides an alternative orthodoxy to both the religious orthodoxy of Protestant Biblicism and the economic orthodoxy of capitalist individualism. Second, Catholicism provides a potential justification for democracy that is grounded in a communitarian ethic rather than an individualistic ethic of accumulation. Third, a careful consideration of Catholicism, which was in many ways the ultimate religious bogeyman for nineteenth-century American Protestants, helped to open the door for a wider-ranging consideration of disparate non-Protestant religious traditions, from Eastern Orthodox Christianity, Judaism, and Islam, all of which fall within the monotheistic tradition, to even more unfamiliar traditions for nineteenth-century American Protestants such as Buddhism and Hinduism.

Much of Protestant writing about Catholicism from the early nineteenth century emphasizes the utter corruption and otherness of the Church of Rome from a Protestant point of view. Monks are inquisitors, conspirators, repressed sex maniacs who abandon their vows with gusto, or a combination of the three. (We might consider Matthew Lewis's *The Monk*, Maria Monk's *Awful Disclosures*, and even Catherine Maria Sedgwick's *Hope Leslie* as exemplars of this tendency, alongside stories like Poe's "The Pit and the Pendulum.")[29] Nuns are either victims or prison-keepers. What distinguishes both *Clarel* and *The Damnation of Theron Ware* from this strand in American Protestant writing about Catholicism is an attraction to the beauties of the Catholic liturgy combined with a sneaking suspicion that Catholicism may, on some points at least, be in a position to instruct Protestant theology students.

In *Clarel*, the character identified only as the Dominican represents the clearest example of the role of Catholicism as an alternative orthodoxy to Protestantism.[30] (It is perhaps indicative of the development in Melville's thought that a religious order associated with Gothic horror in *Benito Cereno* becomes the voice wedding reason, belief, and democracy in *Clarel.*) He is introduced after Rolfe, Vine, and Derwent (two American religious seekers and a Broad Church Anglican priest, respectively) join in singing the "*Ave maris stella*" despite their initial reservations. The Dominican overhears them, and comments "Ah Rome, your tie! May child clean part? / Nay, tugs the mother at the heart!" (*Clarel* 2.25.1–2). This initiates an intense discussion of the relationship of Catholicism to the modern world, with the Dominican continuing to develop the maternal and domestic metaphors with which he began and arguing that Catholicism can support a version of democracy that eschews crass individualism. He argues that Catholicism's divine origin can be demonstrated best by the appeal that it makes to the human heart:

> Crafty is Rome, you deem? Her art
> Is simple, quarried from the heart.
> Rough marbles, rudiments of worth
> Ye win from ledges under earth.
> Ye trim them, fit them, make them shine
> In structures of a fair design.
> Well, fervors as obscure in birth—
> Precious, though fleeting in their dates—
> Rome culls, adapts, perpetuates
> In ordered rites. . . .
> . . . Each hope, each fear
> Between the christening and the bier
> Still Rome provides for, and with grace
> And tact which hardly find a place
> In uninspired designs. (*Clarel* 2.25.35–54)

For the Dominican, Catholicism provides a means of ordering humanity's spiritual impulses so that happiness is maximized. Moreover, the Dominican argues, the order associated with Catholicism is essential, not inimical to democracy. In response to Rolfe's queries about democracy, the Dominican reveals that he has served as an elected legislator and describes himself as "A champion of true liberty— / God's liberty for one and all— / Not Satan's license. Mine's the state / of a staunch Catholic democrat" (2.25.78–81). He acknowledges that this position may seem paradoxical to his American interlocutors, but he suggests that the roots of his democratic theory lie in the church's acceptance of human equality, which is manifested particularly by the possibility that any monk may ultimately become pope. The Dominican's arguments bear a distinct resemblance to those put forward by John Henry Newman and other Catholic converts from the Oxford Movement in England as well as those associated with the American convert Orestes Brownson. For him, democracy and Catholicism come together so naturally as to be inseparable.[31]

The other major Catholic character in the poem, Ungar, is a much more complicated case. Ungar is a lapsed Catholic who sees the collapse of the faith as inevitable, but he is infuriated by the individualism, imperialism, and shallowness of late nineteenth-century Anglo-American culture. (I'm tempted to regard him as a prototype for Graham Greene.)[32] Ungar's view of the fate of nineteenth-century American economic and spiritual individualism is summed up in his final speech to Rolfe, Vine, and Clarel. Individualism becomes "self's base little fallacy" and the expansion of America leads only to "an Anglo-Saxon China"—that is, an empire in place of a republic (*Clarel* 4.22.135, 137). Perhaps the most important and least emphasized point that may be made with regard to Ungar is that his outsider status makes him an oppressor as well as a victim. Ungar eviscerates the Anglo-American imperial ideal, but as Melville made clear in the "Prose Supplement" to *Battle-Pieces*, those who, like Ungar, fought for the Confederacy fought for the idea of a white, Anglo-Saxon empire. Moreover, as a Turkish mercenary, Ungar is currently an imperial occupier likely to be resented by the Arab population of Palestine. Melville's use of Ungar is thus rife with signals warning the eagle-eyed reader to approach this figure with caution.

Ungar's case, however, is not without its merits. Although he willfully obscures the culpability of the Confederacy in the Civil War (which, as we have seen, Melville himself did not do), his critique of Anglo-Saxonism and imperialism in later nineteenth-century America surely comes close to Melville's own views on the subject, and they anticipate the later jeremiads of Mark Twain in relation to these tendencies.[33] Ungar's greatest contribution to Melville's picture of religious difference is the sheer ethical ambiguity of his position. He is able to make a valid and powerful critique of Anglo-American society, at the same time that his critique is undermined by the fact that he has himself been complicit in the very worst of the behavior he describes. And this is, of course, the point. For

Melville in the 1870s there is no character who can possibly have the position necessary to justify the sort of pure righteous indignation that Melville in the 1840s allowed Tommo to express in relation to the missionaries in Polynesia. *Clarel* is the work of a man with a sense of the ambiguities of the moral life that surpasses that of the author of *Typee* and *Omoo* in the 1840s and even that of the author of *Moby-Dick*, "Bartleby," *Benito Cereno*, and *The Confidence-Man* in the 1850s.

Ungar's response to his loss of faith in American exceptionalism and his need for a more capacious alternative is to link the story of Jesus's passion to all those who are suffering. He argues:

> . . . This type's assigned
> To one who, sharing not man's mind
> Partook man's frame; whose mystic birth
> Wrecked him on this reef of earth
> Inclement and inhuman. Yet,
> Through all the trials that beset,
> He leaned on an upholding arm—
> Foreknowing, too, reserves of balm.
> But how of them whose souls may claim,
> Some link with Christ beyond the name,
> Which share the fate, but never share
> Aid or assurance, and nowhere
> Look for requital? Such there be
> In by-lanes o'er the world you see
> The Calvary faces. (*Clarel* 4.10.34–47)

Ungar's idea of the incarnation in this passage is rather unorthodox (he is, after all, a lapsed Catholic), but these lines nonetheless resemble the efforts of twentieth-century liberation theologians to identify Christ with the oppressed in every culture, using a central element of Catholic spirituality, meditation on the sufferings of Jesus, to create a universal sense of solidarity with the suffering. This sense of universal solidarity becomes the core of Melville's engagement with questions of religious pluralism in *Clarel*.

This emphasis on the ecumenical possibilities of suffering brings Melville's work into contact with another of his contemporaries who might seem much more conventionally religious than him. Harriet Beecher Stowe is known primarily as the author of *Uncle Tom's Cabin*, but her work also included texts that centered on New England's maritime development, including both the East Indies trade and the slave trade. In what is perhaps the finest of these novels, *The Minister's Wooing*, religious, cultural, and national difference is layered throughout the text, and the context for understanding difference is always framed by suffering, loss, and the human response to these universal realities. The novel is the story of a young woman, Mary Scudder, who has grown up as a devoted adherent of New England Calvinism and her encounter with three possible suitors: the sophisticated cosmopolitan and skeptic Aaron Burr, the cerebral theologian and uncompromising moralist Samuel Hopkins, and the almost Melvillean sailor James Marvyn.[34]

The novel reaches an emotional crescendo with the narrator's reflections on the meaning of Mary's sufferings after James's apparent loss at sea. Here it is worth quoting at length, as Stowe's narrator combines lyrical emotional intensity with an obsessive need to make meaning out of loss, and the narrator is able to do so by constructing a sort of universal religion out of suffering:

> And yet sorrow is godlike, sorrow is grand and great, sorrow is wise and far-seeing. Our own instinctive valuations, the intense sympathy that we give to the tragedy which God has inwoven into the laws of Nature, show us that it is with no slavish dread, no cowardly shrinking, that we should approach her divine mysteries. What are the natures that cannot suffer? Who values them? From the fat oyster, over which the tide rises and falls without one pulse upon its fleshy ear, to the hero who stands with quivering nerve parting with wife and child and home for country and God, all the way up is an ascending scale, marked by an increasing capacity to suffer; and when we look at the head of all being, up through principalities and powers and princedoms, with dazzling orders and celestial blazonry, to behold by what emblem the Infinite Sovereign has chosen to reveal himself, we behold, in the midst of the throne, "a lamb as it had been slain."
>
> Sorrow is divine. Sorrow is reigning on the throne of the universe, and the crown of all crowns has been one of thorns.[35]

The series of meditations that Stowe devotes to sorrow and suffering indicate that she has come to regard the capacity for suffering as the clearest indication of an individual's humanity, and as the closest approach that humans can make to divinity. Worth noting here is that suffering transcends doctrine: the God Stowe portrays in the passage is not defined by incomparable divine sovereignty, but rather by incomparable divine anguish.

When we put *Clarel* in conversation with Stowe's *The Minister's Wooing*, we see how much Melville's enormous poem has in common with broader nineteenth-century American concerns with grief and loss. Thinking of *Clarel* as a poem that comes at questions of religious difference through the problem of suffering also shows us the degree to which Melville's entire career is bound together by common themes. In *Moby-Dick*, Job and Solomon provide a frame for theodicy and the problem of human suffering. In *Pierre*, *The Encantadas*, *Benito Cereno*, "Bartleby, the Scrivener," and *The Confidence-Man*, suffering, its reasons, and its relief play central thematic parts.

The question of suffering brings us to a consideration of how Melville's work connects with that of another important transatlantic and transdisciplinary interlocutor. Perhaps the single biggest change in the religious world and in Melville's own religious outlook during the writing of *Clarel* was the emergence of Charles Darwin's model of evolution by means of natural selection as the most elegant and coherent explanation for the development of species in the natural world, including the human species. The fact that Melville explicitly discusses evolutionary biology in the epilogue and hints at it as well as directly confronting the new geology in the character of Margoth, the lapsed Jewish geologist who casts doubt on all of the other characters' religious positions, suggests that Darwin had made a significant difference for Melville in his later years.

In the epilogue, Melville writes, "If Luther's day expand to Darwin's year, / Shall that exclude the hope, foreclose the fear" (*Clarel* 4.35.1–2). He goes on to reflect on the question of suffering—the new wrinkle in theodicy, as it were—raised by the long, slow development of the human species through evolution. The human predicament in relation to the new science is stated poignantly: "And tantalized and apprehensive Man / Appealing—wherefore ripen us to pain? / Seems there the spokesman of dumb Nature's train" (*Clarel* 4.35.20–2). Melville again engages in one of his characteristically layered reflections: the question posed by human beings—why allow us consciousness and thus allow us to suffer?—no longer presupposes a personal divine interlocutor because of the expansion of Luther's day to Darwin's year, and at the same time, it gains a special poignancy. There is no teleological need to the evolutionary process to bestow consciousness upon human beings, and yet it is nonetheless present; hence suffering. The new forms of religious difference enabled by modern science merely make the perennial questions that confront the religious more vexing, but the questions do not go away. Faith and doubt are not resolved, but deepened, fragmented, and intensified. The epilogue thus reveals the interplay of faith and doubt and connects the impulses that gave birth to Protestantism with the impulses that were paving the way for a post-Protestant society.[36]

Melville, All Souls, and Religious Liberalism

Melville's interaction with the new geology and the new biology through his representation of Margoth and his allusions to Darwin brings us full circle. If Melville shared with the liberal Christianity and Unitarianism of his time a respect for science even when it undermined old certainties, how do we situate Melville himself with regard to the religious liberalism that formed such an important part of his context in his later years? The question of how to view Melville's relationship to Unitarianism has yet to be resolved and will surely not be resolved definitively here. The fact that *Clarel* is so deeply engaged with the questions that the congregation at All Soul's was also concerned with suggests at the very least that we cannot simply assume that Melville's decision to join All Soul's was made out of a desire to conciliate Elizabeth independent of any real personal conviction. Likewise, Melville's possible awareness of and receptiveness to themes from Henry Whitney Bellows's preaching undermines assumptions about Melville's lack of respect for Elizabeth's beliefs and intellect. If we are to believe (and there seems no reason not to) family members' testimony to the effect that Melville rarely attended All Soul's in the period when he was writing *Clarel*, surely we must also accept that Elizabeth was a major source of information on the intellectual ferment taking place in that church.

The Melville who was received into membership at All Soul's nearly a decade after the writing of *Clarel* had been engaged in an intellectual dialogue with the concerns of Unitarianism for decades. He was not a doctrinaire adherent to everything that the ministers at All Soul's taught, but he did not need to be in order to join. The Unitarian Church of the 1880s was a more open ecclesial polity than that which expelled Emerson, and it had a long history of tolerating variations in belief so long as they did not generate disharmony. Melville would have found a community of difference not unlike the one that he describes in *Clarel*: in Melville's Holy Land and in Melville's church, seekers of divergent beliefs engaged in discussions that illuminated the critical debates at the core of Christian belief and practice as the nineteenth century drew to a close.

We can speculate profitably, I believe, about what Melville sought at All Soul's. It is easy to lionize Melville as the ultimate fearless individual religious seeker, contemptuous of traditional answers to perennial questions and eager to seek out answers of his own. It seems to me that this is an accurate picture, so far as it goes. And yet, there is another side to Melville that emphasizes the communal and the relational, and suggests that nothing is more tragic than to surrender fully one's ability to interact fruitfully with other human beings. As much as Melville exalts and embodies intellectual and spiritual independence, he also writes lyrically about the experience of community. We often remember that Dutch Reformed Calvinism was the faith of Melville's mother; it is sometimes less easy to remember that Unitarianism was the faith of his father, as well as the religious tradition into which Melville married. Melville's uncertain movement between Calvinism and Unitarianism and his flirtation with High Church Episcopalianism and Catholicism mirrored his family's continuing history.[37]

So, once again, was Melville a Unitarian? The answer may be a qualified yes. Melville simultaneously held views that on a scale of theological liberalism and conservatism would fall well to the left and well to the right of mainstream Unitarianism. The evidence is overwhelming that whatever else Melville may have disbelieved, the Calvinist emphasis on human depravity was never something with which he could fully dispense. The melancholy that affects so many of his characters is the melancholy of men and women who live in a fallen world that cannot simply be defined out of existence by hope or optimism. The ecclesial structure of the Catholic Church, meanwhile, seems to have held considerable appeal for Melville toward the end of his life, and he seems to have found considerable beauty and power in Catholic devotional art and literature and the stories of the saints. The liturgy of the Episcopal Church seems also to have appealed powerfully to his sense of reverence for beauty. In this, Melville was at least as much a representative of the literary culture of his time as he was an outlier from it. Harriet Beecher Stowe decorated her home in Hartford with paintings of the Virgin Mary, and Mark Twain wrote a surprisingly non-ironic biography of Joan of Arc. All Soul's Church, meanwhile, situated itself on the boundary between various theological and ecclesiological traditions in ways that could not help but appeal to Melville.

Melville would not undertake so ambitious a work as *Clarel* again. The poetry that followed often has a fragmentary, unfinished feel to it. It also, however, illustrates that *Clarel* was no more a stopping place for Melville's art and thought than was *The Confidence-Man*, or *Moby-Dick*, or *Typee*. Perhaps nothing illustrates more stunningly the fluidity of Melville's thought in the years and months preceding his death than the greatest of all his posthumous works, *Billy Budd*. The story of the final years of Melville's life and career as a verbal artist is clearest and most compelling when we view his poetry and prose from the period together, and it is to this late efflorescence of poetry and prose that we turn in the final chapter.

Chapter 6

✦

"I Too Am Uncertain": The Doubtful Testament of *Billy Budd* and Melville's Later Poetry

One of the paradoxes of Melville's work is the seeming seductiveness exercised by celibacy upon his imagination. Associations with celibacy contribute to the appeal of Dunkers, Shakers, and Catholic monastic orders at various points in Meville's poetry and prose. These associations have, as we have seen, been connected by scholars with Melville's own sexuality via suggestions about his possible homosexuality or bisexuality, and they have also been connected with suggestions of misogyny on Melville's part.[1] These tantalizing possibilities come together with one of Melville's most characteristic epistemological themes in his markings and annotations in the seventh chapter of the First Epistle to the Corinthians. Melville marks a series of Paul's arguments for celibacy, but at the end of the chapter, he leaves with a note that is characteristically Melvillean in its ambiguity. Having scored the verse that reads, "But she is happier if she so abide, after my judgment: and I think also that I have the spirit of God," Melville underlined the two words "I think" and wrote a two-line remark in the bottom margin. Most of this remark has been irretrievably erased, but what remains reads "I too am uncertain" (*MMO* 65). As is so often the case with Melville, the locus of his uncertainty is itself in doubt: does he mean that he is uncertain about the relative merits of celibacy and marriage? Or about Paul's possession of the spirit of Christ? What is clear is that Melville's restlessness and sense of fully impassioned and engaged doubt is a central strand in his career, and as we turn to the last chapter of Melville's story, we find that this uncertainty is intensified rather than resolved. This appears in relation both to questions of theological dialogue and difference and to questions of sexuality in Melville's late and unpublished work. Melville's reading thus not only continues to inform his work in his later career; it actually intensifies its effects in his later years.

More than any of Melville's other works, *Billy Budd* has at times appeared to be self-generated and radically disconnected from the rest of Melville's career. *Billy Budd* was Melville's only major posthumously published work, and the way it emerged generated some of the most venerable mythologies in Melville criticism. As Wyn Kelley has recently pointed out, the conventional story that *Billy Budd* was discovered by Raymond Weaver in a breadbox in the Melville family attic is a distortion—in fact the women in Melville's family, first his widow, and then his granddaughter, Eleanor Melville Metcalf, had carefully preserved these materials, and passed them on to Weaver because they believed he would do them justice.[2] Nonetheless, the romance of a forgotten manuscript emerging from a breadbox three decades after its author's death, and proving to be a masterpiece worthy of being considered alongside *Moby-Dick*, which was at that very historical moment being rediscovered as the great nineteenth-century American novel, had proved an irresistible piece of Melville mythology.

Perhaps the most misleading part of the myth that has grown up around *Billy Budd* is the idea that it represents a belated return to fiction after a "long quietus" (to use Raymond Weaver's famous expression) during which Melville gave up on writing altogether.[3] In this telling, a disillusioned Melville gave up on writing in 1857 with the publication of *The Confidence-Man*, and returned to create one magnificent deathbed novella, which should be read as a sort of "last will and testament," defining the ultimate shape of his artistic and philosophical vision. Melville scholars have long acknowledged that the "long quietus" did not in fact exist: the years from 1857 to 1891 were years of constant writing, reading, and poetic experimentation for Melville. Despite this acknowledgment, however, the tendency to move quickly over Melville's poetry in pursuit of a final moment of artistic brilliance and incisive cultural comment in *Billy Budd* has proved persistent.

The two previous chapters have hinted at the inadequacy of such an approach: the scope and ambition, not to mention the artistic and philosophical development, that appear in *Battle-Pieces* and *Clarel* forbid their being excluded from a thorough accounting of Melville's career. Neither *Battle-Pieces* nor *Clarel*, however, have suffered from anything like the neglect extended to Melville's two last published collections of poems, *John Marr and Other Sailors, with Some Sea-Pieces* (1889) and *Timoleon, etc.* (1891), and his unpublished *Weeds and Wildings, with a Rose or Two*. Melville's uncollected poetry from his later years has been still more egregiously ignored by many scholars. William Shurr and William Bysshe Stein both published important discussions of Melville's poetic career that took these works into account in the early 1970s, and more recently Douglas Robillard, Dennis Berthold, Elizabeth Renker, and Hershel Parker have all pointed out from a range of vantage points the value of these collections. What remains to be established is the precise nature of the relation of the poems from Melville's last years to the rest of his career as a writer, and particularly the way in which they connect *Billy Budd* to the rest of Melville's career.[4]

The thread that connects the later poetry and *Billy Budd* to the long trajectory of Melville's career, from *Typee* through *Moby-Dick* and "Bartleby, the Scrivener" to *Clarel* is the obsession with religious difference that unifies Melville's entire body of work. This point of connection does not, however, imply uniformity. In the final years of his life, Melville was finding a new set of concepts to probe the questions of religious difference with which he had always wrestled, and he likewise found a new set of artistic tools with which to work. The questions that Melville posed in *Billy Budd* brought the uncertainties associated with religious difference into closer contact than ever before with matters of human prudence and judgment. Melville's last years were spent seeking to understand how just authority could be possible in an unjust world. Rather than setting up oppositions between ethics and doctrine, as he did in the later 1850s; or between narrow dogmatism and expansive pluralism, as he did in the 1840s and early 1850s; or even among a range of discrete religious or political positions, as he did in the 1860s and 1870s; Melville here dealt with religiously, philosophically, and morally complex individuals whose moral quandaries manifested themselves in ways that could be resolved neither by taking a position on exclusivism versus pluralism nor by accepting or rejecting the moral codes of the Sermon on the Mount, but rather by means of a sort of moral reflection that is both informed by an understanding of difference and capable of decisive moral choice.

In this, Melville anticipates one of the most frequently encountered questions in the twenty-first-century literature classroom: that of presentism and the possibility of moral judgment in relation to those who live at different times than ours and according to different codes than ours. Melville's treatment of moral, ethical, and religious questions in his later poetry and *Billy Budd* neither dissolve into relativism nor ossify into orthodoxy. He considers a substantial range of moral and religious options, and works his way to evaluative positions that are nuanced and, often, courageous. What Melville requires of belief in his later work, then, is not so much solidity as agility. Faith and ethics must be strong enough to endure, and ductile enough to be reimagined in contexts that seem to defy their strictures.

John Marr and Other Sailors

In order to trace the development of the ethical and multi-religious sensibility found in *Billy Budd*, it is necessary to trace Melville's development through his later poetry—a body of work that is tantalizingly fragmented, but which includes some of the most daring and unexpected moments in Melville's entire body of work. Melville's later poetry includes two published collections: *John Marr and Other Sailors, with Some Sea-Pieces*, and *Timoleon, etc.*; and two unpublished collections: *Weeds and Wildings, with a Rose or Two* and *Marquis de Grandvin*, with a number of uncollected poems and the unfinished work *The Burgundy Club* outstanding.

In the prose preface to *John Marr and Other Sailors, with Some Sea-Pieces*, we read the story of a seeker who finds his sources of meaning in both the expanses of the Midwestern prairie and the vaster expanses of the oceans of the world. John Marr, we are told, is a longtime sailor who since 1838 has resided in the prairies near "where the Mound-Builders of a race only conjecturable had left their pottery and bones, one common clay, under a terrace serpentine in form" (*PP* 195). The reference to the Mound-Builders is telling: Melville is interested in the layers of cultures reflected in Marr's region. Several pages after his reference to the Mound-Builders, Melville refers to the history of violence and displacement of native peoples that also shaped the prairie region, describing them as "almost exterminated in their recent and final war with regular white troops, a war waged by the Red Men for their native soil and natural rights" (*PP* 197). Marr is an American of European descent, but his reality is shaped by the indigenous history of the prairie. Echoes of Melville's review of Parkman's *The California and Oregon Trails* should be kept in view here, as well as his extensive treatment of Pacific Island cultures in his early novels. Also worthy of note is the fact that Marr is an outsider of sorts: the dwellers in the prairies generally have little concern with the ocean, and are "narrowly religious" and while "kindly at need," lacking in geniality, so his reveries about his erstwhile comrades tend to fall on deaf ears. This discussion of Marr serves to frame the collection as a whole: these poems are the reminiscences of a lonely man whose past at sea is more real to him than his present on the prairie, and the poems are an attempt to reconnect with the "phantoms" of the sailors he had known: "He invokes these visionary ones, striving, as it were, to get into verbal communion with them, or under yet stronger illusion, reproaching them for their silence" (*PP* 199). The collection thus invokes in a very touching way Melville's continual engagement with solitude and communion.

In the verse portion of *John Marr and Other Sailors*, Melville experiments extensively with creating voices that are significantly different from his own. Perhaps the most frequently discussed poem in the collection, "Bridegroom Dick," presents us with a figure who both resembles Melville himself and is a distinct "type" among sailors. The speaker in this poem addresses himself to his aging wife, and he reflects on the cruel contradictions that the Civil War forced upon his fellow sailors:

> Sentiment, ay, while suspended hung all,
> Ere the guns against Sumter opened there the ball,
> And partners were taken, and the red dance began,
> War's red dance o' death!—Well, we to man,
> We sailors o' the North, wife, how could we lag?—
> Strike with your kin, and you stick to the Flag!
> But to the sailors o' the South that easy way was barred.
> To some, dame, believe, (and I speak what I know)
> Wormwood the trial, and the Uzzite's black shard;
> And the faithfuller the heart, the crueler the throe.
> Duty? It pulled with more than one string,
> This way and that, and anyhow a sting.
> The Flag and your kin, how be true unto both?
> If either plight ye keep, then ye break the other troth.
> But elect here they must, though the casuists were out:
> Decide—hurry up—and throttle every doubt. (lines 109–24)

Bridegroom Dick's reflection here emphasizes the pain of uncertainty in the face of differing imperatives. The sailors who must choose whether to fight against their nation or their family are compared to Job ("the Uzzite"), and their very moral strength comes to be a source of suffering for them. Nor is a state of suspension an option: without the moral guidance offered by "casuists," these men must make an irrevocable decision. This imperative to choose without complete information and without authoritative guidance is among the most painful aspects of the struggle with questions of difference for Melville.

If "Bridegroom Dick" can stand as a representative for the titular first part of the collection, the segment of "Sea-Pieces" that illustrates most decisively the religious cast of the collection as a whole is the brief collection of poems entitled "Pebbles."[5] Here, Melville finds in the sea a visible representation of the moral and spiritual uncertainties that have shaped his career. The first poem starts by keeping the physicality of the sea clearly in sight: "Though the Clerk of the Weather insist, / And lay down the weather law,

/ Pintado and gannet they wist / That the winds blow whither they list / In tempest or flaw" (lines 1–5). Melville sets up an opposition between the spurious certainties imposed by human will (the "Clerk of the Weather" and the "weather law") and the absolute imperviousness of the winds to human control. His use of two seabirds, the pintado, or cape petrel, and the gannet, creates a telling contrast: humans believe that they can control nature, whereas seabirds that soar where the winds take them have adapted themselves to nature. Although it is lightly submerged, there is also a religious element to this image: in the King James translation of Jesus's dialogue with Nicodemus in the Gospel of John, Jesus states that "the wind blows where it will," implying in context that the spirit of God cannot be controlled by human regulations. Putting the natural imagery of the poem into conversation with the religious element implied by the allusion, we can see that Melville's suggestion here is that the question of meaning in human existence is ultimately ineffable. The Clerk of Weather is impertinent in his pretensions to control the wind, and religious attempts to categorize the substance of faith are likely to find this substance infinitely elusive.

The poems that follow build on the foundational uncertainty of the opening piece in "Pebbles." If the first poem moves from the brute facts of the sea to spiritual insinuations, the second moves from an explicit discussion of dogma to the suggestion that the sea is the source of our metaphors for the spirit. The poem begins, "Old are the creeds, but stale are the schools / Revamped as the mode may veer" (lines 1–2). Here we see a theme that connects this poem to Melville's interrogation of faith, doubt, and difference in *Clarel*, and indeed to Henry Whitney Bellows's stated desire to reinvigorate liberal Christianity. The ancient creeds of the Christian faith are set against the contemporary inability to give them a construction that can matter in the world of the 1880s, and the solution that the poem nostalgically yearns for is an escape from time itself: when a sailor listens to the voice of the sea in a conch shell, he find that the sound remains the same as always. He reflects regarding the sound of the conch: "The Seas have inspired it, and Truth, / Truth varying from sameness never" (lines 9–10).

Following this identification of the voice of the sea with a timeless truth in the second poem, the third poem dwells upon the incommensurability of the human desire to find ourselves in nature with the sheer vastness and power of the sea, but does so using metaphors that point us back to our inability to speak of the sea without making use of images drawn from land: unlike the Blue Ridge mountains ("Blue Ridge" here constitutes a characteristic Melvillean pun), we humans are flattered by no echo from the sea, the truth of which is fundamentally inhuman: "For echo the seas have none; / Nor aught that gives back man's strain— / The hope of his heart, the dream in his brain" (lines 4–6). The fourth poem consists of just two lines, but it represents an important turn in Melville's treatment of the place of humanity in the cosmos. The speaker reflects: "On ocean where the embattled ships repair / Man, suffering inflictor, sails on sufferance there" (lines 1–2). The fifth provides a kind of riposte, as the sea responds that it is "Pleased, not appeased, by myriad wrecks in me" (line 3). The sixth poem contains a reassertion of human values expressed in the specifically religious terms most frequently invoked by Melville throughout his career:

> Curled in the comb of yon billow Andean,
> Is it the Dragon's heaven-challenging crest?
> Elemental mad ramping of ravening waters—
> Yet Christ on the Mount, and the dove in her nest! (lines 1–4)

The power of the sea is here imagined as the revolt of Satan described in the New Testament Book of Revelation, and the description of the waves as Andean mountains reinforces the degree to which the ocean's power dwarfs human fears and desires. And yet, humanity asserts itself in the final line, with the moral teaching of Christ on the one hand, and humanity's survival of Noah's flood in the Hebrew scriptures on the other. This leads into the final poem in the sequence, which "laud[s] the inhuman sea," finding a balance between human aspiration and the way in which the sea makes all such aspiration small. Thus with a passage reminiscent of Pip's and Ishmael's visions of infinity Melville closes his published engagement with the sea.

Wrestling with Art in *Timoleon*

Melville ranges broadly through questions of religious and cultural difference in his final published collection of poetry, *Timoleon*, a collection that incorporates work from the last thirty years of his career as a writer. In the concluding portion of the collection, a grouping of poems entitled "Fruits of Travel from Long Ago," Hershel Parker has meticulously documented the evidence that numerous poems from *Timoleon* were initially written and intended for a collection meant to be published in 1860 under the simple title "Poems," but languished for decades before their publication in *Timoleon*.[6] Melville thus produced these poems over an extended period of time, but what is especially noteworthy is the unity of vision that this volume communicates despite the vast expanse of Melville's career that is associated with these poems.

Religious difference is always in the background in this collection, but in a few poems it becomes especially explicit. The poem that captures most thoroughly the thematic interplay of faith and art is a brief piece with the simple title "Art." In this poem, Melville brings the aesthetic and the religious together. In a piece reminiscent of his reflections on Milton's artistic process in the lecture "Statues in Rome," Melville suggests that art is fundamentally dependent on the meeting of apparent opposites:

> In placid hours well-pleased we dream,
> Of many a brave unbodied scheme.
> But form to the lend, pulsed life create,
> What unlike things must meet and mate;
> A flame to melt—a wind to freeze;
> Sad patience—joyous energies;
> Humility—yet pride and scorn;
> Instinct and study; love and hate;
> Audacity—reverence. These must mate,
> And fuse with Jacob's mystic heart,
> To wrestle with the angel—Art. (lines 1–11)

The piece encapsulates perfectly Melville's insistence on the analogy between the visual and the verbal arts, and particularly illustrates the tensions between faith and doubt and solitude and sociability that provide so much of the energy that drives Melville's work. Here, Milton's Satan ("audacity," "hate," "pride," "scorn") and the Christ of the Sermon on the Mount ("humility," "reverence," "sad patience") are both present, and both are necessary for the artist's work. Melville's tendency to move between expressions of admiration for self-sacrifice and expressions of enthusiasm for egotism and self-assertion, between admiration for the Hebrew and Christian sense of the vanity of human existence and the classical virtues that he suggested that this sense undermined is explained more clearly and concisely here than anywhere else in his work. If Melville relishes difference throughout his work, he does so ultimately in the service of art.

As discussed in the previous chapter, the short poem "Buddha" illustrates both the range of Melville's religious interests and the syncretic method with which he handled these interests. Several other poems from the collection provide a complementary view of Melville's syncretic mode. "Shelley's Vision" provides an understanding of Melville's philosophical thought through the lens of his engagement with British romantic poetry.

Here Melville imagines Shelley as a counterpart to Saint Stephen, the first martyr of the book of Acts in the New Testament. In this poem, Shelley, who as a historical figure was widely reviled for his unorthodox religious views, has internalized the attacks to the point where he is ready to stone his own shadow. It is at this point that he has the vision alluded to in the title: "When lo, upon that sunlit ground / I saw the quivering phantom take / The likeness of St. Stephen crowned: / Then did self-reverence awake" (lines 8–11). Shelley, an atheist, has here found grounds for "self-reverence" in his realization that he, like the biblical Saint Stephen, is a kind of religious martyr. Difference and analogy function in tandem here: Shelley's and Stephen's points of view on doctrinal questions are irrevocably opposed, and yet in some sense their moral courage and willingness to suffer on behalf of their own visions of the truth makes them analogues for each other.

Melville's attraction to the prophetic and mysterious likewise appears in the intriguingly titled piece "Fragments of a Lost Gnostic Poem of the 12th Century." Gnosticism was a heretical rival to Christianity, and given Melville's persistent interest throughout his career in heretics and religious minorities more generally, it is no surprise that they stimulated his imagination. The two fragments are also characteristic of Melville's artistic method in that they present the reader with a kind of diptych: there are two short, four-line stanzas, which present a complementary understanding of human effort. Notably, the gnostic speaker in this poem shares the Hebrew and Christian sense of the vanity of human endeavor:

> Found a family, build a state,
> The pledged event is still the same:
> Matter in end will never abate
> His ancient, brutal claim. (lines 1–4)

This first half of the poem is a flat statement of the evanescence of human effort and desire. Death and decay await, no matter what the scope of human accomplishment. The second stanza teases out the implications of all this:

> Indolence is heaven's ally here,
> And energy the child of hell:
> The Good Man pouring from his pitcher clear
> But brims the poisoned well. (lines 5–8)

The Blakean resonances of the poem are unmistakable, with the connection between hell and energy a clear echo of Blake's *The Marriage of*

Heaven and Hell.[7] Melville is up to his own sort of marriage of heaven and hell here, albeit somewhat distinct from Blake's: hellish energy is contrasted, not to constraining reason, as in Blake, but to passivity: restlessness and rest both have roles to play for Melville, and this rift between ceaseless action and passive acceptance is another of the ways in which Melville identifies religious difference that transcends doctrinal and confessional boundaries.

Melville's fascination with difference is strikingly evident even, and perhaps especially, when he is at his most whimsical. "Herba Santa," a comic piece in praise of tobacco, fits this pattern beautifully. Indeed, whimsy and blasphemy are never far from each other in this poem, which opens its second stanza with a reflection on Christianity's shortcomings as a religion of peace:

> Shall code or creed a lure afford
> To win all selves to Love's accord?
> When Love ordained a supper divine
> For the wide world of man,
> What bickerings o'er his gracious wine!
> Then strange new feuds began. (lines 8–13)

As he had done in work going back to *Typee*, Melville identifies love and forgiveness as the ethical core of Christianity, and reflects on the distance of Christian practice from this ethical core. Like the insufficiently evangelized missionary woman in *Typee*, the Christian church in "Herba Santa" has flouted forgiveness while acting in the name of the Prince of Peace. This paradox points Melville back to an alternative tradition: the smoking of the peace pipe among indigenous peoples in the Americas. Here, Melville's career comes full circle: his early assertion in *Typee* that cannibals may be the moral superiors of Christians when judged by the standard of the Sermon on the Mount is reasserted here with the same sort of genial good humor that obtained in his earliest novels. This captures one of the most compelling attributes of Melville's later poetry: in brief, lyrical, and reflective pieces, he underscores thematic elements and formal devices that have been central to his entire career.

Melville's Unpublished and Uncollected Poetry

Despite the speed with which Melville published collections of poetry in the years immediately preceding his death, he left a substantial amount of unpublished, uncollected, or unfinished material at the time of his death. *Weeds and Wildings, with a Rose or Two*, a collection compiled shortly before Melville's death for his wife Elizabeth, is in two parts, the longer of which consists of poems that are held together loosely by references to gardening, and the shorter of which uses roses in particular for their defining motif.[8] He also left a number of uncollected poems that shed light on matters of faith and difference in his work.

One poem that can stand in for the beauties, complexities, and ambivalences of the collection is "Rosary Beads." The title image from the series of poems calls attention implicitly to questions of religious difference and dialogue: the rosary is used in both the Islamic and Roman Catholic traditions as an aid to prayer, and aspects of the poems point toward both traditions while finally associating them with neither. The rose poems use a form of religious imagery that can be associated with the Persian poetry for Sa'di's *Gulistan* or Omar Khayyam's *Rubaiyat*, both available to Melville in translation, or the rose imagery associated with the Virgin Mary in the Catholic tradition.[9] Melville's fascination with both Muslim and Catholic devotional practices is particularly evident in "Rosary Beads," but here as elsewhere in this collection, the spiritual impulse is turned firmly toward the natural world. The roses in this poem are concrete, physical roses, not spiritualized concepts, and the "rose-priests" are gardeners and vendors of flowers. The first fragment, "The Accepted Time," echoes in its title a biblical passage which calls for repentance and conversion: as Melville would have read in his King James New Testament, 2 Corinthians 6.2 reads in part "Now is the accepted time. Behold, now is the day of salvation." As in the Catholic devotion of the Rosary, readers are asked to meditate on this particular concept as a response to a physical object. A Catholic praying the Rosary will meditate on a specific mystery from the life of Christ for the space of ten beads (a decade) while repeating a Hail Mary at each bead, and it is not uncommon for a brief verse to be read out at the start of each decade to guide the meditation. Here, the title serves to state the "mystery," and the four-line verses provide a guide to meditation for the reader. The verse that follows the title "The Accepted Time" is in tension with the title's implicit call for repentance and spiritual conversion. The verse commands: "Adore the Roses; nor delay / Until the rose-fane fall, / Or ever their censers cease to sway: / 'Today!' the rose-priests call" (lines 1–4). This whimsical quatrain brings together Catholic liturgical imagery in which the fragrance of the roses is compared to incense, echoes of evangelical Protestant revival sermons in which sinners are urged to repent of their sins before it is too late, and the carpe diem verse tradition associated in English with seventeenth-century poets like Robert Herrick and Andrew Marvell. The reader is asked to delight in the physical world, not in spite of, but because of, its evanescence.

The second stanza picks up the superficially light-hearted and profoundly poignant use of syncretism in praise of the roses. Under the heading, "Without Price," which recalls the idea from the Gospels of the Kingdom of Heaven as the Pearl of Great Price and the invitation at the opening of the fifty-fifth chapter of Isaiah to obtain bread "without price" we read:

Have the Roses. Needs no pelf
The blooms to buy,
Nor any rose-bed to thyself
Thy skill to try:
But live up to the Rose's light,
Thy meat shall change to roses red,
Thy bread to roses white. (lines 5–11)

Here we see the roses as a kind of gratuitous gift of beauty. The idea of meat and bread changing to roses plays loosely off the change of bread to the body of Christ in transubstantiation in the same way that the poem as a whole plays off of the relationship between the metaphorical flowers of the rosary and literal roses.

In the third stanza, Melville engages in a more concrete sort of reflection upon evanescence, with the grim meditation "Grain by grain the desert drifts / Against the Garden-Land: / Hedge well thy roses, heed the stealth / Of ever-creeping land" (lines 12–14). The fragility of the roses is set in stark opposition to the inevitable spread of the desert and enjoins the reader to defend these possessions, which in the previous stanza seem so gratuitous and prodigal in their beauty. The "Rosary Beads" of the title thus involve a reflection on mortality and significance like that associated with the mysteries of the Catholic rosary, but unmoored from doctrinal connections. Melville's description of the roses allows his readers to meditate profoundly on the numinous aspects of beauty, while leaving to the side questions of dogma.

Among Melville's uncollected poems is "A Reasonable Constitution," which again points to Melville's awareness of uncertainty as inescapable. In this brief, four-line poem, Melville's speaker addresses the founders of a new regime: "What though Reason forged your scheme? / Twas Reason dreamed the Utopia's dream: / Tis dream to think that Reason can / Govern the reasoning creature, man" (lines 1–4). Evident here is Melville's love of paradox. Reason and fantasy are revealed to be, not opponents, but complementary and necessary adjuncts to each other. Moreover, humanity's capacity for "reasoning" (with a lowercase "r") is the very thing that in this poem subverts the possibility that "Reason" (with a capital "R") can resolve the paradoxes of human experience. "Reasoning" here refers not only to ratiocination, but to the human tendency to generate self-serving "reasons"—as in Benjamin Franklin's celebrated observation, "So useful a thing it is to be a Reasonable Creature"—because reason can allow one to do precisely as one pleases.[10] Indeed, Franklin and his fellow founders are almost certainly in view here, as well as the nineteenth-century European revolutionaries to whom they were often compared. Melville asserts that Reason in the abstract is ultimately an unreasonable delusion, a standpoint that reflected his doubts that ratiocination could ultimately triumph completely over human interests, including those that are perennially destructive—hence the value of doubt for Melville.

"Rammon" is one of the most tantalizing portions of Melville's entire literary corpus, and this little-known prose fragment demonstrates how determinative religious difference was for the shape of Melville's career. The story is framed with a characteristic touch of uncertainty, as Melville's speaker notes, "In touching upon historical matters the romance and the poet have generously been accorded a certain license, elastic in proportion to the remoteness of the period embraced and consequent incompleteness and incertitude of our knowledge" (*CP* 411). He therefore feels free to put forward a parable of sorts about a figure associated with the biblical narrative but "not mentioned in canonic Scripture" (*CP* 411). "Rammon" is the putative story of the youngest and frailest of the sons of Solomon. Throughout his career, Melville had shown a great deal of interest in this wisest and most magnificent of Israel's kings, from his tendency to score references to the Queen of Sheba in his copy of *The New Testament and Psalms* to his meditation on the wisdom of "unchristian Solomon" in the "Try-Works" chapter of *Moby-Dick*. Here, Melville takes seriously the idea that Solomon had come into contact with world religions other than Judaism as a result of Israel's trade with other parts of the ancient world. Melville argues that Solomon was a "very lax Hebrew" who was heavily influenced by thought from a variety of religious traditions around the world. Rammon suffers early in life from a realization of the vanity of human existence and the fact that evil is "like good . . . an irremovable element" (*CP* 411). These realizations inclined Rammon toward a suicidal desire for "the cessation of being" (*CP* 411). Rammon's initial impulse is to rest in the knowledge that death will eventually come for him, but he becomes disturbed by his conversations with a loquacious

Queen of Sheba, who brings to Rammon's attention the doctrines of Buddhism regarding reincarnation and also the details of the Buddha's own exemplary life. Melville was clearly in the midst of a substantial rethinking of the relationship of Western and Eastern modes of thought, one which allowed him to think of traditions like Buddhism as interlocutors with Christianity from a standpoint of equality:

> But the wonderful conceptions of Prince ——— [Siddhata?] were backed by something equally marvelous, his personality and life. These singularly appealed to Rammon also born a Prince, and conscious too that rank had not hardened his heart as to the mass of mankind, toilers and sufferers, nor in any wise intercepted a just view of the immense spectacle of things.
>
> But, in large, his thought of the Buddha partook of that tender awe with which, long after Rammon's time, the unconventional Christians were impressed by the story and character of Christ. It was not possible therefore for him to regard any doctrine, however repugnant to his understanding and desire, authentically ascribed to so transcendent a nature. (*CP* 412)

Melville's reflections on Rammon serve to illuminate much about his broader understanding of religious faith and theological reflection. Rammon is drawn to the Buddha by his character, just as the early Christians were drawn to Jesus by a similar sense of admiration for his.

As in *Clarel*, the encounter with world religions is paralleled by the encounter with the natural world and the natural sciences. In "Pontoosuce," one of the most lyrical of his late, uncollected poems, Melville wrestled forthrightly with the problem of death and evanescence. The problems of mortality and loss are fundamental to religious and philosophical thought in all its varieties, and Melville confronts these crucial and clarifying existential problems directly in this poem. Using language and imagery reminiscent of "The Piazza," Melville describes the romance and beauty of Nature in the early lines of the poem, and then confronts what the geological record tells us about human transience:

> The workman dies, and after him, the work;
> Like to those pines whose grave I trace,
> Statue and statuary fall upon their face:
> In very aramanths the worm doth lurk,
> Even stars, Chaldaeans say, have left their place,
> Andes and Apalachee tell

Of havoc ere our Adam fell,
And present Nature as a moss doth show
On the ruins of the Nature of the aeons of long ago. (lines 51–59)

Melville reflects here on the changes wrought in belief by what discoveries in geology and biology had meant in displacing humanity from the central position of life on earth and on the degree to which these new revelations reinforce the idea of the vanity of existence. Despite the melancholy tone here, at the end of the poem, he reinforces a response to unsettling changes in belief that has been consistent throughout his work: evanescence, change, and uncertainty become things to be revered, not despised, as the poem closes, first (in inverted commas) with an address from a mysterious woman who seems to represent the response of the soul and of nature to his gloomy reflections, and then his own response to her consolation:

"Since light and shade are equal set
And all revolves, nor more ye know;
Ah why should tears the pale cheek fret
For aught that waneth here below.
Let go, Let go!"

With that, her warm lips thrilled me through,
She kissed me, while her chaplet cold
Its rootlets brushed against my brow,
With all their humid clinging mould.
She vanished, leaving fragrant breath
And warmth and chill of wedded life and death. (lines 86–97)

The concluding stanzas of the poem thus suggest that the apparent antimonies of life and death, hope and terror, faith and doubt, are ultimately complementary rather than opposed, and we see something of Ishmael's equanimity and the equanimity of the narrator of the epilogue of *Clarel* emerging as Melville's stance toward the spiritual, moral, and intellectual struggles of his life.

In the myriads of fragmentary images Melville provides in his later poems of his understanding of faith, a remarkably consistent picture emerges. What Melville values beyond all doubt is a sense of kindness, empathy, and unwillingness to do harm that he is able to associate with sources as diverse as the Sermon on the Mount, Zoroastrian and Muslim ethical teachings, the life and teachings of the Buddha, the esoteric philosophy of the Rosicrucians, and the lessons taught by nature itself. When we consider that the later years of Melville's life coincided with the time spent in London by a young Indian lawyer named Mohandas Gandhi, we can see the degree to which these impulses made Melville a representative figure in the later nineteenth-century—at least among the more adventuresome and profound thinkers of the period.[11]

As William Dillingham has suggested, the new directions in Melville's reading in his last days are as significant as anything that we know about Melville from this period.[12] Schopenhauer was joined in Melville's library by a variety of texts concerned with philosophical and religious questions. Prominent among these texts, of course, is Alger's *The Solitudes of Nature and Man* (1882), the text with which this study begins. We come full circle with this mention of Alger's ruminations on solitude. What we clearly know, from both Melville's marginalia and the scope of his work as rehearsed throughout this volume is that his treatment of religious experience, in all its widely differing modes, gives expression to his own ceaseless efforts to create a sense of truth and meaning in the fragmented moral universe of the nineteenth century.

Platonism, Calvinism, and the Fall in *Billy Budd*

We know something else as well: this aging man, who read Schopenhauer, who wrote about Buddhism and roses, who told stories of the sea to his granddaughter as she tugged on his beard, who jokingly claimed to the other men at his barber's shop to have fathered an illegitimate child during his time in the Marquesas, was also working on one of the most haunting pieces of prose in American literary history. Melville's last work of prose is, of course, the story of a simple-minded sailor caught up in the most complex of human machinations and the most complex of questions about human justice and moral law, to his ultimate detriment and destruction.

What has the silent Billy Budd to do with so complex and vexed a subject as religious difference? Surely Billy is himself no theologian, but he is described and analyzed in terms that are as relentlessly theological as they are ineluctably mythical. Early in the novella, we read the following description:

> By his original constitution aided by the co-operating influences of his lot, Billy in many respects was little more than a sort of upright barbarian, much such as Adam presumably might have been ere the urbane serpent wriggled himself into his company.

> And here be it submitted that apparently going to corroborate the doctrine of man's Fall, a doctrine now popularly ignored, it is observable that where certain virtues pristine and unadulterated peculiarly characterize anybody in the external uniform of civilization, they will upon scrutiny seem not to be derived from custom or convention, but rather to be out of keeping with these, as if indeed exceptionally transmitted from a period prior to Cain's city and citified man. The character marked by such qualities has to an unvitiated taste an untampered-with flavor like that of berries, while the man thoroughly civilized, even in a fair specimen of the breed, has to the moral palate a questionable smack as of a compounded wine. (*BB* 53)

Melville is up to something rather tricky here. The passage seems to affirm the doctrine of the Fall of humanity as expressed in Western Christian theology broadly and Calvinist theology in particular, but in fact it neatly undoes this very affirmation: Original Sin, in the Augustinian and later Calvinist understanding, inheres in all human beings, regardless of their "citified" status, and Original Sin is passed down, not from Cain (who is in any case tangential to the genealogies of the book of Genesis), but rather from Adam and Eve themselves. Billy, and other "untampered-with" souls, seem precisely to have escaped this Fall, thus calling into question the doctrine of Original Sin, not, as the opening of the paragraph seems to suggest, reinforcing it. The reference that follows to "Caspar Hauser, wandering dazed in any Christian capital of our time," likewise underscores that the narrator, while apparently affirming the Fall and Original Sin, is actually casting doubt on both (*BB* 53). Here the celebrated case of a young man who reached adulthood without human contact is invoked to suggest that civility and Christendom are in league with "fallen" elements of the human condition, rather than functioning as remedies for a universal state of reprobation. Billy's unfallen state thus depends on the existence of the theological perception of a Fall, at the same time that it denies its completeness and absoluteness. Without the idea of a fallen world, the very innocence by which Billy's character is defined would make no sense: he gains his power as an archetype precisely because of his state as an exception to the general woe of humankind.

Billy's characterization also depends on the sort of racial and ethnic universalism that Melville introduced in his first novels and continued to develop throughout his career. In *Typee* and *Omoo*, Melville had argued for the moral superiority of indigenous societies in the South Pacific over the materialistic societies of western Europe and North America. In *Mardi*, Melville suggests that the Christianity of the Sermon on the

Mount may only be practiced in as yet undiscovered islands in the South Pacific. The tendency reaches its apotheosis with the divine Queequeg in *Moby-Dick*. Billy partakes of this strand in Melville's work in that he, because of his innocence, has escaped the corruption of Western civilization. Notably, Billy is contextualized and described in terms reminiscent of *Typee* and *Omoo*: he is innocent and beautiful and somehow outside of the scope of modern European civilization. It is impossible to miss the echoes of, for example, the physical description of Marnoo as well as the later moral description of Queequeg. Moreover, Billy is particularly distinguished by his harmlessness, by the utter absence of malice in his personality. This absence of malice does not of course prevent his engaging in a violent act, but even in the case of his killing of Claggart, the act is triggered by malice, and the malice is not Billy's own.

What is noticeable throughout *Billy Budd* is that the sacred hovers in the background, never taking over the foreground, but also never absenting itself from the picture. Melville's narrator, when describing Nelson's conduct at the Battle of Trafalgar, says:

> At Trafalgar Nelson on the brink of opening the fight sat down and wrote his last brief will and testament. If under the presentiment of the most magnificent of all victories to be crowned by his own glorious death, a sort of priestly motive led him to dress his own person in the jeweled vouchers of his own shining deeds; if thus to have adorned himself for the altar and the sacrifice were indeed vainglory, then affectation and fustian is each more heroic line in the great epics and dramas, since in such lines the poet but embodies in verse those exaltations of sentiment that a nature like Nelson, the opportunity being given, vitalizes into acts. (*BB* 58)

The passage is a description of a famous moment in warfare, but the central metaphor is that of a priest dressing himself for a sacrifice. As discussed in the first chapter of this study, Melville in his copy of *The Holy Bible with Apocrypha* noted the correlations between the robes of the Aaronic priesthood and the vestments of a nineteenth-century Catholic priest. In this passage, Nelson is behaving in a manner emblematic of both the priesthood described in the Hebrew scriptures and the priesthood in the nineteenth-century Catholic Church. Like an Aaronic priest carrying out his duties in conformity with the Levitical code, Nelson has arrayed himself in beautiful, artistically designed robes in order carry out a sacrifice; like the sacrifice of the Mass celebrated by Catholic priests, Nelson's sacrifice is of a human being, with Nelson himself being offered as Christ is offered in the sacrament of the bread and wine. In a way, then, religion, and religious difference in particular, functions in a manner similar to the image of the sun through the clouds that is provided at the end of the novella. The text as a whole is "irradiated" with theological content, even as it avoids the sort of explicit sermons that Father Mapple and Fleece provide in *Moby-Dick*.

This presence of the sacred is evident in the characterization of Claggart and Captain Vere as well as Billy. Like Billy, Claggart presents a theological and ethical conundrum, and like Billy, his characterization seems to affirm the Calvinist version of the Fall of humanity while challenging it on a more profound level. In describing Claggart, Melville is careful to emphasize precisely the degree to which Claggart is unaccountable, somehow left out of any calculation that we may use in describing our moral universe. Claggart represents precisely that "malice" that the new Rosicrucians reject and that the "herba santa" is said to dissipate. Notably, Melville finds the resources for writing about Claggart in two seemingly contradictory modes of thought. He draws upon the theological tradition of Calvinism within Christianity to suggest that Claggart is an example of a fundamental depravity in human nature, and then draws back in order to suggest that Claggart is in fact a special case, not a representative of the wider human condition. He uses Plato to suggest that Claggart's depravity may be simply his own. Melville thus invokes Calvinist theology, with its apparatus of sin and damnation to suggest the seriousness of the problem with Claggart, providing a kind of hellish aura for the man, and then uses Plato's concepts to distance his own presentation of Claggart from the very supernaturalism that he invokes.

What Melville does with Calvinism and Platonism in this instance is to mine both systems for a vocabulary to describe the indescribable. Here, despite what is often described as the more measured approach of *Billy Budd* relative to his earlier works, Melville mixes systems syncretically with a level of confidence that surpasses the bravado of *Moby-Dick*. In Melville's earlier work, his syncretism announces itself with fanfare; here it is interwoven with the very fabric of his text. The concept of depravity is the crux of the matter here, and Melville's narrator leads his readers to and fro across the boundary between Calvinist theology, with its intimations of universal depravity, and Platonic philosophy, which defines depravity more narrowly. Here as elsewhere, taking seriously Melville's interest in Unitarian thought may be helpful. Melville is often regarded as either a sharp critic of religion generally or as an exponent of more rigorous forms of religion as opposed to the alleged laxity of more liberal forms like Unitarianism. There is a measure of truth in both perceptions, but here as elsewhere in Melville's corpus, it is necessary to keep in mind the degree to which the religious liberalism he criticizes often also assumes the role of Melville's own default stance.

What does it mean, after all, to place Calvinism and Platonism into interpretive dialogue with each other? On one level, this is characteristic of a vexed dialogue between Jerusalem and Athens that is built into the very structure of the New Testament, and of which Melville would have been aware as a result of the efforts of nineteenth-century historical criticism of the Bible. The patristic writer Tertullian tried to separate Greek philosophy and Christian theology with his famous aphorism, "What has Athens to do with Jerusalem?" but from the Gospel of John to Saint Augustine of Hippo, Platonism was inextricably connected to Christian thought, and where Platonism lost some of its hold on Christian thought during the Middle Ages, it was pushed aside by another influence from Athens, that of Aristotle.[13] Dante, whom Melville read and annotated, makes the intellectuals of classical antiquity a major portion of the figures he classes as virtuous pagans in *The Divine Comedy*.[14] Perhaps even more tellingly, in Melville's copy of the New Testament, passages which refer to specific Greek philosophers are scored and annotated, and there are similar invocations of philosophy in his marginalia to the Apocrypha. What this suggests is Melville's interest in the syncretism internal to Christianity itself, and when he gives his narrator in *Billy Budd* an extended discussion of depravity in relation to contrasting Platonic and Calvinist concepts, Melville is by no means unaware of the genealogy by which Calvinism can be seen as an offspring of Platonism, most specifically through the admiration of Calvin for the Augustinian heritage that was one of the aspects of the Catholic tradition that Calvin retained, however much of medieval Catholicism Calvin rejected.

The figure who mediates among Calvinism and Platonism, liberalism and martial law, is the commander of Billy's ship and the judge in Billy's trial, Captain Vere. For Vere at sea, there can be no absolute distinction between Jerusalem, Athens, and even Newgate (the site of public executions in eighteenth-century England). He must balance the theological demands of Christian charity with the ethical demands of philosophy, and his mandate as a captain at sea in a time of war insists that neither can preempt the brutal realities of martial law in a time of extreme danger. Vere argues in his judgment of Billy that the moral and ethical teachings of Christianity, and indeed of the various world religions that Melville invokes in *Billy Budd* and elsewhere, cannot apply at sea in a time of martial law.

Captain Vere is a truly marvelous character, and ranks with Ishmael and Bartleby as the finest that Melville ever created. He is distinct from both, in that unlike the taciturn Bartleby, he is voluble, and unlike Ishmael, who often presents us with an alter ego for Melville himself, he is a truly independent character, and cannot be presumed at any time to be speaking for Melville. Vere shares with Captain Ahab and the Jesus of the quotation from Goethe that Melville copied onto the inside cover of his copy of *The New Testament and Psalms* a determined independence that can only be described as godlike. At the same time, Vere presents us with the image of a man wrestling with his conscience out loud, thinking through the fundamental moral as well as legal issues posed by Billy Budd's trial, and blending a variety of philosophical and religious approaches to truth and justice as he does so. When Vere considers Billy's crime, he draws on a variety of legal and moral sources, and what is most noteworthy is the manner in which he dispenses with moral arguments that transcend the law. We find a particularly bitter irony here, then: "Starry Vere," the man of thought and of spiritual and intellectual aspiration in the novella, has thought his way out of these very aspirations. Vere presents us with the special danger of the intellect when it becomes corrosive with regard to the moral and ethical demands of a shared humanity, but subservient to the particularized demands of duty in one time, place, and nationality.

Those who dismiss Vere as acting in bad faith miss the point, I believe, as do those who accept the narrator's portrait of Vere as wholly admirable and godlike. Vere is actually something much more interesting than either of these opposed visions: he is the human being who experiences the freedom of uncertainty, but who ultimately finds himself bound by that same uncertainty. As admirable as Vere's intellectual courage is, virtually everyone else on the *Bellipotent* comes to a conclusion that is more intuitively just and more in keeping with visceral human standards of decency. The paradox of Captain Vere is that he is driven by the remorseless logic of his social position to rule his own most worthy characteristics to be irrelevant to the administration of justice. Captain Vere is a good man who is forced to remorselessly suppress his own goodness, a saint who cannot but sin in the most absolute terms by putting to death, with his own full knowledge, an innocent man whom he loves as a son.

The thematic centrality of uncertainty in *Billy Budd* is highlighted by the report at the end of the narrative, and the report highlights these themes in ways that complement the treatment of uncertainty in the representation of Captain Vere. Melville's reader has a clear sense of the relative moral status of Billy and Claggart: Claggart however ambiguous in other respects, is unambiguously depraved, and Billy is simply innocent, regardless of his legal guilt in the case of Claggart's death. The report, however, states with pompous certainty the absolute reverse of everything the reader knows. Billy is manifestly a criminal, Claggart a hero, and Vere an agent of rightfully vengeful justice. The opposition between truth and legality, and the certainty that no one who does not have an inside narrative can truly understand the truth of the matter highlights just how complex Melville's sense of uncertainty is. Truth is not unknowable in *Billy Budd*, but its distortion seems like a virtual inevitability.

The report's uncertainty (or misguided air of certainty) is not strictly religious, but it does correspond in fruitful ways with the reports that undergird the teachings of various religions. When we read the conclusion of *Billy Budd*, we have before us a seemingly definitive statement of truth that is undermined by the entire "inside narrative" we have just read. One of the most liturgically and doctrinally important passages from the book of Isaiah from a Christian theological perspective begins "Who hath believed our report, and to whom hath the arm of the Lord been revealed?" (Isaiah 53.1). Melville echoed the plaintive tone of this passage in his early letters to Hawthorne during the writing of *Moby-Dick*, writing:

> But Truth is the silliest thing under the sun. Try to get a living by the Truth—and go to the soup societies. Heavens! Let any clergyman try to preach the truth from its very stronghold, the pulpit, and they would ride him out of his church on his own pulpit bannister. It cannot be doubted that all Reformers are bottomed on the truth, more or less, and to the world at large are not reformers almost universally laughing-stocks? (*Corres.* 191)

The enormous gap between received opinion and the truth had obsessed Melville throughout his entire career as a writer, and the report in the concluding pages of *Billy Budd* represents a highly concentrated treatment of this characteristic Melvillean theme. Ultimately, the newspaper reports that demonize Billy and sanctify Claggart serve to highlight the elusiveness of truth: whatever report one receives may be deceptive, and the truth itself may appear incredible. This takes us back to Melville's foundational and career-long obsession with religious difference in a way that keeps religious difference from appearing as a mere abstraction outside the self, but rather highlights the idea that uncertainty is at the heart of human selfhood.

Using religious difference as our model for understanding *Billy Budd* also opens up a consideration of the intersection of two perennial strands of inquiry in relation to Melville's last major prose work: the theological approach taken by a large number of critics in the 1930s, 1940s, and

1950s, and the legal studies approach taken by scholars from the late 1960s to the present.[15] For Melville, the "Law" is never to be understood without some shade of the term's theological resonances, and theology cannot escape the suspicion that it is an insubstantial projection of a human will for order and predictability. Thus, Captain Vere's law and that of the "Clerk of the Weather" from "Pebbles" are not so distant from each other. If human and divine law are both indistinguishable (or at the least barely distinguishable) from the content of human wishes, the human intellectual, spiritual, and moral experience is vertiginous indeed, and our quest for solidity in matters of conscience is as unspeakably precarious as Melville suggests in passages ranging from "The Whiteness of the Whale" in *Moby-Dick* to the poem "The Apparition" in *Battle-Pieces*.

Students of law and students of theology have found much to comment on in *Billy Budd* but they have too often failed to speak to one another. The intersection of the two in *Billy Budd* is particularly rich, however. Melville's critique of the law in *Billy Budd* is driven by the failure of the laws made by human societies to square with the deepest moral and ethical intuitions of those same societies. His critique of Christian doctrine and the biblical text is driven by a similar doubt about the larger shape of the Christian religion and its practices and institutions to live up to the most profound moral insights from which Christianity was a vessel. The discussion of legal discourse in *Billy Budd* is thus intimately linked to Melville's encounter with religious difference, and it seems that the interpenetration of these two elements in his thought provide extensive possibilities for ongoing inquiry.

What then, is Melville's final testament in *Billy Budd* and the later poetry? The early days of scholarship on Melville's posthumous novella found scholars divided on the question of how *Billy Budd* in particular might function as a last will and testament for Melville, with some arguing that it formed at last an affirmative "testament of acceptance" and others arguing that it seemed to be more like a testament of "resistance" or of "irony."[16] Others resisted the idea that *Billy Budd* could by itself form a final testament at all and instead located Melville's final bequest in his unpublished poetry. One of the most persuasive suggestions on this score came in 1969 from John T. Frederick, who suggested that Melville's little known and little discussed poem "Pontoosuce" (which is discussed above, however, in relation to its valedictory tone and its orientation toward immortality and evanescence) is in fact the clearest statement of Melville's final attitude toward all the matters that obsessed him throughout his career.[17] This satisfies me to a degree, but it seems to miss something of the unfinished state of Melville's thought at the time of his death. When Melville went to sleep for the final time, *Billy Budd* was not completed, and indeed it never will be completed in a finally authorized form, however much we owe to the heroic efforts of scholars like Raymond Weaver, Harrison Hayford, and Merton Sealts in recovering it. *Weeds and Wildings, with a Rose or Two* was as yet unpublished, as were many of Melville's most fascinating later poems, "Pontoosuce" not excluded. Rather than speaking of final testaments, it seems more prudent to conclude that Melville died intestate—his legacy endlessly fertile because its contradictions remained unresolved, and endlessly suggestive because of his continual impulse toward resolution.

In his most famous letter to Hawthorne, Melville asked, "Lord, when shall we be done growing?" The implied answer, of course, is "never," and Melville's last works make it clear that he was not wrong on this score, in particular with regard to himself. We do Melville, and ourselves, a disservice if we do not acknowledge the consistent growth and change, both as an artist and as a religious thinker, that always appears in his work. It may be satisfying to our own preferences to create a mental snapshot of Melville as a proto-atheist, or an early agnostic, or a Christian longing for the capacity for belief, or a kind of anonymous Buddhist or Hindu or Muslim or Zoroastrian or Jew, or as a kind of postmodern pagan, or as a modern-day Stoic, or as a sybaritic Epicurean; as a Reformed Protestant, or a crypto-Catholic, or (perhaps most accurately) as an ambivalent Unitarian; but ultimately Melville is all of those conflicting things and none. When we try to pin him down, he eludes us, maintaining, like his own greatest characters (including a certain whale), his fundamental inscrutability to the last. We are unable to catch him because he does not mean to be caught, nor does he believe that human nature lends itself to such facile categorization. In the famous passage from *Moby-Dick* where Ahab (or Ishmael; the scholarly jury is still out) reflects on the progression of human existence, it is worth noting that even "manhood's pondering repose of If" is but a temporary way station. Boyhood's faith and adolescent doubt may yet return for those who have seemingly attained repose, and ultimately no certainty and no uncertainty is ever truly final. In this sense, Melville's most representative statement of a final "testament" may have appeared neither in *Billy Budd* nor even in the last poems in *Timoleon* and his unpublished manuscripts, but in the seven-poem sequence "Pebbles" at the end of *John Marr and Other Sailors*: the wisdom that Melville imparts is precisely that of the pintado and the gannet: the winds, conceived as natural process, metaphor for the spirit, and some combination of both, "blow whither they list." To one degree or another, all of Melville's late work, *Billy Budd* included, reprises this theme, leaving us with a testament that casts doubt on the very act of searching for a testament and equal doubt on the possibility of abandoning the search.

What Melville leaves us with, then, is the "sacred uncertainty" that he described with such muted eloquence in the prose "Supplement" to *Battle-Pieces*, and we continue, patiently, to excavate his literary remains because the uncertainty that haunted and elevated him haunts and elevates us too. In one of the most stirring passages of *Moby-Dick*, Ishmael reflects on the glories and terrors of incompleteness:

> But now I leave my cetological System standing thus unfinished, even as the great Cathedral of Cologne was left, with the crane still standing on the top of the uncompleted tower. For small erections may be finished by their first architects; grand ones, true ones, ever leave the copestone to posterity. God keep me from ever completing anything. This whole book is but a draught—nay, but the draught of a draught. Oh, Time, Strength, Cash, and Patience! (*M-D* 145)

Ishmael's plea for "time, strength, cash, and patience" rings with special pathos in light of Melville's last push to finish *Billy Budd*. Here, however, Ishmael, and behind him Melville's authorial persona, refer not to the valedictory drafting of *Billy Budd*, but to the great artistic triumph of Melville's youth. The glory of *Moby-Dick*, Ishmael suggests, is precisely its quality of being a work seemingly in progress, after its publication, and by now, long after its author's death. The cathedral at Cologne in the mid-nineteenth century provided a view of astonishing and unfinished grandeur: it was a monument that stunned and dazzled its viewers, and the fact that it still remained under construction until 1880 after centuries only meant that it could not be contained within the scope of its own time of construction.[18] If necessity left some of Melville's last works in an unfinished state, leaving the copestone for the scholars who recovered his work in the 1920s and the family members who preserved it, in a broader sense, all of Melville's work shares a level of aspiration that exceeds its own formal existence.

Touchingly, in one of his final letters, Melville revisited the matter of incompleteness again, writing to Archibald MacMechan, a Canadian professor of English who was one of the very first academic admirers of *Moby-Dick*, that "I have latterly come into possession of unobstructed leisure, but only just as, in the course of nature, my vigor sensibly declines. What little of it is left, I husband for certain matters as yet incomplete, and which indeed may never be completed" (*Corres.* 519). Melville thus declined an opportunity to consolidate the reputation of already completed work in order to allow for more labor on work that remained incomplete. This choice seems full of meaning for our summation of Melville's career and his effect upon his readers. The age of faiths and doubts of which Melville was an early and formidable critic, prophet, and poet, continues, incomplete and uncompletable, and like the cathedral of Cologne and Melville's own literary labors, we revel and lament in its, and our, incompletion.

NOTES

Introduction

1. For a narrative of Melville's work on and near publication of *Poems*, see Hershel Parker, *Melville: The Making of the Poet* (Evanston, Ill.: Northwestern University Press, 2007), 6–7.

2. "Portrait of Herman Melville," Joseph Oriel Eaton, 1870.

3. Jacques Derrida, *Writing and Difference*, trans. Alan Bass (Chicago: University of Chicago Press, 1978).

4. M. H. Abrams, *Natural Supernaturalism: Tradition and Revolution in Romantic Literature* (New York: W. W. Norton, 1973), 12.

5. William James, *The Will to Believe* (1896), in *Writings, 1878–1899* (New York: Library of America, 1992).

Chapter 1

1. The most important work on Melville's reading, sources, and marginalia has been carried out by Merton M. Sealts in *Melville's Reading* (Madison: University of Wisconsin Press, 1966; rev. and enlarged ed., Columbia: University of South Carolina Press, 1988); Mary K. Bercaw Edwards in *Melville's Sources* (Evanston, Ill.: Northwestern University Press, 1987); Wilson Walker Cowen in *Melville's Marginalia* (dissertation, Harvard University, 1965; New York: Garland, 1987); Steven Olsen-Smith, Peter Norberg, and Dennis C. Marnon in *Melville's Marginalia Online*, http://melvillesmarginalia.org; Gail S. Coffler in *Melville's Allusions to Religion* (New York: Praeger, 2004) and *Melville's Classical Allusions* (Westport, Conn.: Greenwood, 1985); Robin Grey in *Melville & Milton* (Pittsburgh: Duquesne University Press, 2004); and Jay Leyda in *The Melville Log*, 2 vols. (New York: Harcourt, 1951).

2. Leyda, *The Melville Log*, 1:273.

3. Brian Foley, "Herman Melville and the Example of Sir Thomas Browne," *Modern Philology* 81, no. 3 (1984): 265–77.

4. F. O. Matthiessen, *American Renaissance: Art and Expression in the Age of Emerson and Whitman* (New York: Oxford University Press, 1941); John Wenke, *Melville's Muse: Literary Creation and the Forms of Philosophical Fiction* (Kent, Ohio: Kent State University Press), 18.

5. Sir Thomas Browne, *Religio Medici and Urne-Buriall*, ed. Stephen Greenblatt and Ramie Targoff (New York: New York Review of Books, 2012), 10.

6. Browne, *Religio Medici*, 7.

7. My treatment of the marginalia here draws on my work on the introduction and notes to a new edition of Melville's marginalia in *The New Testament of our Lord and Saviour Jesus Christ: Translated out of the Original Greek; and . . . The Book of Psalms, Translated out of the Original Hebrew* (New York: American Bible Society, 1844). The introduction has appeared, and the notes are to appear at *Melville's Marginalia Online*, ed. Steven Olsen-Smith, Peter Norberg, and

Dennis C. Marnon. *Melville's Marginalia Online* will ultimately be the definitive venue for viewing and citing published versions of Melville's marginalia; for materials not yet available there, I have made use of Cowen's *Melville's Marginalia*; Mark Heidmann's revisions to Cowen's transcription (in "The Markings in Melville's Bibles," *Studies in the American Renaissance* [1990]: 342), and my own consultation of the New Testament volume, AC85.M4977.Zz844b, by permission of Houghton Library. Portions of this chapter were previously published as "One's Own Faith: Melville's Reading of *The New Testament and Psalms*" in *Leviathan* (2008).

8. For discussions of Melville's religious thought, see Jonathan Cook, *Inscrutable Malice: Theodicy, Eschatology, and the Biblical Sources of Moby-Dick* (Dekalb: Northern Illinois University Press, 2012); Bradley Johnson, *The Characteristic Theology of Herman Melville: Aesthetic, Politics, Duplicity* (London: Wipf and Stock, 2011); Ilana Pardes, *Melville's Bibles* (Berkeley: University of California Press, 2008); Walter D. Kring, *Herman Melville's Religious Journey* (Pentland, N.C.: Pentland, 1998); T. Walter Herbert, *Moby-Dick and Calvinism: A World Dismantled* (New Brunswick, N.J.: Rutgers University Press, 1977); Lawrence Buell, "Moby-Dick as Sacred Text," in *New Essays on Moby-Dick*, ed. Richard Brodhead (New York: Cambridge University Press, 1986); James Duban, *Melville's Major Fiction: Politics, Theology and Imagination* (Dekalb: Northern Illinois University Press, 1983); Lawrance Thompson, *Melville's Quarrel with God* (Princeton, N.J.: Princeton University Press, 1952); William Braswell, *Melville's Religious Thought* (Durham, N.C.: Duke University Press, 1943); Joseph Knapp, *Tortured Synthesis: The Meaning of Herman Melville's* Clarel (New York: Philosophical Library, 1971); Ronald Mason, *The Spirit above the Dust* (New York: Appel, 1951); Vincent Kenny, *Herman Melville's Clarel: A Spiritual Autobiography* (New York: Archon, 1973); Stan Goldman, *Melville's Protest Theism: The Hidden and Silent God in Clarel* (Dekalb: Northern Illinois University Press, 1993); Alfred Kazin, *God and the American Writer* (New York: Knopf, 1997); Jenny Franchot, "Melville's Traveling God," in *The Cambridge Companion to Herman Melville*, ed. Robert S. Levine (New York: Cambridge University Press, 1998); and William Potter, *Melville's Clarel and the Intersympathy of Creeds* (Kent, Ohio: Kent State University Press, 2005). For more broadly philosophical approaches, see Paul Brodtkorb, *Ishmael's White World: A Phenomenological Reading of Moby-Dick* (New Haven, Conn.: Yale University Press, 1965); Merton M. Sealts, *Pursuing Melville:1940–1980* (Madison: University of Wisconsin Press, 1982); Harrison Hayford, *Melville's Prisoners* (Evanston, Ill.: Northwestern University Press, 2003); Bainard Cowan, *Exiled Waters: Moby-Dick and the Crisis of Allegory* (Baton Rouge: Louisiana State University Press, 1982); Robert Zoellner, *Salt-Sea Mastodon: A Reading of Moby-Dick* (Berkeley: University of California Press,1973); John Wenke, *Melville's Muse: Literary Creation and the Forms of Philosophical Fiction* (Kent, Ohio: Kent State University Press, 1995); and Charles Olson, *Call Me Ishmael* (Reynal, 1947). William Dillingham's career as a Melvillean is spanned by four books that also touch extensively on Melville's position in intellectual history: *An Artist in the Rigging: The Early Work of Herman Melville* (Athens: University of Georgia Press, 1972); *Melville's Short Fiction, 1853–1856* (Athens: University of Georgia Press, 1977); *Melville's Later Novels* (Athens: University of Georgia Press, 1986); and *Melville & His Circle:*

The Last Years (Athens: University of Georgia Press, 1996). Most recently, Dawn Coleman's *Preaching and the Rise of the American Novel* (Columbus: Ohio State University Press, 2013) places Melville in the context of the nineteenth-century American sermon, and Martin Kevorkian's *Writing beyond Prophecy: Emerson, Hawthorne, and Melville after the American Renaissance* (Baton Rouge: Louisiana State University Press, 2013) attends to the religious aspects of Melville's later work. John Lardas Modern's *Secularism in Antebellum America* (Chicago: University of Chicago Press, 2011) relies heavily on a reading of *Moby-Dick*.

9. James Duban, "'Visible Objects of Reverence': Quotations from Goethe in Melville's Annotated *New Testament*," *Leviathan: A Journal of Melville Studies* 9, no. 2 (June 2007): 1–23; Clare Spark, *Hunting Captain Ahab: Psychological Warfare and the Melville Revival*, 2nd ed. (Kent, Ohio: Kent State University Press, 2006.)

10. See Sacvan Bercovitch, *The American Jeremiad* (Madison: University of Wisconsin Press, 1978); and Emory Elliott, "Art, Religion, and the Problem of Authority in *Pierre*," in *Ideology and Classic American Literature* (New York: Cambridge University Press, 1988) for influential discussions of Plinlimmon's pamphlet.

11. Nathalia Wright, *Melville's Use of the Bible* (Durham, N.C.: Duke University Press, 1949); Mark Heidmann, "The Markings in Melville's Bibles," *Studies in the American Renaissance* (1990): 34–98.

12. Duban, "'Visible Objects of Reverence,'" 1–23.

13. William Ellery Channing, "Likeness to God," in *Transcendentalism: A Reader*, ed. Joel Myerson (New York: Oxford University Press, 2000), 3–20; Ralph Waldo Emerson, *The Divinity School Address*, in Myerson, 230–45.

14. For more on Melville and Milton, see Robin Grey's *Melville & Milton* (Pittsburgh: Duquesne University Press, 2004). See also Henry Pommer, *Milton and Melville* (Pittsburgh: University of Pittsburgh Press, 1950).

15. Grey, *Melville & Milton*, 119.

16. Ibid., 121

17. Ibid., 122

18. Ibid., 127

19. Ibid., 158

20. Ibid., 145

21. For Melville and English and German romanticism, see Leon Chai, *The Romantic Foundations of the American Renaissance* (Ithaca, N.Y.: Cornell University Press, 1987); and Jonathan Arac, *Commissioned Spirits: The Shaping of Social Motion in Dickens, Carlyle, Melville, and Hawthorne* (New York: Columbia University Press, 1979).

22. Henry David Thoreau, *Walden, Civil Disobedience, and Other Writings*, ed. John Rossi (New York: Norton, 2008), 76.

23. Melville biography has been a rich field from the start, and a few of these studies have been highly useful to me. The first full-length literary biography, and one with substantial religious overtones, was Raymond Weaver's *Herman Melville: Mariner and Mystic* (New York: Doran, 1921). Other landmarks that are still useful to revisit include Lewis Mumford, *Herman Melville: A Study of His Life and Vision*, rev. ed. (New York: Harcourt, 1962); Leon Howard, *Herman Melville: A Biography* (Berkeley: University of California Press, 1951); and Newton

Arvin, *Herman Melville* (New York: Sloane, 1950). Jay Leyda's *The Melville Log* (1950) remains an essential source of information about Melville's day-to-day activities and artistic development, and the expanded version on which Hershel Parker has been laboring for many years is eagerly anticipated. The definitive Melville biography at present is Hershel Parker's two-volume *Herman Melville: A Biography* (Baltimore: Johns Hopkins University Press, 1996; 2004). Andrew Delbanco's *Melville: His World and Work* (New York: Knopf, 2005) is helpful in relation to the intersection of religion, art, and American culture in Melville's work. Several books that are not biographies strictly speaking but also range broadly across the scope of Melville's work are Warner Berthoff's *The Example of Melville* (Princeton, N.J.: Princeton University Press, 1962) and Milton R. Stern's *The Fine Hammered Steel of Herman Melville* (Urbana-Champaign: University of Illinois Press, 1957). The most substantial work on Melville's reading and sources appears in Mary K. Bercaw's *Melville's Sources* (1987) and Merton M. Sealts's *Melville's Reading* (1966, rev. and expanded, 1988). Sealts and Steven Olsen-Smith published a cumulative supplement in *Leviathan* in 2004.

Chapter 2

1. For the history of nineteenth-century American evangelicalism and revivalism, see Nathan O. Hatch, *The Democratization of American Christianity* (New Haven, Conn.: Yale University Press, 1988); and Mark Noll, *America's God: From Jonathan Edwards to Abraham Lincoln* (New York: Oxford University Press, 2002). For nineteenth-century missionary networks, see Ian R. Tyrrell, *Reforming the World: The Creation of America's Moral Empire* (Princeton, N.J.: Princeton University Press, 2010).

2. For the history of the Transcendentalist encounter with Asian religion and philosophy, see Carl T. Jackson, *The Oriental Religions and American Thought* (Westport, Conn.: Greenwood, 1981); Arthur Versluis, *American Transcendentalism and Asian Religions* (New York: Oxford University Press, 1993) and *The Esoteric Origins of the American Renaissance* (New York: Oxford University Press, 2001); Malini Johar Schueller, *U.S. Orientalisms: Race, Nation, Gender in Literature, 1790–1890* (Ann Arbor: University of Michigan Press, 1998).

3. For discussions of the early novels and of Melville and the Pacific more generally, see T. Walter Herbert, *Marquesan Encounters: Melville and the Meaning of Civilization* (Cambridge, Mass.: Harvard University Press, 1980); Jill Barnum, Wyn Kelley, and Christopher Sten, eds., *"Whole Oceans Away": Melville and the Pacific* (Kent, Ohio: Kent State University Press, 2007); Alex Calder, "The Thrice Mysterious Taboo," *Representations* 67 (1999): 27–43; Juniper Ellis, "Melville Literary Cartographies of the South Seas," *Massachusetts Review: A Quarterly of Literature, the Arts and Public Affairs* 38, no. 1 (1997): 9–29; and Paul Lyons, *American Pacificism* (New York: Routledge, 2008). For the classic treatment of this element in Melville's career, see Charles R. Anderson, *Melville in the South Seas* (New York: Columbia University Press, 1939).

4. Titus Coan, *Life in Hawaii: An Autobiographic Sketch of Missions Life and Labors* (Honolulu, 1882), 100.

5. Anderson, *Melville in the South Seas*; David Porter, *Journal of a cruize made to the Pacific Ocean by Captain David Porter, in the United States frigate Essex, in the years 1812, 1813, and 1814: Containing descriptions of the Cape de*

Verd Islands, coasts of Brazil, Patagonia, Chili, and Peru, and of the Gallapagos Islands: Also, a full account of the Washington groupe of islands, the manners, customs, and dress of the inhabitants, &c. &c.: Illustrated with fourteen engravings, in two volumes (New York: Bradford and Inskeep, 1815); C. S. Stewart, *Journal of a Residence in the Sandwich Islands during the years 1823, 1824, and 1825: Including descriptions of the natural scenery, and remarks on . . . to the great volcano of Kirauea in Hawaii* (London, 1828); William J. Ellis, *Polynesian Researches during a Residence of Nearly Six Years in the South Sea Islands* (1829; reprint ed. New York: Cambridge University Press, 2013).

6. Rufus Wilmot Griswold, "The Heroism of the Knights Errant and of the Female Missionaries of North America," *Godey's Ladies Book*, vol. 37 (1848): 61–69; Miron Winslow, *A Memoir of Mrs. Harriet L. Winslow: Thirteen Years a Member of the American Mission in Ceylon* (New York: American Tract Society, 1840); Leonard Wood, *A Sermon Preached at Haverhill (Mass.) in Remembrance of Mrs. Harriet Newell, Wife of Rev. Samuel Newell, Missionary in India, who died at the Isle of France, November 30, 1812, To which are appended Memoirs of Her Life (*Boston: Samuel T. Armstrong, 1814).

7. See Lesslie Newbigin, *Foolishness to the Greeks: The Gospel and Western Culture* (Grand Rapids, Mich.: William B. Eerdman's, 1986) for an outline of this turn in missiology.

8. Walt Whitman, *Song of Myself*, in *Walt Whitman: Poetry and Prose*, ed. Justin Kaplan (New York: Library of America, 1982); Thoreau, *Walden.*

9. See Ann Radcliffe, *The Italian* (Oxford: Oxford World Classics, 2008), for an example of the use of cathedrals in the English Gothic tradition.

10. See Brian Higgins and Hershel Parker, *Herman Melville: The Contemporary Reviews* (New York: Cambridge University Press, 1995), for examples of sharply critical reviews of Melville's early novels in the missionary press.

11. Henry T. Cheever, *Life in the Sandwich Islands, or, The Heart of the Pacific, as it was and is* (London: Richard Bentley, 1851); Howard, *Herman Melville, A Biography.*

12. For a recent treatment of the history of the American Board of Commissioners for Foreign Missions, see Tyrrell, *Reforming the World.*

13. Coan, *Life in Hawaii*, 199–200.

14. Parker, *Herman Melville: A Biography*, 2:397.

15. For Titus Coan's connection with Finney, see Coan, *Life in Hawaii*, 49.

16. Charles Grandison Finney, *Memoirs of Rev. Charles G. Finney, Written by Himself* (New York: Fleming H. Revell, 1876), 20.

17. The most extensive critical discussion of *Mardi* is Merrell Davis's *Mardi: A Chartless Voyage* (New Haven, Conn.: Yale University Press, 1949). For *Redburn*, see William Gilman's *Melville's Early Life and Redburn* (New York: New York University Press, 1951). For source material on *White-Jacket*, see Howard P. Vincent, *The Tailoring of Melville's White-Jacket* (Evanston, Ill.: Northwestern University Press, 1970). For the sources of *Moby-Dick*, see Howard P. Vincent, *The Trying-Out of Moby-Dick* (Carbondale: Southern Illinois University Press, 1965).

18. On Melville and Islam, see Timothy Marr, *The Cultural Roots of American Islamicism* (New York: Cambridge University Press, 2006); Schueller, *U.S. Orientalisms*; Brian Yothers, *The Romance of the Holy Land in American Travel*

Writing, 1790–1876 (Burlington, Vt.: Ashgate, 2007); Hilton Obenzinger, *American Palestine: Melville, Mark Twain, and the Holy Land Mania* (Princeton, N.J.: Princeton University Press, 1999).

19. H. Bruce Franklin, *The Wake of the Gods: Melville's Mythology* (Palo Alto, Calif.: Stanford University Press, 1963); Vincent, *The Trying-Out of Moby-Dick*.

20. Robert Knox, *An Historical Relation of Ceylon* (1681), 3rd rpt. edition, ed. S. D. Saparamadu (Dehiwala, Sri Lanka: Tisara Prakasakayo, 1981).

21. Walt Whitman, "Out of the Cradle Endlessly Rocking," in *Walt Whitman: Poetry and Prose*, ed. Justin Kaplan (New York: Library of America, 1982).

22. H. B. Kulkarni, *Moby-Dick, A Hindu Avatar: A Study of Hindu Myth and Thought in Moby-Dick* (Logan: Utah State University Press, 1970).

23. Franklin, *The Wake of the Gods: Melville's Mythology*.

24. Christopher Sten uses this passage in both the title and the epigraph of his intricate study of Melville as a novelist, *The Weaver-God, He Weaves: Melville and the Poetics of the Novel* (Kent, Ohio: Kent State University Press, 1996). For a particularly useful reading of the passage in the context of Melville's wide use of the body of the whale and the scientific discourse of the period, see Samuel Otter, *Melville's Anatomies* (Berkeley: University of California Press, 1999), 156–58.

25. Ralph Waldo Emerson, "The Over-Soul," in *Emerson: Selected Essays*, ed. Larzer Ziff (New York: Penguin, 1982).

26. Dorothee Metlitsky Finkelstein, *Melville's Orienda* (New Haven, Conn.: Yale University Press, 1961).

27. Cyrus R. K. Patell has addressed the issue of Fedallah's Zoroastrianism in his essay "Cosmopolitanism and Zoroastrianism in *Moby-Dick*," in *The Turn around Religion in America: Literature, Culture, and the Work of Sacvan Bercovitch*, ed. Nan Goodman and Michael P. Kramer (Burlington, Vt.: Ashgate, 2006, 19–36).

28. William Braswell, *Melville's Religious Thought: An Essay in Interpretation* (Durham, N.C.: Duke University Press, 1943).

29. For a much more extensive, and very insightful, reading of Fleece's sermon, see Cook, *Inscrutable Malice*, 167–76.

30. Thoreau, *Walden*, 218.

Chapter 3

1. John Evans, *Evans' Sketch of the Christian Denomination*, ed. James Aikman (Edinburgh: Peter Brown, 1837), 275–76.

2. For an extended interpretation of *Pierre*, see Hershel Parker and Brian Higgins, *Reading Melville's Pierre, or the Ambiguities* (Baton Rouge: Louisiana State University Press, 2007).

3. For more on the religious ferment in early nineteenth-century New York, see Hatch, *The Democratization of American Christianity*; and Daniel Walker Howe, *What Hath God Wrought: The Transformation of America, 1815–1848* (New York: Oxford University Press, 2007).

4. Parker, *Herman Melville: A Biography*, 1:350.

5. Ibid., 2:53–69.

6. For recent critical discussions of *Israel Potter*, see Robert S. Levine, "The Revolutionary Aesthetics of *Israel Potter*," in *Melville and Aesthetics*, ed. Samuel Otter and Geoffrey Sanborn (Basingstoke, Eng.: Palgrave, 2011); and Edgar Dryden, *Monumental Melville* (Palo Alto, Calif.: Stanford University Press, 2005).

7. For a recent critical discussion of "The Piazza," see Peter Balaam, "'Piazza to the North': Melville Reading Sedgwick," in *Melville and Women*, ed. Haskell Springer and Elizabeth Schultz (Kent, Ohio: Kent State University Press, 2006).

8. For religiously or philosophically oriented discussions of Bartleby, see Branka Arsic, *Passive Constitutions: 7½ Times Bartleby* (Palo Alto, Calif.: Stanford University Press, 2007); and Franklin, *The Wake of the Gods*. For a useful and critical survey of Bartleby scholarship through the late 1980s, see Dan McCall, *The Silence of Bartleby* (Ithaca, N.Y.: Cornell University Press, 1989).

9. For extended discussions of *Benito Cereno*, see Eric Sundquist, "*Benito Cereno* and New World Slavery," in *Reconstructing American Literary History*, ed. Sacvan Bercovitch (Cambridge, Mass.: Harvard University Press, 1986); Carolyn Karcher, *Shadow over the Promised Land: Slavery, Race, and Violence in Melville's America* (Baton Rouge: Louisiana State University Press, 1980); Andrew Delbanco, *Melville: His World and Work* (New York: Knopf, 2005); Emily Miller Budick, *Engendering Romance: Women Writers and the Hawthorne Tradition, 1850–1990* (New Haven, Conn.: Yale University Press, 1994); and Greg Grandin, *The Empire of Necessity: Slavery, Freedom, and Deception in the New World* (New York: Metropolitan Books, 2014).

10. Jenny Franchot, *Roads to Rome: The Antebellum Protestant Encounter with Catholicism* (Berkeley: University of California Press, 1994).

11. On romantic racialism, see George Fredrickson, "Romantic Racialism" in Harriet Beecher Stowe, *Uncle Tom's Cabin, or, Life Among the Lowly*, 2nd Norton Critical Edition, ed. Elizabeth Ammons (New York: Norton, 2010). Stowe's *Uncle Tom's Cabin* serves as a leading example of the use of this tendency in nineteenth-century popular culture.

12. For more on Johannes Tetzel, see Heiko Oberman, *Luther: Man between God and the Devil* (New Haven, Conn.: Yale University Press, 2006), 187–90.

13. Merton M. Sealts reconstructed the lectures that Melville gave in the 1850s in his *Melville as Lecturer* (Cambridge, Mass.: Harvard University Press, 1957).

14. For Melville's treatment of Italy, see Dennis Berthold's magisterial *American Risorgimento: Herman Melville and the Cultural Politics of Italy* (Columbus: Ohio State University Press, 2009). For Melville's classical and religious allusions, see Coffler, *Melville's Classical Allusions* and *Melville's Allusions to Religion*.

15. The most significant book-length studies on *The Confidence-Man* are Tom Quirk, *Melville's Confidence Man: From Knave to Knight* (Columbia: University of Missouri Press, 1982); Jonathan A. Cook, *Satirical Apocalypse: An Anatomy of Melville's The Confidence-Man* (Westport, Conn.: Greenwood,1996); Edgar Dryden, *Melville's Thematics of Form: That Great Art of Telling the Truth* (Baltimore: Johns Hopkins University Press, 1967); and Franklin's *In the Wake of the Gods*. These are classics in the study of this novel, as is Elizabeth Foster's introduction to the Hendricks House edition of *The Confidence-Man*. John Bryant, *Melville and Repose: The Rhetoric of Humor in the American Renaissance* (New York: Oxford University Press, 1993), is especially strong on the use of humor in the novel and the ways in which Melville fits into nineteenth-century-American traditions of humor and storytelling.

16. Cook, *Satirical Apocalypse*, 12.

17. Merlin Bowen, *The Long Encounter: Self and Experience in the Writings of Herman Melville* (Chicago: University of Chicago Press, 1960), 257

18. Manco Capac is a central figure in Inca mythology. Franklin's *The Wake of the Gods* provides commentary on the role of this figure for *The Confidence-Man*. For more on his role in Inca religion and myth, see Paul Richard Steele, *Handbook of Inca Mythology* (New York: ABC-Clio, 2004).

19. Karl Rahner, *Theological Investigations*, vol. 6. (New York: Darton, Longman, and Todd, 1969). The concept of "anonymous Christianity" both allows for the salvation of non-Christians within a Christian theological framework and privileges Christianity as the truest kind of faith.

20. Elizabeth Foster, *The Confidence-Man: His Masquerade* (New York Hendricks House, 1949).

21. William James, *Pragmatism: A New Name for Some Old Ways of Thinking* (New York: Longmans, 1907), 38.

22. Hershel Parker's argument regarding the metaphysics of Indian-hating is found in the second Norton Critical Edition of *The Confidence-Man* that he coedited with Mark Niemayer (New York: W. W. Norton, 2005), 493–501.

23. For Carlyle on the Victorian ethic of work, see Thomas Carlyle, *Past and Present* (London: Chapman and Hall, 1843), 207–11.

24. Thoreau, *Walden*, 76.

25. Melville refers to the Book of Mormon and the Mormon church on two occasions in *The Confidence-Man*: in his catalog of passengers of the *Fidele* and in his account of the founding of the town of "New Jerusalem."

26. Cook, *Satirical Apocalypse*, 72.

27. Charles Taylor, *A Secular Age* (Cambridge, Mass.: Harvard University Press, 2007).

Chapter 4

1. Abraham Lincoln, "Second Inaugural Address," in *The Portable Abraham Lincoln*, ed. Andrew Delbanco (New York: Penguin, 2009).

2. For discussions of Melville in relation to the Civil War, see Stanton Garner, *The Civil War World of Herman Melville* (Lawrence: University of Kansas Press, 1993); Randall Fuller, *From Battlefields Rising: How the Civil War Transformed American Literature* (New York: Oxford University Press, 2011); and Daniel Aaron, *The Unwritten War: American Writers and the Civil War* (New York: Knopf, 1973). For a discussion of Melville's relation to pacifism, see Joyce Sparer Adler, *War in Melville's Imagination* (New York: New York University Press, 1981). For treatments of *Battle-Pieces*, see Helen Vendler, "Melville and the Lyric of History," *Southern Review* 35, no. 3 (1999): 579–94; Rosanna Warren, "Dark Knowledge: Melville's Poems of the Civil War," *Raritan: A Quarterly Review* 19, no. 1 (1999): 100–121; Faith Barrett, "'They Answered Him Aloud': Popular Voice and Nationalist Discourse in Melville's Battle-Pieces," *Leviathan: A Journal of Melville Studies* 9, no. 3 (2007): 35–49; and Cody Marrs, "A Wayward Art: Battle-Pieces and Melville's Poetic Turn," *American Literature: A Journal of Literary History, Criticism, and Bibliography* 82, no. 1 (2010): 91–119.

3. Parker, *Melville: The Making of the Poet.*

4. Garner, *The Civil War World of Herman Melville.*

5. David S. Reynolds, *John Brown, Abolitionist: The Man Who Killed Slavery, Sparked the Civil War, and Seeded Civil Rights* (New York: Knopf, 2006).

6. On Melville's Unionism, see Garner, *The Civil War World of Herman Melville*, 5.

7. On Nathaniel Hawthorne's "Chiefly about War Matters, by a Peaceable Man," see Brenda Wineapple, *Hawthorne: A Life* (New York: Random House, 2010), 348–54.

8. Garry Wills, *Lincoln at Gettysburg: The Words That Remade America* (New York: Simon and Schuster, 1992).

9. William Dean Howells, Review of *Battle-Pieces* in *The Atlantic Monthly*, February 1867, 252–53, in *Herman Melville: The Contemporary Reviews*, ed. Brian Higgins and Hershel Parker (New York: Cambridge University Press, 1995), 526.

10. Elizabeth Renker, "Melville the Realist Poet," in *The Blackwell Companion to Herman Melville*, ed. Wyn Kelley (Malden, Mass.: Blackwell, 2008), 482–96.

11. Vendler, "Melville and the Lyric of History"; Warren, "Dark Knowledge: Melville's Poems about the Civil War."

12. Edgar Allan Poe, "The Rationale of Verse," in *Edgar Allan Poe: Essays and Reviews*, ed. G. R. Thompson (New York: Library of America, 1984), 26–70.

13. On the identification of "man's foulest crime," see Garner, *The Civil War World of Herman Melville*, 61.

14. Thomas Carlyle, *Sartor Resartus* (1833), ed. Kerry McSweeney and Peter Sabor (New York: Oxford University Press, 2008). Carlyle's concept of the "everlasting yea" and the "everlasting nay" seem to be echoed in Melville's poem.

15. See Garner, *The Civil War World of Herman Melville*.

16. For more on the draft riots of 1863, see Garner, *The Civil War World of Herman Melville*, 276.

17. For discussions of ekphrasis in Melville's work, see Berthold, *American Risorgimento*; Robert K. Wallace, *Melville & Turner: Spheres of Love and Fright* (Athens: University of Georgia Press, 1992); the superb collection edited by Christopher Sten, *Savage Eye: Melville and the Visual Arts* (Kent, Ohio: Kent State University Press, 1991); and Douglas Robillard, *Melville and the Visual Arts: Ionian Form, Venetian Tint* (Kent, Ohio: Kent State University Press, 1997).

18. George Fredrickson, "Romantic Racialism," in the Norton Critical Edition of *Uncle Tom's Cabin*.

19. The family motif is a common one in nineteenth-century slave narratives and in abolitionist fiction: in addition to *Uncle Tom's Cabin*, see for example Harriet Jacobs, *Incidents in the Life of a Slave Girl*, ed. Frances Smith Foster and Nellie Y. McKay (1859; New York: W. W. Norton, 2000); Lydia Maria Child, *A Romance of the Republic*, 1867, ed. Dana Nelson (Lexington: University of Kentucky Press, 1997); and Solomon Northup, *Twelve Years a Slave* (1853; New York: Penguin, 2012).

20. Extended treatments of Melville and race include Samuel Otter and Robert S. Levine, *Frederick Douglass and Herman Melville: Essays in Relation* (Amherst: University of Massachusetts Press, 2008); Robert K. Wallace, *Douglass and Melville: Anchored Together in Neighborly Style* (New Bedford, Mass.: Spinner, 2005); Carolyn Karcher, *Shadow Over the Promised Land* (Baton Rouge: Louisiana State University Press, 1980); Sterling Stuckey, *African Culture and Melville's Art: The Creative Process in Benito Cereno and Moby-Dick* (New York: Oxford University

Press, 2009); and Eric Sundquist, *To Wake the Nations: Race in the Making of American Literature* (Cambridge, Mass.: Harvard University Press, 1993).

21. Thoreau, *Walden*, 39.

22. Edgar Allan Poe, "The Fall of the House of Usher," in *Edgar Allan Poe: Poetry and Tales*, ed. Patrick F. Quinn (New York: Library of America, 1984), 325–27.

23. Robert Southey, "The Lover's Rock," in *The Poetical Works of Robert Southey* (New York: D. Appleton, 1839).

24. Washington Irving, *The Alhambra, in The Works of Washington Irving* (Philadelphia: Lea and Blanchard, 1840).

25. See Jacobs, *Incidents in the Life of a Slave Girl*; Child, *A Romance of the Republic*; and Northup, *Twelve Years a Slave*.

26. James M. McPherson, *Battle-Cry of Freedom: The Civil War Era* (New York: Oxford University Press, 1988), 209.

Chapter 5

1. For Melville's acquisition of books in preparation for writing *Clarel*, see the "Historical and Critical Note" in the Northwestern Newberry Edition of *Clarel*. For further discussion of Clarel, see Samuel Otter, "How Clarel Works," in *A Companion to Herman Melville*, ed. Wyn Kelley, 467–81 (New York: Blackwell, 2005); Helen Vendler, "Desert Storm," review of *Clarel*, by Herman Melville, and *Journals*, by Herman Melville, *New Republic*, December 7, 1992, pp. 39–42; Walter Bezanson, "Historical and Critical Note" to the Northwestern-Newberry edition of *Clarel* (1991), itself a revision of his introduction to the 1960 Hendricks House edition of *Clarel*; Vincent Kenny, *Herman Melville's Clarel: A Spiritual Autobiography*; Stan Goldman, *Melville's Protest Theism: The Hidden, Silent Voice of God in Clarel* (Dekalb: Northern Illinois University Press, 1993); William Potter, *Melville's Clarel and the Intersympathy of Creeds*; Obenzinger, *American Palestine*; Yothers, *The Romance of the Holy Land*; Robert Milder, "Unworldly Yearners: Agnostic Spirituality in *Clarel*," in *Exiled Royalties: Melville and the Life We Imagine* (New York: Oxford University Press, 2006); Dryden, *Monumental Melville*; Kevorkian, *Writing beyond Prophecy*. Portions of this chapter were originally published in *Poe Studies* in 2006 as "Terrors of the Soul: Religious Pluralism, Cosmic Exaltation, and Epistemological Dread in Poe, Hawthorne, and Melville."

2. James Duban is one of a small number of Melville scholars to discuss Bellows's theology, writing about him briefly in *Melville's Major Fiction: Politics, Theology, and Imagination*. Forthcoming work on Bellows by Dawn Coleman promises to make Bellows a more standard part of the conversation on Melville and religion.

3. Ralph Waldo Emerson, "The American Scholar," in *Transcendentalism: A Reader*, ed. Joel Myerson (New York: Oxford University Press, 2000).

4. See Walter Kring and Jonathan S. Carey, "Two Discoveries Concerning Herman Melville," *Proceedings of the Massachusetts Historical Society* 87 (1975): 136–41.

5. For the discoveries regarding Bellows's plot to stage a kidnapping of Elizabeth Shaw Melville in order to help her extricate herself from her marriage, see Kring and Carey, "Two Discoveries Concerning Herman Melville."

6. For more on Bellows, see Henry Warner Bowden, *Dictionary of American Religious Biography* (Westport, Conn.: Greenwood, 1993), 46–47.

7. Parker, *Herman Melville: A Biography*, vols. 1 and 2; Leyda, *The Melville Log*. Parker is in the process of developing a digital version of *The Melville Log* that will be still more extensive than its print predecessors. What is clear from the massive biographical labors behind these volumes is that if Melville had been a regular churchgoer, we would know it by now.

8. Henry Whitney Bellows, *Restatements of Christian Doctrine, in Twenty-Five Sermons* (New York: American Unitarian Association, 1870), 8–9.

9. Ibid., 41.

10. Lydia Maria Child, *The Progress of Religious Ideas through Successive Ages*, vol. 1 (New York: C. S. Francis, 1855), 1.

11. The motto for Child's work is from James Russell Lowell's poem "God Sends His Teachers Unto Every Age," a frequently anthologized piece reprinted well after Child's own work, for example, in Robert Maynard Leonard, *The Pageant of English Poetry* (Oxford: Oxford University Press, 1911), 297.

12. Ralph Waldo Emerson, "Brahma" (1857), in *Emerson's Prose and Poetry*, ed. Joel Porte and Saundra Morris (New York: Norton, 2001), 464; Thoreau, *Walden*, 71.

13. Brownson, *Charles Elwood, or, The Infidel Converted.*

14. For more on Brownson's numerous conversions, see Arthur Schlesinger, *Orestes A. Brownson: A Pilgrim's Progress* (1939), reprint ed. (New York: Octagon, 1963).

15. Edgar Allan Poe, "Mesmeric Revelation" (1844), in *Works: Tales and Sketches, 1843–1849*, reprint ed. edited by Thomas Ollive Mabbott, Eleanor D. Kewer, and Maureen Cobb Mabbott (Urbana-Champaign: University of Illinois Press, 2000), 1033–34.

16. Ibid., 1034.

17. Edgar Allan Poe, *Eureka* (1848), in *Poetry, Tales, and Selected Essays*, ed. G. R. Thompson and Patrick Quinn (New York: Library of America, 1984), 1358.

18. See Hatch, *The Democratization of American Christianity.*

19. Nathaniel Hawthorne, "The Celestial Railroad" (1843), in *Hawthorne: Selected Tales and Sketches*, 3rd ed. (New York: Rinehart, 1970), 475.

20. Ibid., 485.

21. Schueller, *U.S. Orientalisms*, 128.

22. Edward Robinson, *Biblical Researches in Palestine* (London: John Murray, 1841); Bayard Taylor, *The Lands of the Saracen* (New York: Putnam, 1855).

23. William Potter, *Melville's Clarel and the Intersympathy of Creeds* (Dekalb: Northern Illinois University Press, 2004).

24. For more on Warder Cresson, see Hilton Obenzinger, *American Palestine* (1999); and Yothers, *The Romance of the Holy Land.*

25. For more on anti-Catholicism in the antebellum United States, see Franchot, *Roads to Rome* (1994); and Susan M. Griffin, *Anti-Catholicism in Nineteenth-Century Fiction* (New York: Cambridge University Press, 2004).

26. See Angela Conrad, *The Wayward Nun of Amherst* (New York: Garland, 2000), for a discussion of Emily Dickinson's interest in medieval Catholic women. See Joan Hedrick, *Harriet Beecher Stowe: A Life* (New York: Oxford University Press, 1994), for more on the complexities of Stowe's religious identifications.

27. Harold Frederic, *The Damnation of Theron Ware (*1892), ed. Clay Motley (New York: Barnes and Noble, 2006).

28. See Henry Adams, *Mont-Saint-Michel and Chartres* [1905] (Boston: Houghton Mifflin, 1933), for an example of this sort of treatment of Catholicism.

29. See Matthew Lewis, *The Monk* [1794] (New York: Oxford University Press, 2008) and Maria Monk, *Awful Disclosures of the Hotel Dieu Nunnery* [1836] (Hamden, Conn.: Archon, 1962), for British and American examples of hostile representations of Catholic clergy and nuns.

30. For an alternative reading of the Dominican as a figure for satire rather than as a figure who speaks for Melville, see Dennis Berthold, *American Risorgimento: Herman Melville and the Cultural Politics of Italy* (2009).

31. John Henry Newman, *Apologia Pro Vita Sua* [1865–66] (New York: Dover, 2005).

32. Graham Greene, *The Quiet American* (New York: Penguin, 1957).

33. Mark Twain, "To the Person Sitting in Darkness" [1901], in *The Portable Mark Twain*, ed. Tom Quirk (New York: Penguin, 2004), 491–508.

34. Harriet Beecher Stowe, *The Minister's Wooing* [1859], in *Harriet Beecher Stowe: Three Novels: Uncle Tom's Cabin, or, Life Among the Lowly; The Minister's Wooing; Oldtown Folks* (New York: Library of America, 1982).

35. Ibid., 744.

36. For influential readings of the epilogue, see Edgar Dryden, *Monumental Melville* (2005); Vincent Kenny, *Herman Melville's Clarel: A Spiritual Autobiograhy* (1973); and Hilton Obenzinger, *American Palestine* (1999). My own *The Romance of the Holy Land in American Travel Writing, 1790–1876* also takes up the matter of the epilogue.

37. For more on Melville's Episcopalian connection via his brother-in-law John Hoadley, see Parker, *Herman Melville: A Biography*, 2:94.

Chapter 6

1. For discussions of Melville's sexuality, see Robert K. Martin, *Hero, Captain, Stranger* (Chapel Hill: University of North Carolina Press, 1986); James Creech, *Closet Writing / Gay Reading: The Case of Melville's Pierre* (Chicago: University of Chicago Press, 1993); Caleb Crain, "Lovers of Human Flesh: Homosexuality and Cannibalism in Melville's Novels," *American Literature: A Journal of Literary History, Criticism, and Bibliography* 66, no. 1 (1994): 25–53; Jana Argersinger and Leland Person's collection, *Hawthorne and Melville: Writing a Relationship* (Athens: University of Georgia Press, 2008). For extended discussions of misogyny in Melville's work, see Cowen, *Melville's Marginalia*; and Elizabeth Renker, *Strike through the Mask: Herman Melville and the Scene of Writing* (Baltimore: Johns Hopkins University Press, 1995). For a response to these claims of misogyny, see Laurie Robertson-Lorant's essay "Melville and the Women in His Life" in *Melville and Women*, ed. Haskell Springer and Elizabeth Schultz (Kent, Ohio: Kent State University Press, 2006).

2. Kelley discusses this matter in "Out of the Breadbox: Eleanor Melville Metcalf and the Melville Legacy," *Leviathan* 13, no. 1 (2011), 21–33. For a broader set of discussions of Melville's often underestimated relationship to women's experience in the nineteenth century, see Elizabeth Schultz and Haskell S. Springer, eds., *Melville and Women* (Kent, Ohio: Kent State University Pres, 2006).

3. For Raymond Weaver's "long quietus" view, see his biography, *Herman Melville: Mariner and Mystic.*

4. The most extensive discussions of Melville's late poetry can be found in William Shurr, *The Mystery of Iniquity* (Lexington: University of Kentucky Press, 1972); William Bysshe Stein, *The Poetry of Melville's Late Years: Time, History, Myth, and Religion* (Albany: State University of New York Press, 1970); Dryden, *Monumental Melville*; and Robert Milder, *Exiled Royalties: Melville and the Life We Imagine* (New York: Oxford University Press, 2006). Douglass Robillard's introduction to his selection of *The Poems of Herman Melville* (Kent, Ohio: Kent State University Press, 2000) is the fruit of extensive reflection over the course of a long career. Elizabeth Renker has argued quite persuasively in "Melville the Realist Poet" in *The Blackwell Companion to Herman Melville*, ed. Wyn Kelley (Malden, Mass.: Blackwell, 2008), that Melville's poetry has been ignored by many critics because of a broader tendency among Americanists to neglect realist poetry in particular. Hershel Parker's *Melville: The Making of the Poet* leaves no doubt that poetry held a central place in Melville's imagination throughout his career.

5. One of the best discussions of the "Pebbles" sequence is found in Edgar Dryden's *Monumental Melville*, where Dryden explores the relationship between human legal and linguistic authority and nature.

6. Parker, *Melville: The Making of the Poet*, 7.

7. William Blake, *The Marriage of Heaven and Hell*, in *The Portable William Blake*, ed. Alfred Kazin (New York: Penguin, 1977).

8. For the most comprehensive discussion of Melville's use of rose imagery, along with one of the most insightful discussions of the relationship between the later poetry and *Billy Budd*, see Robert Milder's "Old Man Melville: The Rose and the Cross" in *New Essays on Billy Budd*, ed. Donald Yannella (New York: Cambridge University Press, 2002). John Bryant's introduction to his edition of Melville's *Tales, Poems, and Other Writings* (New York: Modern Library, 2002) also includes a very useful discussion of these poems. Martin Kevorkian has work in progress on the subject that will further expand the range of discussion on this important body of work.

9. For Melville's reading of Sa'di's *Gulistan* and *The Rubaiyat of Omar Khayyam*, see *Melville's Marginalia Online*, http://melvillesmarginalia.org.

10. Benjamin Franklin, *Autobiography (*1793; New York: Oxford World Classics), 36.

11. Mahatma Gandhi, *An Autobiography: Or the Story of My Experiments with the Truth*, trans. Mahadev Desai (Boston: Beacon Hill, 1957).

12. William Dillingham, *Melville & His Circle: The Last Years* (Athens: University of Georgia Press, 1996.

13. For more on Platonism in Christianity, see Jaroslav Pelikan, *The Christian Tradition: A History of the Development of Doctrine*, vol. 1. (Chicago: University of Chicago Press, 1971).

14. See Melville's annotated copy of Dante Alighieri, *The Divine Comedy*, at *Melville's Marginalia Online*, http://melvillesmarginalia.org.

15. For discussions of law and literature in *Billy Budd*, see the very influential special issue of the *Cardozo Review of Law and Literature* (vol. 1, no. 1 [1089]) devoted to *Billy Budd*, including articles by Michael Hancher, Richard Weisberg,

and Richard Posner. See also Barbara Johnson, "Melville's Fist: The Execution of Billy Budd," *Studies in Romanticism* 18, no. 4 (1979): 567–99; Deak Nabers, *Victory of Law: The Fourteenth Amendment, the Civil War, and American Literature, 1852–1867* (Baltimore: Johns Hopkins University Press, 2006); Wai-Chee Dimock, *Residues of Justice: Literature, Law, and Philosophy* (Berkeley: University of California Press, 1997); and Jeffrey Westover, "The Impressments of Billy Budd," *Massachusetts Review: A Quarterly of Literature, the Arts and Public Affairs* 39, no. 3 (1998): 361–84.

16. For the "testament of acceptance" controversy, see E. L. Grant Watson, "Melville's Testament of Acceptance," *New England Quarterly* 6, no. 2 (1933): 319–27; Charles Weir, Jr., "Malice Reconciled: A Note on *Billy Budd*," *University of Toronto Quarterly* 13 (1944): 276–85; Phil Withim, "Billy Budd: Testament of Resistance," *Modern Language Quarterly* 20 (1959): 115–27; and Lawrance Thompson, *Melville's Quarrel with God* (Princeton, N.J.: Princeton University Press, 1952).

17. John T. Frederick, *The Darkened Sky; Nineteenth-Century American Novelists and Religion* (South Bend, Ind.: University of Notre Dame Press, 1969).

18. "History of the Building," *Der Koelner Dom*, http://www.koelner-dom.edu.

SELECTED BIBLIOGRAPHY

Aaron, Daniel. *The Unwritten War: American Writers and the Civil War*. New York: Knopf, 1973.

Abrams, M. H. *Natural Supernaturalism: Tradition and Revolution in Romantic Literature*. New York: W. W. Norton, 1973.

Adler, Joyce. *War in Melville's Imagination*. New York: New York University Press, 1981.

Alter, Robert. *Pen of Iron: American Prose and the King James Bible*. Princeton, N.J.: Princeton University Press, 2010.

Anderson, Charles R. *Melville in the South Seas*. New York: Columbia University Press, 1939.

Argersinger, Jana L., and Leland S. Person, eds. *Hawthorne and Melville: Writing a Relationship*. Athens: University of Georgia Press, 2008.

Arsic, Branka. *Passive Constitutions, or, 7½ Times Bartleby*. Stanford, Calif.: Stanford University Press, 2007.

Arvin, Newton. *Herman Melville*. New York: Sloane, 1950.

Baird, James. *Ishmael*. Baltimore: Johns Hopkins University Press, 1956.

Balaam, Peter. *Misery's Mathematics: Mourning, Compensation, and Reality in Antebellum American Literature*. New York: Routledge, 2009.

———. "'Piazza to the North': Melville Reading Sedgwick." In *Melville and Women*, edited by Elizabeth A. Schultz, and Haskell S. Springer, 60–81. Kent, Ohio: Kent State University Press, 2006.

Barnum, Jill, Wyn Kelley, and Christopher Sten, eds. *"Whole Oceans Away": Melville and the Pacific*. Kent, Ohio: Kent State University Press, 2007.

Barrett, Faith. "'They Answered Him Aloud': Popular Voice and Nationalist Discourse in Melville's Battle-Pieces." *Leviathan: A Journal of Melville Studies* 9, no. 3 (2007): 35–49.

Baym, Nina. "The Erotic Motif in Melville's *Clarel*." *Texas Studies in Literature and Language: A Journal of the Humanities* 16 (1974): 315–28.

Bell, Millicent. "Pierre Bayle and Moby Dick." *PMLA* 66, no. 5 (1951): 626–48.

Bellows, Henry Whitney. *Restatements of Christian Doctrine, in Twenty-Five Sermons*. New York, 1860.

Bercaw, Mary K. *Melville's Sources*. Evanston, Ill.: Northwestern University Press, 1987.

Bercaw Edwards, Mary K. *Cannibal Old Me: Spoken Sources in Melville's Early Works*. Kent, Ohio: Kent State University Press, 2009.

Bercovitch, Sacvan. *The American Jeremiad*. Madison: University of Wisconsin Press, 1978.

Berthoff, Warner. *The Example of Melville*. Princeton, N.J.: Princeton University Press, 1962.

Berthold, Dennis. *American Risorgimento: Herman Melville and the Cultural Politics of Italy*. Columbus: Ohio State University Press, 2009.

Bezanson, Walter E. "Introduction." In *Clarel, A Poem and Pilgrimage in the Holy Land*. New York: Hendricks House, 1960.

———. "*Moby-Dick*: A Work of Art" (1950). In *Moby-Dick: A Norton Critical Edition*, edited by Hershel Parker and Harrison Hayford, 2nd ed., 641–56. New York: Norton, 2001.

Bowen, Merlin. *The Long Encounter: Self and Experience in the Writings of Herman Melville*. Chicago: University of Chicago Press, 1960.

Braswell, William. *Melville's Religious Thought: An Essay in Interpretation*. Durham, N.C.: Duke University Press, 1943.

Brodtkorb, Paul. *Ishmael's White World: A Phenomenological Reading of Moby-Dick*. New Haven, Conn.: Yale University Press, 1965.

Brodwin, Stanley. "Herman Melville's *Clarel*: An Existential Gospel." *PMLA* 86, no. 3 (1971): 375–87.

Browne, Ray B. *Melville's Drive to Humanism*. Lafayette, Ind.: Purdue University Press, 1971.

Brownson, Orestes. *Charles Elwood, or the Infidel Converted*. Boston: Little and Brown, 1840.

Bryant, John. *A Companion to Melville Studies*. New York: Greenwood, 1986.

———. *Melville and Repose: The Rhetoric of Humor in the American Renaissance*. New York: Oxford University Press, 1993.

Bryant, John, Mary K. Bercaw Edwards, and Timothy Marr, eds. *Ungraspable Phantom: Essays on Moby-Dick*. Kent, Ohio: Kent State University Press, 2006.

Bryant, John, and Robert Milder, eds. *Melville's Evermoving Dawn*. Kent, Ohio: Kent State University Press, 1997.

Buell, Lawrence. "*Moby-Dick* as Sacred Text." In *New Essays on "Moby-Dick,"* edited by Richard H. Brodhead, 53–72. London: Cambridge University Press, 1986.

Calder, Alex. "'The Thrice Mysterious Taboo': Melville's *Typee* and the Perception of Culture." *Representations* 67 (1999): 27–43.

Cardozo Studies in Law and Literature. Special issue on *Billy Budd*, vol. 1, no. 1 (1989).

Chai, Leon. *The Romantic Foundations of the American Renaissance*. Ithaca, N.Y.: Cornell University Press, 1987.

Cheever, Henry T. *Life in the Sandwich Islands, or, The Heart of the Pacific, as It Was and Is*. London: Richard Bentley, 1851.

Child, Lydia Maria. *The Progress of Religious Ideas: Through Successive Ages*. New York: C. S. Francis, 1855.

Coan, Titus. *Life in Hawaii: An Autobiographic Sketch of Missions Life and Labors*. Honolulu, Hawaii, 1882.

Coleman, Dawn. *Preaching and the Rise of the American Novel*. Columbus: Ohio State University Press, 2013.

Cook, Jonathan A. *Inscrutable Malice: Theodicy, Eschatology, and the Biblical Sources of Moby-Dick*. Dekalb: Northern Illinois University Press, 2012.

———. *Satirical Apocalypse: An Anatomy of Melville's "The Confidence-Man."* Westport, Conn.: Greenwood, 1996.

Cowan, Bainard. *Exiled Waters: Moby-Dick and the Crisis of Allegory*. Baton Rouge: Louisiana State University Press, 1982.

Cowen, Walker, ed. *Melville's Marginalia*. New York: Garland, 1987.

Crain, Caleb. "Lovers of Human Flesh: Homosexuality and Cannibalism in Melville's Novels." *American Literature: A Journal of Literary History, Criticism, and Bibliography* 66, no. 1 (1994): 25–53.

Creech, James. *Closet Writing / Gay Reading: The Case of Melville's Pierre*. Chicago: University of Chicago Press, 1993.

Davis, Merrell R. *Melville's "Mardi": A Chartless Voyage*. New Haven, Conn.: Yale University Press, 1952.

Delbanco, Andrew. *Melville: His World and Work*. New York: Knopf, 2005.

Dettlaff, Shirley M. "Ionian Form and Esau's Waste: Melville's View of Art in *Clarel*." *American Literature* 54, no. 2 (1982): 212–28.

Dillingham, William B. *An Artist in the Rigging: The Early Work of Herman Melville*. Athens: University of Georgia Press, 1972.

———. *Melville & His Circle: The Last Years*. Athens: University of Georgia Press, 1996.

———. *Melville's Later Novels*. Athens: University of Georgia Press, 1986.

———. *Melville's Short Fiction, 1853–1856*. Athens: University of Georgia Press, 1977.

Dimock, Wai-Chee. *Residues of Justice: Literature, Law, Philosophy*. Berkeley: University of California Press, 1996.

Dryden, Edgar A. *Melville's Thematics of Form: The Great Art of Telling the Truth*. Baltimore: Johns Hopkins University Press, 1968.

———. *Monumental Melville: The Formation of a Literary Career*. Stanford, Calif.: Stanford University Press, 2004.

Duban, James. *Melville's Major Fiction: Politics, Theology, and Imagination*. DeKalb: Northern Illinois University Press, 1983.

————. "'Visible Objects of Reverence': Quotations from Goethe in Melville's Annotated *New Testament*." *Leviathan: A Journal of Melville Studies* 9, no. 2 (June 2007): 1–23.

Elliott, Emory. "Art, Religion, and the Problem of Authority in *Pierre*." In *Ideology and Classic American Literature*, edited by Sacvan Bercovitch and Myra Jehlen, 337–51. New York: Cambridge University Press, 1988.

Ellis, Juniper. "Melville's Literary Cartographies of the South Seas." *Massachusetts Review: A Quarterly of Literature, the Arts and Public Affairs* 38, no. 1 (1997): 9–29.

Finkelstein, Dorothee Metlitsky. *Melville's Orienda*. New Haven, Conn.: Yale University Press, 1961.

Finney, Charles Grandison. *Memoirs of Rev. Charles G. Finney, Written by Himself*. New York: Fleming H. Revell, 1876.

Foley, Brian. "Herman Melville and the Example of Sir Thomas Browne." *Modern Philology* 81, no. 3 (1984): 265–77.

Foster, Elizabeth Sophia. Introduction to *The Confidence-Man—His Masquerade*, by Herman Melville, xiii–xcv. Edited by Elizabeth Sophia Foster. New York: Hendricks House, 1954.

Franchot, Jenny. "Melville's Traveling God." In *The Cambridge Companion to Herman Melville*, edited by Robert S. Levine, 157–85. New York: Cambridge University Press, 1998.

———. *Roads to Rome: The Antebellum Protestant Encounter with Catholicism*. Berkeley: University of California Press, 1994.

Franklin, H. Bruce. *The Wake of the Gods: Melville's Mythology*. Palo Alto, Calif.: Stanford Universiy Press, 1963.

Frederick, John T. *The Darkened Sky: Nineteenth-Century American Novelists and Religion*. South Bend, Ind.: University of Notre Dame Press, 1969.

Fuller, Randall. *From Battlefields Rising: How the Civil War Transformed American Literature*. New York: Oxford University Press, 2011.

Garner, Stanton. *The Civil War World of Herman Melville*. Lawrence: University Press of Kansas, 1993.

Gilman, William H. *Melville's Early Life and Redburn*. New York: New York University Press, 1951.

Goldman, Stan. *Melville's Protest Theism: The Hidden and Silent God in Clarel*. DeKalb: Northern Illinois University Press, 1993.

Grey, Robin. *Melville & Milton: An Edition and Analysis of Melville's Annotations on Milton*. Pittsburgh: Duquesne University Press, 2004.

Gunn, Giles, ed. *A Historical Guide to Herman Melville*. New York: Oxford University Press, 2005.

Haberstroh, Charles. *Melville and Male Identity*. Rutherford, N.J.: Fairleigh Dickinson University Press, 1980.

Hancher, Michael. "Billy Budd: Famous Last Words." *Cardozo Studies in Law and Literature* 1, no. 1 (1989): 109–21.

Hardwick, Elizabeth. *Herman Melville*. New York: Viking, 2000.

Harvey, Bruce A. *American Geographics: U.S. National Narratives and the Representation of the Non-European World, 1830–1865*. Palo Alto, Calif.: Stanford University Press, 2001.

Hatch, Nathan. *The Democratization of American Christianity*. New Haven, Conn.: Yale University Press, 1989.

Hawthorne, Nathaniel. "The Celestial Railroad." (1843). In *Hawthorne: Selected Tales and Sketches*, 3rd edition. New York: Rinehart, 1970.

Hayford, Harrison. "'Loomings': Yarns and Figures in the Fabric." In *Artful Thunder: Versions of the Romantic Tradition in American Life*, edited by Howard P. Vincent, 119–38. Kent, Ohio: Kent State University Press, 1975

———. *Melville's Prisoners*. Evanston, Ill.: Northwestern University Press, 2003.

Heidmann, Mark. "The Markings in Herman Melville's Bibles." *Studies in the American Renaissance* (1990): 341–98.

Herbert, T. Walter. *Marquesan Encounters: Melville and the Meaning of Civilization*. Cambridge, Mass.: Harvard University Press, 1980.

———. *Moby-Dick and Calvinism: A World Dismantled*. New Brunswick, N.J.: Rutgers University Press, 1977.

Higgins, Brian, and Hershel Parker. *Herman Melville: The Contemporary Reviews*. Cambridge, Eng.: Cambridge University Press, 1995.

Howard, Leon. *Herman Melville, a Biography*. Berkeley: University of California Press, 1951.

Hsu, Hsuan. "War, Ekphrasis, and Elliptical Form in Melville's Battle-Pieces." *Nineteenth Century Studies* 16 (2002): 51–72.

Jackson, Carl T. *The Oriental Religions and American Thought: Nineteenth-Century Explorations*. Westport, Conn.: Greenwood Press, 1981.

Johnson, Barbara. "Melville's Fist: The Execution of *Billy Budd*." *Studies in Romanticism* 18, no. 4 (1979): 567–99.

Johnson, Bradley. *The Characteristic Theology of Herman Melville: Aesthetics, Politics, Duplicity*. London: Wipf and Stock, 2011.

Karcher, Carolyn L. *Shadow Over the Promised Land: Slavery, Race, and Violence in Melville's America*. Baton Rouge: Louisiana State University Press, 1980.

Kazin, Alfred. *God & the American Writer*. New York: Alfred A. Knopf, 1997.

Kelley, Wyn. *Melville's City: Literary and Urban Form in Nineteenth-Century New York*. New York: Cambridge University Press, 1996.

———. "Out of the Breadbox: Eleanor Melville Metcalf and the Melville Legacy." *Leviathan: A Journal of Melville Studies* 13, no. 1 (2011): 21–33.

Kenny, Vincent S. *Herman Melville's Clarel: A Spiritual Autobiography*. Hamden, Conn.: Archon, 1973.

Kevorkian, Martin. *Writing beyond Prophecy: Emerson, Hawthorne, and Melville after the American Renaissance*. Baton Rouge: Louisiana State University Press, 2013.

Knapp, Joseph G. *Tortured Synthesis: The Meaning of Melville's "Clarel."* New York: Philosophical Library, 1971.

Koffler, Judith Schenck, and Robin West. "The Feminine Presence in *Billy Budd*." *Cardozo Studies in Law and Literature* 1, no. 1 (1989): 1–20.

Kring, Walter Donald. *Herman Melville's Religious Journey*. Raleigh, N.C.: Pentland, 1997.

Kring, Walter Donald, et al. *The Endless, Winding Way in Melville: New Charts by Kring and Carey*. Glassboro, N.Y.: Melville Society, 1981.

Kring, Walter Donald, and Jonathan S. Carey. "Two Discoveries Concerning Herman Melville." *Proceedings of the Massachusetts Historical Society* 87 (1975): 136–41.

Kulkarni, Hemant Balvantrao. *Moby-Dick: A Hindu Avatar, A Study of Hindu Myth and Thought in Moby-Dick*. Logan: Utah State University Press, 1970.

LaRue, L. H. "Paradox and Interpretation." *Cardozo Studies in Law and Literature* 1, no. 1 (1989): 97–108.

Ledbetter, Jack W. "The Trial of Billy Budd, Foretopman." *American Bar Association Journal* 58 (1972): 614–18.

Leyda, Jay. *The Melville Log: A Documentary Life of Herman Melville*. New York: Harcourt, Brace, 1951.

Lyons, Paul. *American Pacificism: Oceania in the U.S. Imagination*. New York: Routledge, 2006.

Mailloux, Steven. "Judging the Judge: *Billy Budd* and 'Proof to all Sophistries.'" *Cardozo Studies in Law and Literature* 1, no. 1 (1989): 83–88.

———. "Political Theology in Douglass and Melville." In *Frederick Douglass and Herman Melville: Essays in Relation*, edited by Robert S. Levine and Samuel Otter, 159–80. Chapel Hill: University of North Carolina Press, 2008.

Marr, Timothy. *The Cultural Roots of American Islamicism*. New York: Cambridge University Press, 2006.

Marrs, Cody. "A Wayward Art: Battle-Pieces and Melville's Poetic Turn." *American Literature: A Journal of Literary History, Criticism, and Bibliography* 82, no. 1 (2010): 91–119.

Martin, Robert K. *Hero, Captain, and Stranger: Male Friendship, Social Critique, and Literary Form in the Sea Novels of Herman Melville*. Chapel Hill: University of North Carolina Press, 1986.

Mason, Ronald. *The Spirit above the Dust: A Study of Herman Melville*. London: J. Lehmann, 1951.

Matthiessen, F. O. *American Renaissance: Art and Expression in the Age of Emerson and Whitman*. New York: Oxford University Press, 1941.

McCall, Dan. *The Silence of Bartleby*. Ithaca, N.Y.: Cornell University Press, 1989.

McPherson, James M. *Battle Cry of Freedom: The Civil War Era*. New York: Oxford University Press, 1988.

"Melville the Poet." Edited by Elizabeth Renker and Douglas Robillard. Special issue. *Leviathan: A Journal of Melville Studies* 9, no. 3 (2007).

Melville's Marginalia Online. Edited by Steven Olsen-Smith, Peter Norberg, and Dennis Marnon. http://melvillesmarginalia.org.

Metcalf, Eleanor Melville. *Herman Melville, Cycle and Epicycle*. Cambridge, Mass.: Harvard University Press, 1953.

Milder, Robert. *Exiled Royalties: Melville and the Life We Imagine*. New York: Oxford University Press, 2006.

———. "Old Man Melville: The Rose and the Cross." In *New Essays on Billy Budd*, ed. Donald Yannella. New York: Cambridge University Press, 2002.

———. "'The Ugly Socrates': Melville, Hawthorne, and the Varieties of Homoerotic Experience." In *Hawthorne and Melville: Writing a Relationship*, edited by Leland S. Person, 71–111. Athens: University of Georgia Press, 2008.

Modern, John Lardas. *Secularism in Antebellum America*. Chicago: University of Chicago Press, 2011.

Mumford, Lewis. *Herman Melville: A Study of His Life and Vision*. Revised editon. New York: Harcourt, Brace, 1962.

Nabers, Deak. *Victory of Law: The Fourteenth Amendment, the Civil War, and American Literature, 1852–1867*. Baltimore: Johns Hopkins University Press, 2006.

New, Elisa. "Bible Leaves! Bible Leaves! Hellenism and Hebraism in Melville's *Moby-Dick*." *Poetics Today* 19, no. 2 (1998): 281–303.

Noll, Mark. *America's God: From Jonathan Edwards to Abraham Lincoln*. New York: Oxford University Press, 2002.

Obenzinger, Hilton. *American Palestine: Melville, Twain, and the Holy Land Mania*. Princeton, N.J.: Princeton University Press, 1999.

———. "Wicked Books: Melville and Religion." In *A Companion to Herman Melville*, edited by Wyn Kelley, 181–96. New York: Blackwell, 2005.

Olsen-Smith, Steven, Peter Norberg, and Dennis Marnon, eds. *Melville's Marginalia Online.*

Olsen-Smith, Steven, and Merton M. Sealts. "*A Cumulative Supplement to* Melville's Reading" *(1988). Leviathan: A Journal of Melville Studies* 6, no. 1 (2004): 55–77. Olson, Charles. *Call Me Ishmael*. New York: Reynal and Hitchcock, 1947.

Otter, Samuel. "How *Clarel* Works." In *A Companion to Herman Melville*, edited by Wyn Kelley, 467–81. New York: Blackwell, 2005.

———. *Melville's Anatomies*. Berkeley: University of California Press, 1999.

Otter, Samuel, and Geoffrey Sanborn, eds. *Melville and Aesthetics*. New York: Palgrave, 2011.

Pardes, Ilana. *Melville's Bibles*. Berkeley: University of California Press, 2008.

Parker, Hershel. *Herman Melville: A Biography*. Vol. 1. Baltimore: Johns Hopkins University Press, 1997.

———. *Herman Melville: A Biography*. Vol. 2. Baltimore: Johns Hopkins University Press, 2002.

———. *Melville: The Making of the Poet*. Evanston, Ill.: Northwestern University Press, 2008.

———. *Reading Billy Budd*. Evanston, Ill.: Northwestern University Press, 1990.

———. *The Recognition of Herman Melville: Selected Criticism since 1846*. Ann Arbor: University of Michigan Press, 1967.

Parker, Hershel, and Harrison Hayford, eds. *Moby-Dick: A Norton Critical Edition*. 2nd edition. New York: W. W. Norton, 2001.

Poe, Edgar Allan. "Mesmeric Revelations" (1844). In *Works: Tales and Sketches, 1843–1849*. Reprint ed. edited by Thomas Ollive Mabbott, Eleanor D. Kewer, and Maureen Cobb Mabbott. Urbana-Champaign: University of Illinois Press, 2000.

———. *Eureka* (1848). In *Poetry, Tales, and Selected Essays*. Ed. G. R. Thompson and Patrick Quinn. New York: Library of America, 1984.

Pommer, Henry. *Milton and Melville*. Pittsburgh: University of Pittsburgh Press, 1950.

Potter, William. *Melville's "Clarel" and the Intersympathy of Creeds*. Kent, Ohio: Kent State University Press, 2004.

Renker, Elizabeth. "Herman Melville, Wife Beating, and the Written Page." *American Literature: A Journal of Literary History, Criticism, and Bibliography* 66, no. 1 (1994): 123–50.

———. "Melville the Realist Poet." In *A Companion to Herman Melville*, edited by Wyn Kelley, 482–96. Malden, Mass.: Blackwell, 2005.

———. *Strike through the Mask: Herman Melville and the Scene of Writing*. Baltimore: Johns Hopkins University Press, 1996.

Robertson-Lorant, Laurie. "Melville and the Women in His Life." In *Melville and Women*, edited by Elizabeth A. Schultz, and Haskell S. Springer, 15–37. Kent, Ohio: Kent State University Press, 2006.

———. *Melville: A Biography*. New York: Clarkson Potter, 1996.

Robillard, Douglas. *Melville and the Visual Arts: Ionian Form, Venetian Tint*. Kent, Ohio: Kent State University Press, 1997.

Sanborn, Geoffrey. *The Sign of the Cannibal: Melville and the Making of a Postcolonial Reader*. Durham, N.C.: Duke University Press, 1998.

———. "Whence Come You, Queequeg?" *American Literature: A Journal of Literary History, Criticism, and Bibliography* 77, no. 2 (2005): 227–57.

———. *Whipscars and Tattoos: The Last of the Mohicans, Moby-Dick, and the Maori*. New York: Oxford University Press, 2011.

Schueller, Malini Johar. *U.S. Orientalisms: Race, Nation, and Gender in Literature, 1790–1890*. Ann Arbor: University of Michigan Press, 1998.

Sealts, Merton M. *Melville as Lecturer*. Cambridge, Mass.: Harvard University Press, 1957.

———. *Melville's Reading*. Revised and enlarged edition. Columbia: University of South Carolina Press, 1988.

———. *Melville's Reading: A Check-List of Books Owned and Borrowed*. Madison: University of Wisconsin Press, 1966.

———. *Pursuing Melville, 1940–1980: Chapters and Essays*. Madison: University of Wisconsin Press, 1982.

Sedgwick, William Ellery, and Sarah Cabot Sedgwick. *Herman Melville: The Tragedy of Mind*. Cambridge, Mass.: Harvard University Press, 1944.

Sherrill, Rowland A. *The Prophetic Melville: Experience, Transcendence, and Tragedy*. Athens: University of Georgia Press, 1979.

Shurr, William. *The Mystery of Iniquity: Melville as Poet, 1857–1891*. Lexington: University Press of Kentucky, 1972.

Snyder, Sharon L., and David T. Mitchell. *Cultural Locations of Disability*. Chicago: University of Chicago Press, 2006.

Solove, D. J. "Melville's Billy Budd and Security in Times of Crisis." *Cardozo Law Review* 26, no. 6 (2005): 2443–70.

Spark, Clare. *Hunting Captain Ahab: Psychological Warfare and the Melville Revival*. 2nd edition. Kent, Ohio: Kent State University Press, 2006.

Stein, William Bysshe. *The Poetry of Melville's Late Years; Time, History, Myth, and Religion*. Albany: State University of New York Press, 1970.

Sten, Christopher. "City of Hope and Fear: Douglass and Melville in the Nation's Capital." *Leviathan: A Journal of Melville Studies* 10, no. 2 (2008): 23–36.

———. "Melville's Cosmopolitanism: A Map for Living in a (Post-)Colonialist World." In *Melville "Among the Nations,"* edited by Sanford E. Marovitz and A. C. Christodoulou, 38–48. Kent, Ohio: Kent State University Press, 2001.

———. *Savage Eye: Melville and the Visual Arts*. Kent, Ohio: Kent State University Press, 1991.

———. "Vere's Use of the 'Forms': Means and Ends in *Billy Budd*." *American Literature* 47, no. 1 (1975): 37–51.

———. *The Weaver-God, He Weaves: Melville and the Poetics of the Novel*. Kent, Ohio: Kent State University Press, 1996.

Stern, Milton R. *The Fine Hammered Steel of Herman Melville*. Urbana: University of Illinois Press, 1957.

Stewart, Randall. *American Literature and Christian Doctrine*. Baton Rouge: Louisiana State University Press, 1958.

Stone, Geoffrey. *Melville*. Great Writers of the World series. New York: Sheed and Ward, 1949.

Stuckey, Sterling. *African Culture and Melville's Art: The Creative Process in "Benito Cereno" and "Moby-Dick."* Oxford: Oxford University Press, 2009.

Sundquist, Eric J. "*Benito Cereno* and New World Slavery." In *Reconstructing American Literary History*, edited by Sacvan Bercovitch, 93–122. Cambridge, Mass.: Harvard University Press, 1986.

———. "Suspense and Tautology in *Benito Cereno*." *Glyph: Textual Studies* 8 (1981): 103–26.

———. *To Wake the Nations: Race in the Making of American Literature*. Cambridge, Mass.: Belknap Press of Harvard University Press, 1993.

Taylor, Charles. *A Secular Age*. Cambridge, Mass.: Harvard University Press, 2007.

Thompson, Lawrance Roger. *Melville's Quarrel with God*. Princeton, N.J.: Princeton University Press, 1952.

Thoreau, Henry David. *Walden, Civil Disobedience, and Other Writings*. Edited by John Rossi. New York: W. W. Norton, 2008.
Tyrrell, Ian R. *Reforming the World: The Creation of America's Moral Empire*. Princeton, N.J.: Princeton University Press, 2010.
Vendler, Helen. "Desert Storm." Review of *Clarel*, by Herman Melville, and *Journals*, by Herman Melville. *The New Republic*, December 7, 1992, pp. 39–42.
———. "Melville and the Lyric of History." *Southern Review* 35, no. 3 (1999): 579–94.
Versluis, Arthur. *American Transcendentalism and Asian Religions*. New York: Oxford University Press, 1993.
———. *The Esoteric Origins of the American Renaissance*. New York: Oxford University Press, 2002.
Vincent, Howard Paton. *The Tailoring of Melville's "White-Jacket."* Evanston, Ill.: Northwestern University Press, 1970.
———. *The Trying-Out of "Moby-Dick."* Carbondale: Southern Illinois University Press, 1965.
Wallace, Robert K. *Douglass and Melville: Anchored Together in Neighborly Style*. New Bedford, Mass.: Spinner, 2005.
———. *Melville & Turner: Spheres of Love and Fright*. Athens: University of Georgia Press, 1992.
Wallace, Robert K., and Ivy G. Wilson, eds. "Frederick Douglass and Herman Melville." *Leviathan: A Journal of Melville Studies* 10, no. 2 (2008): 3–83.
Warren, Rosanna. "Dark Knowledge: Melville's Poems of the Civil War." *Raritan: A Quarterly Review* 19, no. 1 (1999): 100–121.
Watson, E. L. Grant. "Melville's Testament of Acceptance." *New England Quarterly* 6, no. 2 (1933): 319–27.
Weaver, Raymond M. *Herman Melville: Mariner and Mystic*. 1920. Reprint, New York: Cooper Square, 1961.
Weir, Charles, Jr. "Malice Reconciled: A Note on *Billy Budd*." *University of Toronto Quarterly* 13 (1944): 276–85.
Weisberg, Richard H. "Accepting the Inside Narrator's Challenge: *Billy Budd* and the 'Legalistic' Reader." *Cardozo Studies in Law and Literature* 1, no. 1 (1989): 27–48.
Wenke, John Paul. *Melville's Muse: Literary Creation and the Forms of Philosophical Fiction*. Kent, Ohio: Kent State University Press, 1995.
Werge, Thomas. "*Moby-Dick* and the Calvinist Tradition." *Studies in the Novel* 1, no. 4 (1969): 484–506.
Westover, Jeff. "The Impressments of *Billy Budd*." *Massachusetts Review: A Quarterly of Literature, the Arts and Public Affairs* 39, no. 3 (1998): 361–84.
Withim, Phil. "Billy Budd: Testament of Resistance." *Modern Language Quarterly* 20 (1959): 115–27.
Wright, Nathalia. *Melville's Use of the Bible*. New York: Octagon Books, 1947.
Yothers, Brian. *Melville's Mirrors: Literary Criticism and America's Most Elusive Author*. Rochester, N.Y.: Camden House, 2011.
———"One's Own Faith: Melville's Reading of *The New Testament and Psalms*." *Leviathan: A Journal of Melville Studies* 10, no. 3 (2008): 39–59.
———. *The Romance of the Holy Land in American Travel Writing, 1790–1876*. Burlington, Vt.: Ashgate, 2007.

———. "Terrors of the Soul: Religious Pluralism, Cosmic Exaltation, and Epistemological Dread in Poe, Hawthorne, and Melville." *Poe Studies / Dark Romanticism* 39 (2006–07, double issue): 136–44.

Zoellner, Robert. *The Salt-Sea Mastodon: A Reading of "Moby-Dick."* Berkeley: University of California Press, 1973.

INDEX

Abrams, M. H., 6
Adams, Henry, 181
agnosticism, 125–26
Ahasuerus, 76
Aikman, James, 99–100
Alger, William Rounseville, 11–13, 49, 206
American Board of Commissioners for Foreign Missions (ABCFM), 54, 67, 75
Anabaptism, 42, 159
Anderson, Charles R., 55
animism, 163
Apocrypha, 43, 124–26; Ecclesiasticus (Sirach), 43, 124, 126–27; 2 Esdras, 43; Wisdom of Solomon, 43
Aratus, 35
Aristotle, 46–47, 210
Arminianism, 31, 42
Astor, John Jacob, 108
Athanasius, 70
Augustine, 70, 210
autos-da-fé, 115–16

Bacon, Francis, 70
Bellows, Henry Whitney, 164–67, 187, 196
Berthold, Dennis, 193
Bible. *See* Apocrypha; New Testament; Old Testament
Blake, William, 140, 199–200
Booth, Edwin, 159
Booth, John Wilkes, 159
Braswell, William, 81
Brown, John, 133–35, 143, 158–59
Brown, William Wells, 157
Browne, Thomas, 16–21, 49
Brownson, Orestes, 168, 178, 180, 183
Bryant, John, 223n15, 229n8
Buddhism, 13, 20, 47, 69, 72–73, 117, 163, 167, 179, 204, 205–6
Bunyan, Paul, 127, 170

Calvinism, 42, 45, 68, 101, 117, 127–28, 188, 207, 209–10
Carlyle, Thomas, 122–23, 143, 225n14; Goethe translations, 23, 36, 123
Catholicism, 17, 19, 31, 35, 42, 188, 191, 201; in *Clarel*, 31–32, 10, 165, 176, 180–84; in Melville's fiction, 62, 64, 65, 84, 108–9, 113–14, 115–16, 165, 182
Cato the Younger, 75
celibacy, 41, 85, 100–101, 121,
Cervantes, Miguel de, 106–7
Channing, William Ellery, 36, 52
Chaucer, Geoffrey, 117
Cheever, Henry T., 66
Child, Lydia Maria, 157, 166–67
Christianity. *See* New Testament; *and individual sects*
Civil War, 3–5, 8, 129, 131–52, 154–61, 183, 195
Coan, Titus, 53–54, 67, 69
Coan, Titus Munson, 67, 69
"Come outers," 117, 166
Cook, Jonathan A., 116, 125
Cowen, Wilson Walker, 15
Cowper, William, 92
Cresson, Warder, 178

Dante Alighieri, 210
Darwin, Charles, 186–87
Democritus, 70
Derrida, Jacques, 5–6
Dickinson, Emily, 93, 180
difference, defined, 5–6
Dillingham, William, 206
Draco, 39, 144
Dryden, Edgar, 115, 125
Duban, James, 23, 36, 226n2
Dunkers, 29, 85, 99–101, 104, 105–6, 191
Dutch Reformed Church, 94–95, 188
Duyckinck, Evert Augustus, 14, 16
Duyckinck, George Long, 16

Edwards, Jonathan, 90, 108
Edwards, Mary Bercaw, 15
Egyptology, 70, 77
Ellis, William, 54–55
Emerson, Ralph Waldo, 11, 12, 36–37, 44, 72, 91, 122–23, 134, 163, 166, 167, 170
Epiminedes, 35
Evangelicalism, 42, 51–52, 54, 56–57, 64, 68

Finkelstein, Dorothee Metlitsky, 69, 80
Finney, Charles Grandison, 67–68
Foley, Brian, 16–17, 20
Foster, Elizabeth S., 115, 118–19
Franchot, Jenny, 109, 115, 180
Franklin, Benjamin, 29, 99, 100–101, 104, 105, 203
Franklin, H. Bruce, 69–70, 77, 115, 117, 118–19, 125
Frederic, Harold, 180
Frederick, John T., 213
Frederickson, George, 146
Fuller, Margaret, 167
fundamentalism, 81

Gandhi, Mohandas, 206
Garner, Stanton, 132, 136, 139, 143
Garrison, William Lloyd, 159
Gifford, Sanford Robinson, 159
Gnosticism, 199
Goethe, Johann Wolfgang von, 91, 122–23, 166; Alger on 11–12; *Autobiography*, 13; *Wilhelm Meister's Apprenticeship*, 36–37, 38, 40, 95, 106, 153, 211; *Wilhelm Meister's Travels*, 23–24
gothicism, 64, 182
Greene, Graham, 183
Grey, Robin, 44
Griswold, Rufus Wilmot, 57

Harper, Frances E. W., 157
Hatch, Nathan, 170
Hauser, Caspar, 207
Hawthorne, Nathaniel, 101–2; *The Blithedale Romance*, 168; "The Celestial Railroad," 168, 169–71; "Chiefly about War Matters," 137; on Melville, 6, 14, 50, 129; Meville's marginalia to, 15. *See also under* Melville, Herman
Hayford, Harrison, 214
Haystack Revival, 51
Hegel, Georg Wilhelm Friedrich, 12
Heidmann, Mark, 35
Herbert, T. Walter, 218n8, 220n3
Herrick, Robert, 202
Higgins, Brian, 66, 104
Hinduism, 20, 47, 69, 70, 75, 77, 117, 163, 166–67
Holy Bible, with Apocrypha: Melville's marginalia to, 30, 35, 43, 91, 124, 166, 208, 210
Howard, Leon, 66
Howells, William Dean, 138, 161
Hsu, Hsuan, 145

Irving, Washington, 154
Islam, 47, 69, 75, 76, 80, 108, 117, 152–54, 163, 167, 175, 176–77, 201, 205

James, William, 8–9, 119
Jesus. *See* New Testament: Gospels and Acts
Jonah. *See under* Old Testament
Jones, John Paul, 106
Judaism, 35, 44, 75, 161, 163, 173, 175, 178
Julian the Apostate, 70

Kelley, Wyn, 192
Knox, Robert, 72
Kulkarni, H. B., 77

Lee, Ann, 85, 99
Lee, Robert E., 149
Lewis, Matthew, 181
Leyda, Jay, 164
Lincoln, Abraham, 8, 131, 137, 159–60
Lowell, James Russell, 167
Lucretius, 45
Luther, Martin, 31, 186

MacMechan, Archibald, 215
Manco Capac, 116–17
Marr, Timothy, 69
Marvell, Andrew, 45, 202
Matthiessen, F. O., 16
Maurice, Thomas, 70, 71
Melville, Elizabeth Shaw, 164–65, 187, 201
Melville, Gansevoort, 67
Melville, Herman: on America, 23, 38–39, 59, 140; on the Eucharist, 89–90, 95–96; Hawthorne and, 14, 40, 53, 89–91, 95–96, 99, 101–2, 143, 212, 214; and the law, 213; married life, 41, 101, 164; on originality, 48–49, 94; pacifism, 5, 142–43, 159; on racism, 120–21, 136–37, 157; religious thought, 5–8, 14–15, 27, 42–44, 70–71, 88–98, 101, 193, 214; skepticism, 8–9, 17; solitude vs. sociability, 11–13, 51, 60–61, 83, 88, 94–95, 194; on travel, 112
FICTION: "Bartleby, the Scrivener," 8, 30, 108, 109, 121, 186, 210–11; *Benito Cereno*, 8, 97, 108–11, 186; *Billy Budd*, 3, 8–9, 24, 38, 40, 64, 73, 111, 115, 162, 189, 191–93, 206–16; *The Confidence-Man*, 7–8, 30–31, 48, 98, 106, 112, 115–29, 131, 163, 186; *The Encantadas*, 32, 97, 153, 186; *Israel Potter*, 7, 29, 85, 99, 101, 103, 105–6,

109; "The Lightning-Rod man," 111–12; *Mardi*, 7, 16, 19–20, 23, 28, 37–38, 47, 49, 62, 69–71, 75, 88, 89, 93, 137, 142, 165, 207; *Moby-Dick*, 3, 7, 9, 16–20, 23, 24, 28–29, 35, 36, 38–40, 42, 45–46, 47, 59, 61, 63, 64, 68, 70, 72, 73–97, 104, 106, 117–19, 125, 137, 149, 161–62, 165, 174, 186, 203, 208–9, 210–11, 213, 214–15; *Omoo*, 7, 36, 52–55, 58, 65–66, 70, 84, 111, 114, 173, 207–8; "The Piazza," 106–8, 109, 204; *The Piazza Tales*, 7, 106; *Pierre*, 7–8, 21, 27, 29–30, 59, 98, 102–5, 121, 128–29, 131, 143, 156; "Rammon," 203–4; *Redburn*, 7, 38–39, 71–73, 89; *Typee*, 7, 19, 27–28, 36, 51, 52–68, 75, 79, 84, 111, 114, 143, 173, 184, 200, 207–8; *White-Jacket*, 7, 28, 38, 43, 59, 71–73, 85, 89, 110, 142–43

LECTURES: "The South Seas," 114; "Statues in Rome," 112–14, 198; "Traveling," 112, 114, 117

NONFICTION: "Hawthorne and His Mosses," 14, 18, 25, 38, 95, 101–3; *Journals*, 44, 174; "Mr. Parkman's Tour," 120, 194; "Prose Supplement" to *Battle Pieces*, 3–4, 49, 62, 135–37, 139, 151, 158, 183, 215

POETRY: "The Accepted Time," 201–2; "America," 148–49; "The Apparition," 149, 213; "Art," 198; *Battle Pieces*, 3–5, 8, 30, 131–62, 163, 192; "Bridegroom Dick," 195; "Buddha," 20, 179, 198; *The Burgundy Club*, 194; *Clarel*, 8, 20, 24, 25–26, 31, 32–33, 39–40, 44, 47, 53, 61, 64–65, 128, 149, 150, 153, 162, 163–89, 192, 196, 204; "The Coming Storm," 159–60; "The Conflict of Convictions," 139–42, 156; "An Epitaph," 148; "Formerly a Slave," 145–47; "Fragments of a Lost Gnostic Poem of the 12th Century," 199–200; "Herba Santa," 200, 209; "The House-Top," 39, 143–44; *John Marr and Other Sailors*, 153, 162, 163, 192, 194–97, 214; "Lee in the Capitol," 8, 132, 149–55, 157–58; *Marquis de Grandvin*, 194; "The Martyr," 160–61; "A Meditation," 155–57; "Misgivings," 138–39, 143, 156; "On the Men of Maine," 147; "On the Slain at Chickamauga," 148; "Pebbles," 195–97, 213, 214; *Poems*, 3, 197; "Pontoosuce," 204–5, 213–14; "The Portent," 133–35, 138, 143, 156, 158; "A Reasonable Constitution," 202–3; "Rosary Beads," 201–2; "Shelley's Vision," 198–99; "The Swamp Angel," 8, 145; *Timoleon*, 112, 153, 162, 163, 182, 192, 194, 197–200; *Weeds and Wildings*, 163, 192, 194, 201, 214; "Without Price," 202

Metcalf, Eleanor Melville, 192

Methodism, 67, 117

Milder, Robert, 226n1, 229n8

Milton, John, 15, 44–46, 70–71, 113, 120, 140, 143, 150, 166, 198

missionary movement, 19, 27–28, 35, 51–62, 65–69, 73, 111, 173, 178, 184, 200

Monk, Maria, 181

Montaigne, Michel de, 59, 70

Mormonism, 123–24, 127

Moses, 44–45

Nelson, Horatio, 208

Newbigin, Lesslie, 60

Newell, Harriet, 57

Newman, John Henry, 183

New Testament: Gospels and Acts, 12, 15, 22–28, 32–33, 34–35, 37, 39–42, 46–47, 60, 63, 68, 92, 95, 109, 121, 145, 149, 160, 184, 196, 199–200, 202, 210; Pauline epistles, 22, 31, 33–34, 35, 39, 40, 41, 43, 70, 101, 118–19, 176, 179, 191, 201; Revelation, 33, 44, 116, 117, 123, 125, 127, 197; Sermon on the Mount, 12, 22, 27–30, 40–41, 46–47, 58, 62–63, 68, 73, 76, 83, 85, 96, 100, 103–4, 110, 114, 119, 121, 127, 141, 155–56, 159, 193, 198, 200, 205, 207–8

New Testament and Psalms: Melville's marginalia to, 17–18, 21–27, 33–34, 36–37, 39–43, 46, 63, 83, 95, 106, 118–19, 123, 153, 156, 166, 191, 203, 210–11

Nile River, 4

Old Testament, 30, 35, 85, 101, 175, 208; Daniel, 86; Ecclesiastes, 40, 91–92, 186; I Kings, 83; Genesis, 197, 198; Isaiah, 212; Job, 40, 43, 78, 86–87, 186, 195; Jonah, 80–82; Psalms, 22, 34, 38, 40–42

Olsen-Smith, Steven, 15, 50

Omar Khayyam, 201

Otter, Samuel, 222n24, 225n20, 226n1

pantheism, 90

Parker, Hershel, 18, 44, 50, 66, 104–5, 118, 120–21, 132, 164, 193, 197

Parker, Theodore, 181
Parkman, Francis, 120
Parsee, 80. *See also* Zoroastrianism
Pascal, Blaise, 12, 92
Plato and Platonism, 43, 170, 209–10
Poe, Edgar Allan, 57, 80, 139, 148, 167–69, 181
Polynesian religions, 53, 61–64, 75, 77, 79, 84
Porter, David, 54–55
Potter, William, 176
presentism, 193
Priestly, Joseph, 108
Proclus Lycaeus, 70
Protestantism, 17, 32, 35, 42, 51, 52, 53–54, 56, 62, 64, 83–85, 102, 111, 115–16, 123, 127, 165, 180
Pyrrho, 70

Quakerism, 29, 59, 84–86, 93–94, 97, 99–100, 118

Rabelais, François, 92
Radical Reformation, 32, 159
Rahner, Karl, 117
Rama, 20, 65
Reconstruction, 4–5, 49, 136–37, 157–58, 160
Reformism, 102, 104
Renker, Elizabeth, 138, 193
Robillard, Douglas, 145, 193
Robinson, Edward, 174
romanticism, 68, 198–99; religion and, 6, 46
Rosicrucianism, 206, 209
Rousseau, Jean-Jacques, 92

Sabbatarianism, 66
Sa'di, 201
Saint-Évremond, Charles de, 36, 37
Schopenhauer, Arthur, 12, 13, 47, 206
Schueller, Malini Johar, 69, 172
Sealts, Merton M., 15, 112, 153–54, 214
Second Great Awakening, 51, 64, 67
Sedgwick, Catherine Maria, 181
Shakerism, 84–86, 99–101, 191
Shakespeare, William, 15, 48, 102, 106, 159–60
Shelley, Percy Bysshe, 46, 166, 198–99
Sheridan, Richard Brinsley, 47–48
Shurr, William, 192
slavery, 4–5, 8, 13, 61, 67, 108–9, 136, 139, 141, 145–46, 151, 153–54, 156–58; antislavery novels, 110, 146, 157, 225n19
Southey, Robert, 153–54
Spark, Clare, 23
Spenser, Edmund, 106–7
Stein, William Bysshe, 192
Sten, Christopher, 79, 222n24, 225n17
Stephen, 199
Stewart, C. S., 54–55
Stoicism, 40
Stowe, Harriet Beecher, 110, 146, 157, 184–86, 188, 223n11
Summary View of the Millennial Church, A, 99
syncretism, 43–44, 73, 75–80, 118, 132, 166–67, 198, 206, 209–10, 214

taboo, 63–65
Taylor, Bayard, 172, 174
Taylor, Charles, 128
Tennyson, Alfred, Lord, 106
Tertullian, 210
Tetzel, Johannes, 112
Thomas à Kempis, 70
Thoreau, Henry David, 44, 47, 61, 72, 93, 122–23, 134, 147, 167
Transcendentalism, 51–52, 79, 102, 104, 122–23, 127–28, 143, 167, 170
Twain, Mark, 59, 172, 183, 188

Unitarianism, 11, 31, 36, 42, 51, 70–71, 127–28, 164–66, 187–88, 209

Vedder, Elihu, 145
Vendler, Helen, 138
Vincent, Howard, 70

Warren, Rosanna, 138
Washington, George, 75
Weaver, Raymond, 50, 192, 214
Wenke, John, 17
Whitman, Walt, 61, 77
Wills, Gary, 137
Winslow, Harriet, 57
Wright, Nathalia, 35

Young, Edward, 92

Zeno, 70
Zoroastrianism, 70, 75, 80, 167, 205